THE FERRARI LEGEND
THE ROAD CARS

THE FERRARI LEGEND
THE ROAD CARS

BY ANTOINE PRUNET

W. W. Norton & Company
New York. London

Table of Contents

Acknowledgements

The documents kindly made available by Industrie Pininfarina, Studio Giovanni Michelotti, Ghia S.p.a., Zagato, Bertone and of course, Ferrari have been an invaluable help.

The best pictures of the four colour sections (Galleria) were made specially by John Lamm thanks to the active participations of Norman Silver, Fred Leydorf, Mike Shenan and John Clinard.

Other enthusiast owners who co-operated to these colour sections are Fernand Maria, Ado Vallaster, David A. Clarke, Maurice Sauzay, Dries Jetten, Peter J. Agg and Harry Payne, Jacques Swaters and Garage Francorchamps, Charles Robert.

This work would certainly never had been possible without advice, suggestions and encouragements of many friends : Jean Badré, Serge Bellu, Gilles Blanchet, Philippe Brugnon, Daniela Cappa, Tom Churchill, Peter Coltrin, Massimo Colombo, Gérard Crombac, Arno Flach, Dries Jetten, Gedovius, David Gunn, Giovanni Michelotti, Corrado Millanta, Christian Moity, Didier Moreau, Giorgio Nada, Marc Nicolosi, Edwin K. Niles, Victor Norman, Jean-Pierre Ori, Dominique Pascal, Christian Philippsen, Jess Pourret, Charles Pozzi, Gerald L. Roush, Maurice Sauzay, Jacques Swaters, Gilles Templier, Mark Arnold Tippetts, Fredi Valentini and Ado Vallaster.

Finally, I would like to thank in advance all the Ferrari enthusiasts, past, present and future, who will be kind enough to let me know any of the mistakes or omissions they could find in this book.

Antoine Prunet
21, rue de Téhéran
75008 PARIS FRANCE
May the 3rd, 1981.

The epic of the automobile is now almost a century old. It is the story of a very long series of constructors, important or unimportant, ignored or famous. Many have disappeared from the list of companies still in production, the result of the enexorable vicissitudes of history. Others still live, more active than ever.

In the book of gold figure two famous marques carrying the names of the two great men who founded them and who personally presided over their singular destinies—the inimitable and legendary Bugatti and Ferrari.

Bugatti was created by the exceptional, imaginative, and genial master of the mechanical arts, the Milanese Ettore Bugatti. The very glorious career of the French marque unrolled between the two World Wars, and it ended for all intents and purposes with the death of its irreplaceable "patron."

The marque Ferrari, on the other hand, was born shortly after the Second World War, in a fashion picking up where Bugatti ended. It was created and is, even today, managed by the incomparable and wise inspirer and organizer of ideas and talents who is Enzo Ferrari.

The Bugattis, in their day, made automotive history, just as Ferrari makes it today. During Bugatti's era several other famous marques built vehicles of great prestige: Mercedes in Germany; Bentley in England; Alfa Romeo in Italy; Hispano-Suiza, Delage, and others in France; Stutz and Duesenberg in the United States. But the Bugattis were "something else." The Alsatian vehicles had "a certain unknown" which inspired the invincible passion with which "Bugattistes" were possessed, to the exclusion of all discussion to the contrary. Today the Bugattis are rare and precious collector's pieces, and the history of the Bugatti marque and of each of the individual models has been made the subject of knowledgeable publications and precisely documented books.

Thus the great analogy which exists between the Ferraris and the Bugattis, for they are of the same "breed"—the exalted and incomparable racing traditions, and the same passions which they inspire in the more civilized automotive enthusiasts. It is the Ferraris, in the same manner, that today always prevail as the top choice of the more refined clients—and this despite the presence of such contemporaries as Mercedes, Jaguar, Aston Martin, Maserati, Lamborghini, Alfa Romeo, Porsche, and others—a choice often made, not for technical or economic reasons, but for "reasons of the heart."

At the same time, the Ferrari marque has become the subject of a body of literature also well documented and quite interesting, with, moreover, a subject matter of one special emphasis or on one certain variety—the monoplaces of all formulas, the two, four, six, eight, or 12 cylinder cars, the sports models, the gran turismo competition versions, the "normal" vehicles (if any Ferrari can be considered "normal")—categories into which the more considerate and learned authors tend to subdivide this large and diverse subject, in order to provide a more profound study of the characteristics of each particular model of Ferrari production.

Thus was born this book, dedicated to the Ferraris which can be defined as being for the "street," that is to say, more accessible to customers desiring to use the car for touring rather than racing. The passionate Ferraristi will find here a documentation apparently without end. The production, both original and varied, from the "magician" of Maranello will appear even more diversified, adapted to the times and the fashions, always centered on progress and tending toward absolute perfection, reflecting the aspirations of their constructor, more severe with himself than with others, anxious for the class of his production, always conceived with the objective of constituting the absolute pinnacle of the immense pyramid which represents the world-wide automotive production.

Count Giovanni Lurani-Cernuschi

I
The Birth of the Legend

Why "The Ferrari Legend?" Why are Ferrari automobiles, today more than ever, the holders of incomparable prestige? Certainly their high performance and their consistent elegance have always placed the products of the Maranello firm in the first rank of exceptional automobiles. But there was something else, some aura, some mystique, to the name Ferrari. Above all this thought of Ferrari as being a "class apart," of being of the nobility, which gave it its dominance, was the result of a special "dowry," the heritage of competition. "For a constructor with standards for competition the normal evolution is as follows: From the Formula 1 to the prototypes; then from the prototypes to the production." Enzo Ferrari stated this principle in 1973, but the celebrated firm that bears his name has always been faithful to it. It can be proven, for example, with the 512 BB, the famous Berlinetta Boxer still in production. Its flat 5 litre 12 cylinder engine was directly derived from the 4.4 presented on the 365 GT4/BB, at the end of 1971. It, in turn, was conceived from the 3 litre that equipped the prototype 312 PB that appeared at the beginnning of 1971 and was crowned Champion of the World at the end of the 1972 racing season. The 312 PB was in its turn derived directly from the monoplace 312 B entered in the Formula 1 Grands Prix in 1970. The heritage of competition cannot only not be denied, but equally the lessons learned by the high standards of competition—as happened with the advantages of the Boxer engine—can find rapid practical applications, as happened when not two years elapsed between the appearance of the Formula 1 monoplace and the presentation of the street vehicle.

Rare today are the automobile manufacturers who have maintained with such consistency and such success this tradition of distinction. Only one other name comes immediately to mind, that of Ettore Bugatti. If desired there are many comparisons that can be made between the creator of the Ferrari and the creator of the Bugatti. It is perhaps superfluous to do so, however, except on the precise point of the application of the lessons of racing to the high performance touring vehicles. Of numerous common convictions that without doubt animated these two legendary figures, this one was most important in making their creations, both symbolized by the thoroughbred, the most admired works in the history of automotive art.

But let us stop our comparisons and return to 1946 and to Maranello, the Emilian town situated on the flat plain of the Po, in the mountain chain of the Appenines, 16 km (10 mi) to the south of Modena.

I·A
The 125 Sport
1947

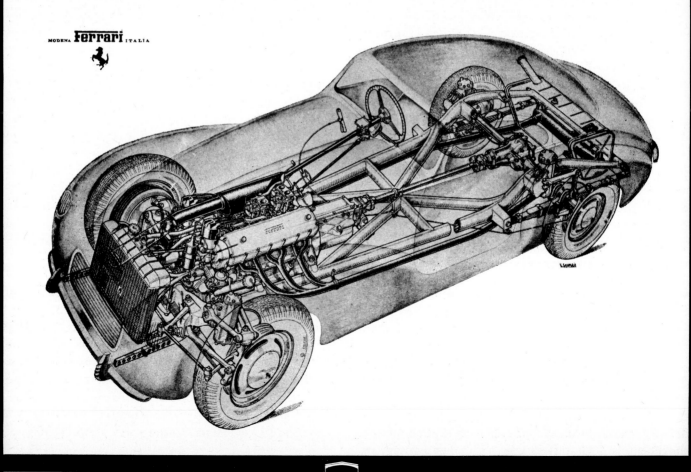

The idea of a touring Ferrari was undoubtedly born at the same time as the ideas which led to the successive appearances of the 125 Sport, on May 11, 1947 at Piacenza, and the 125 Formula 1, on September 5, 1948 at the Grand Prix of Italy. The first detailed information on the projects being developed at Maranello after 1946 was given by the Italian press during the first quarter of 1947. The source for the information was certainly official, judging by the "Modena—Ferrari—Italia" logo which appeared on the documents. This first "press release" was composed of four specially-created, exploded drawings signed by Giovanni Cavara. The bodywork which clothed the drawing of the complete assembly was that of a coupe, but with a rather vague outline in comparison to the sharp detail of the mechanical components shown in the "X-ray" view.

This first available information on the 125 Sport deserves a close look. The details of its conception reveal the ambitions and abilities which motivated the new team at Maranello, a purpose for which the first 125 is ideal even though the form in which it was presented is not the same as the form in which it was actually built.

The basic principles which were considered in the conception of the 125 were constant and can be defined as follows: A continual search for exceptional performance; an intense struggle against weight; and an absolute refusal to accept chance or haphazard solutions.

The search for exceptional performance obviously centered on the engine. The choice of a V-12 may have been the result of a dream—the impressive Packard to which Enzo Ferrari refers in his Memoirs—but the advantages of this configuration are positive and surely did not escape the initiator of this adventure. It is a fact that dividing the cubic capacity of an engine into many fractions results in a large total piston area and permits a reduction in piston stroke, a factor of great power. In decreasing piston linear speed, wear and tear and the loss of efficiency due to friction are also decreased. For the same reasons, the division inherent in 12 cylinders permits high overall engine speed.

The struggle against weight was most obvious in the nature of the materials chosen. Thus, the engine block for the 60° V-12 was made of an aluminum alloy casting. Another advantage of the over-square V-12 is its reduced stroke, which permits a shorter block and therefore a lower overall height for the vehicle, resulting in a lower center of gravity.

The cylinder liners were of the wet type, made of special high-strength steel, and pressed into the block for about a third of their height. A light alloy was also used for the pistons and the connecting rods. The short, strong rods were paired on the six rod journals of the crankshaft, this being possible because of an offset of 20 mm between the two banks of cylinders. An interesting feature of these connecting rods was the angled split of the big end, allowing them to be withdrawn through the top of the block. But even more interesting was the pairing of the rods which allowed a relatively conventional crankshaft. The six

---

The 60° V-12 engine was surely the master trump of the new manufacturer.

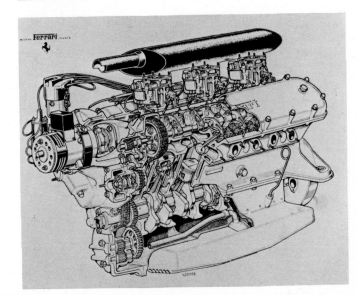

(Left) This X-ray drawing signed by Giovanni Cavara formed part of what appears to have been the first information packet supplied by the new constructor at Maranello. Dating from the Winter of 1946-47, it gave the details of the Ferrari 125 Sport which, however, was almost certainly not built in this exact form.

rod journals were arranged in three planes at 120°, as on a normal, in-line, six-cylinder engine.

The crankshaft itself deserves some special attention. It was made from a solid billet of steel, with well-finished counterbalances and seven main journals allowing an almost equal division of stress on the bearings, and an important reduction in the moment of inertia. As a result there was the almost complete elimination of vibration and torsional stress.

The struggle against weight was also exercised at the top of the engine, with the two cylinder heads being made of Silumin and using pincer springs to control the opening of the 24 valves. Of slightly more importance for the intake than the exhaust, the valves formed an angle of 60°, allowing optimum positioning in the hemispherical combustion chamber.

The camshafts were made of steel and ran on six bearing surfaces, actuating the valves through the intermediary of rocker arms. Each cylinder head was attached to the block by 18 studs, arranged three-by-three around each cylinder. Because of a lack of space this method of attaching the heads was used until the pincer springs were replaced by coil springs.

While each combustion chamber had its own exhaust port opening to the outside of the V, the 12 intake

passages were paired in a Y and opened to the center of the V. These six intake ports were connected to three dual-throat downdraft carburetors. These carburetors, built especially for Ferrari by the firm of Edoardo Weber of Bologna, were of the type 30 DCF (30 representing the inside diameter of the throat; DC signifying double throat or doppio corpo; and F designating the nature of the light alloy used in the carburetor castings).

The baffled oil sump attached to the block at the plane of the crankshaft, and the oil pan was considerably lightened by making it as small as possible and by using aluminum and magnesium alloy in casting it. One pump, gear-driven off the crankshaft, picked up the oil through a primary filter located at the lowest part of the sump and sent it under pressure to the main, self-cleaning filter. In the same housing as this filter was a thermostatic valve which determined, based upon temperature, if the oil could be sent directly to the pressure regulating valve or if it had to

---

Issued with the same series of documents, this drawing of the front section reveals the principal characteristics of the Ferrari—among them the chassis of steel tubes, the V-12 engine, and the "house" hydraulic shock absorbers.

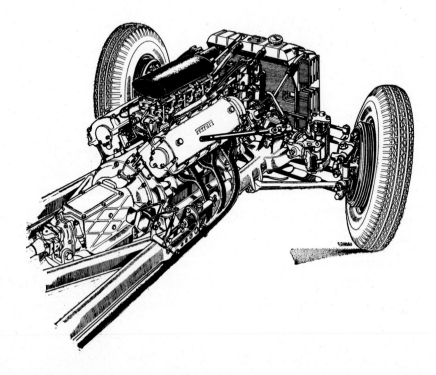

go first to the vertical oil cooler at the front of the vehicle, beside the water radiator.

On the front of the engine a timing case in cast aluminum covered the sprockets controlling the water pump, the generator, and the two camshafts. These sprockets were driven off the crankshaft by a single triple-link chain with a roller adjustment for tension.

Two distributors were positioned vertically at the front of the camshafts and were driven by the camshafts. Each distributor supplied a row of six spark plugs located on the intake side of the cylinder head, inside the V. The two coils were mounted vertically on the same supports as the distributors, and the diaphragm-type fuel pump was driven by a sprocket off the front of the right camshaft.

Finally, neither a fan nor the means of driving one were judged necessary. The size of the radiator, the ease of heat exchange with the small single-cylinder displacement, and the high speeds for which the car was intended are probably the reasons for this omission.

The drawing to the rear section shows the elliptical section of the chassis tubes, the unusual torsion bar, and the Borrani "Cabo Sport" wheels.

The chassis was composed of oval-section manganese chromium steel tubes and, in the interest of lightness without jeopardizing rigidity, its design was reduced to the essentials. Two parallel side members, to which the engine was attached at four points, were connected by two main cross members at the front and rear, with the whole ensemble being reinforced at the center by a solid X-frame of tubes of the same section. At the ends of the two main cross members, brackets were welded to the chassis to serve as mounting points for the shock absorbers and the front suspension.

This front suspension was independent, with four unequal-length A-arms and a semi-elliptical transverse leaf spring. At the rear, the solid rear axle was attached to two parallel leaf springs, the whole assemblage passing under the curved side members.

The Dubonnet-type hydraulic shock absorbers were specially built for Ferrari by the engineer Colombo. They were identical for front and rear, but at the front they acted directly on the upper A-arms while at the rear they controlled the movement of the rear axle through the intermediary of two articulated arms, and were subjected to the control of an anti-roll bar concealed in the chassis cross member.

The transmission was connected directly to the rear

of the engine and was housed in a light alloy case which also enclosed the single-disc clutch mechanism. This case was attached to the chassis' central X-frame at two points. The drawing accompanying the press release clearly shows what appears to be a shift mechanism operated by a lever mounted on the steering column. Some of the very first Ferraris were actually so equipped.

Through a drive shaft and two universal joints, the secondary shaft of the transmission was linked to the differential which contained conical gears and a helicoidal reduction gear. The differential case was cast in light alloy and the axle tubes were in cast steel.

Light alloys were also used for the four drums of the hydraulic brakes, for the rims of the Borrani "Cabo Sport" 15-inch wheels with Rudge hubs and perforated hubcaps (the rest of the wheels being of stamped sheet steel), and for the fuel tank which occupied the space left free between the rear axle and the last chassis cross member.

From this same rear cross member was hung one large muffler with a single outlet. This muffler was the terminus for the two exhaust pipes which followed the chassis side members after having collected the exhaust from the six Y-shaped exhaust manifolds.

In summation, the Ferrari 125 Sport represented a combination of carefully considered solutions which

A symbolic picture: The first Ferrari at the gate of the works at Maranello. It was in this form that the 125 Sport was first presented to the public, at its first competition appearance on May 11, 1947 at Piacenza.

until then had only been applied to extremely sophisticated competition vehicles. In reality, therefore, it is probably just as well that it never left Maranello in that exact form, especially with regard to the berlinetta bodywork which clothed the design and which was carefully described on the descriptive notice. The 125 which was driven by Franco Cortese at Piacenza a short time later—the first true outing of a Ferrari—tended to confirm this. For while it presented the same mechanical characteristics, with a few slight variations, it reverted to a strictly "sport" open bodywork, and its wheelbase was obviously shorter at 2.42 metres.

For the rest of the 1947 season, work was concentrated almost exclusively on the development of the 125 Competition, and a second Ferrari appeared on June 8, at the Roman circuit of Caracalla. It was also a 125, but the bodywork was reduced to a simple two-seater "cigar" with the wheels exposed.

The first increase in displacement arrived with the 159 Sport which contested its first race at Pescara, August 15, driven by Cortese. The bodywork was that of the first roadster, but the bore had been enlarged to 59 mm and the stroke increased to 58 mm, raising the displacement to 1902.84 cc.

At Turin, on October 12, Raymond Sommer won with the 159 for the first time and gave Ferrari its first victory in an international race. The racing season therefore ended on a happy note for the Maranello team, but the year passed without even a hint of the touring Ferrari that had been announced.

Specifications

12 cylinders, in a 60° V

Timing by two overhead camshafts, rocker arms, and valves in a V

Bore and stroke: 55 x 52.5 mm

Total displacement 1496.77 cc (one cylinder displacement 124.73 cc)

Compression ratio: 8:1

Maximum power: 72 hp at 5600 rpm

3 carburetors, Weber 30 DCF, dual-throat, downdraft.

Ignition by two distributors, Marelli S44, and two coils, Superpotente B5

Fuel pump with diaphragm

Self cleaning oil filter

Single-disc dry clutch

Transmission with 5 speeds plus reverse. Direct drive in 4th gear, and 5th overdrive. 3rd and 4th synchronized

Transmission ratios: 1st, 3.09; 2nd, 2.22; 3rd, 1.38; 4th, 1.00; 5th, 0.92; reverse, 3.95.

Rear axle ratio: 4.9

Solid rear axle with anti-roll bar

Hydraulic brakes, pedal actuated, on all four wheels; hand brake on rear wheels only. Drums of 300 mm diameter.

Front suspension by unequal length A-arms and a single transverse semi-elliptic leaf spring.

Rear suspension by two parrallel semi-elliptic leaf springs.

Four hydraulic shock absorbers

Steering box with worm and sector

Wheelbase: 2420 mm

Track: 1255 mm front; 1200 mm rear

Principal dimensions of the three-place berlinetta:

Maximum length	4500 mm
Maximum width	1550 mm
Maximum height	1500 mm
Ground clearance	165 mm

Turning circle: 5200 mm

Weight of chassis with spare wheel, battery, and tools: 570 kg

Dry weight of the three-place berlinetta: 800 kg

Tires: 5.50 x 15

Disc wheels of stamped steel with light alloy rims

Mounting hub Rudge knock-off type

Fuel tank of 75 litres

Maximum speed on level ground of the three-place berlinetta: 155 kmh

Fuel consumption: 12 to 13 litres per 100 km

The 166 Sport
1947-1948

Before the end of 1947 the V-12 Ferrari engine was enlarged to two litres by utilizing a new bore dimension of 60 mm. Thus the Type 166 was born which, like the preceding types, took its designation from the displacement of one cylinder. Because the 1947 racing season had already ended this new engine did not appear in competition until 1948, but the successes obtained in only a few races with the Types 125 and 159 led quite soon to the appearance at Maranello of the first enthusiastic customers for this new breed of thoroughbred, these lively red automobiles displaying above their grills a rectangular badge with a black prancing horse on a yellow background, named Ferrari.

These first customers began arriving during the last months of 1947. Among them were the Besana brothers, Gabriele and Soave, who acquired two 166 Corsas which were to be delivered to them at the beginning of 1948. In actuality, there was not a great supply of reserves at Maranello following the racing season essentially dedicated to the development of the 125.

It was at this same time, in November, that Prince Igor Troubetzkoy, who was just finishing a season with Simca-Gordini, and his friend Count Bruno Sterzi, a fervent racing enthusiast and industrialist from Milan, arrived at Ferrari. Between them they had decided to form a Franco-Italian racing team, Gruppo Inter, and wanted to acquire three Ferraris for the team. They were promised two 166 Corsas in time to compete in the 1948 Targa Florio, which for that year was paired with the Tour of Sicily, scheduled to be run on April 3. But the pair, anxious to acquire one of the automobiles with such an astonishing performance and a magical exhaust note, also received immediate delivery of a Ferrari which was intended to serve them as a "muletto", a training mule.

There are still many details about this car which are unknown today, but its designation as 166 Sport

rather than 166 Corsa leads to the supposition that here was a new generation of Ferrari, an assumption which is confirmed by the serial number assigned to it—001/S. The system of allocating serial numbers at Ferrari was perhaps still rather imprecise at the time, but as will be verified later, the even numbers as a general rule were assigned to competition or racing cars, and the odd numbers to touring or road vehicles.

But to return to this historic 166 Sport (001/S) which, driven by Prince Troubetzkoy, left Maranello one fine day in November, 1947, we think that it was nothing more than another of the 125 Sports mentioned in the preceding chapter. The two-litre engine which powered it was in all likelihood the old 125 bored out from 55 to 60 mm and stroked from 52.5 to 58.8 mm. The chassis, with a 2.42 metre wheelbase, was identical to the earlier car, and only the bodywork differed. The body builder is not known, but the design of the roadster lacks considerable refinement. The rather vertical front was pierced by a rectangular aluminum grill, and the rectilinear fenders merged into a rounded and slightly plunging rear.

Oddly enough, although it was originally destined to serve only as a "muletto", this first 166 Sport had a very successful racing career. This resulted from an accident which occurred before the race, eliminating one of the 166 Corsas newly constructed for Gruppo Inter, requiring Clemente Biondetti and Prince Troubetzkoy to start the 1948 Tour of Sicily and Targa Florio with the "muletto". Good luck, however, was on their side on the 1080 kilometres of Sicilian roads which encompassed the event. The newer Ferraris all succumbed to a defect in the fuel pump and it was the "old" roadster which took the lead and was first across the finish line. A very sporting baptism for what must have been the first touring Ferrari!

In December, 1947, Scuderia Ferrari published its first illustrated sales brochure, detailing separately the 166 Corsa and the 166 Sport. Details given for the Corsa deviated even more from those given for the Sport, which is the one which interests us here. The principal changes were in the areas of carburetion and bodywork. Substituted for the three carburetors was a single Weber dual-throat 32 DCF, mounted on a single manifold which was heated by circulating water

At the same 1948 Mille Miglia, Biondetti and Navone began the long list of Ferrari victories in this prestigious event with this 166 Sport. At least by its odd chassis number—003 S—this Allemano coupe can be considered as the second touring Ferrari.

from the cooling system. All was topped off with a "T" shaped double air filter. As for the bodywork, the catalog depicted it summarily in profile, with characteristics to which we will return shortly.

On May 2, 1948, Clemente Biondetti captured Ferrari's first victory in the most important Italian race, the Mille Miglia. For that occasion he drove a coupe very similar to the one which illustrated the 1947 catalog. Carrozzeria Allemano of Turin bodied this red double-windowed coupe, recognizable by its rectangular grill and by the large "brows" which capped the front wheel arches, a detail which will be seen again in about five years on the Mercedes 300 SL. But in looking back at the design in the brochure several differences are noted: The side windows were sliding (not roll-up) the Borrani Rudge Record wire wheels replaced the Cabo Sport wheels with perforated covers, and the functional air scoop on the hood indicated the presence of three carburetors topped by velocity stacks.

The roadster 001/S also participated in the 1948 Mille Miglia, with Nando Righetti as driver, but he had to retire shortly after the start. In 1950, 001/S was sold to a Sicilian, Stefano La Motta, who obtained a meritorious third place in the Targa Florio that year. After that, all trace of this historic vehicle was lost.

The Allemano coupe which won the Mille Miglia did not reappear in 1948, but several brochures published that year depict a similar coupe with several slight differences, notably, descending door windows, Cabo Sport wheels, and thin blades on the fenders. The main technical specifications announced, 110 hp at 6,000 rpm, three Weber 32 DCF carburetors, and 2.42 metre wheelbase, were rightly those of the 166 Sport, but the designation was given as 166 Inter. In March, 1949, a very similar gray coupe was sold under serial number 003/S to a Milanese, Gianpiero Bianchetti, who later drove it in several races. All trace of 003/S has been lost as well, but it seems almost certain that this coupe and the Mille Miglia winner are one and the same.

In all probability, 001/S and 003/S constitute the total production of the 166 Sport. At least by their serial numbers they can be considered as the first touring Ferraris, or rather "gran turismo".

In 1949 the Allemano coupe 003 S was reconditioned and sold to G.P. Bianchetti of Milan. Here it is seen at the Cisa Pass during the 1949 Mille Miglia.

The 166 Inter
1948-1951

The first automobile show in which Ferrari participated was the one held in Turin, in November, 1948, at the same edge of the Valentino Park where one year earlier Raymond Sommer had won Ferrari's first international victory with a Type 159. Two Ferraris were displayed at the Turin Show, a 166 Mille Miglia barchetta and a 166 Inter coupe. The bodywork of both cars was the work of the Milanese firm Carrozzeria Touring Superleggera, founded in 1926 and directed since then by Felice Bianchi Anderloni and Gaetano Ponzoni. Touring, which before then had exercised their skills on Isotta-Fraschinis, Alfa Romeos, and on the BMW that won the 1940 Mille Miglia, was also, since the 1930s, holder of the "Superleggera" patent. This method, which can be translated literally as "super-light," consisted of a framework of small, lightweight steel tubes to which previously formed panels of bodywork were attached. This evidently permitted a considerable weight advantage in comparison to the wooden framework used by the majority of the pre-World War II body builders.

(Left) Carrozzeria Touring-Superleggera of Milan bodied the first 166 Inters. Here is shown a model (in the background) along with those for a BMW and an Alfa Romeo (at left) and a Ferrari 166 Mille Miglia (at right). The first Carrozzeria Touring 166 Inter coupe was shown at the 1948 Turin Show.

The chassis of the 166 Inter as it was delivered to the body builder. Compare it to the drawing by Cavara on page 14.

The tubular framework of the body constituted the uniqueness of the Superleggera method.

Using this method, Touring created for the 166 MM the "barchetta" body, which became very famous and much copied. For the 166 Inter, which interests us here, they created a four-windowed coupe, reminiscent of certain Alfa Romeos, of integrated design, perhaps a little too high but not lacking elegance. The almost rectangular grill, ornamented by horizontal bars, was slightly inclined towards the rear and was capped by a crease which swept down on each side to pass under the headlights. The front fenders, slightly detached from the hood, faded out on the doors and the design of the rear fenders outlined the wheel arches before dissolving into the trunk, the rear of the car having very rounded lines. The long hood was noticeably higher than the fenders, and the generous dimensions of the roof line allowed a large amount of window area, as well as permitting the addition of two supplementary rear seats.

This new Ferrari coupe, therefore, represented an important evolution, with affinity to the preceding 166 Sport yet appearing at the same time to be a true touring Ferrari. The catalog published at the same time confirmed this. The wheelbase varied according to circumstances between 2.50 metres and 2.62 metres

The unique steering wheel of 015 S is one of these variations; as are the switches on the right.

This design by Touring was adapted with several slight variations to some five 166 Inters. The unique steering of 015S (above) was one of these variations.

and the chassis was reinforced by several supplementary cross members while two exterior side members were added in the center. It was also about this same time that the Colombo shock absorbers were replaced by those of the lever-type, manufactured by Houdaille.

In the engine compartment, the single carburetor and heated intake manifold announced at the end of 1947 made their first appearance. With a compression ratio reduced to 6.8:1, the maximum power announced by the catalog was 90 hp at 5600 rpm, and the maximum speed was 150 km/h (95.6 mph). The same catalog bestowed anew on this Ferrari the designation 166 Sport while the Allemano coupe (003/S) was pictured under the heading 166 Inter, as we have seen in the preceding chapter. In reality, it was the touring coupes which very quickly adopted the designation of 166 Inter.

Touring clothed about five vehicles with bodywork of this same design between the end of 1948 and the middle of 1949. They were 005/S (probably the car displayed at Turin), 007/S, 013/S, 015/S, and 017/S. But, in general, Ferrari sold the chassis bare, and they were bodied to special order, either for a private customer or a dealer, which explains the infinite variations in the design, in the details, and in the mechanical specifications. Thus, for example, 015/S was given a shorter chassis, a carburetor of 36 mm instead of 32, and a power rating of 150 hp. (And it was recently found to have a stroke of 59.5 mm!)

At the end of 1949, a noticeable change occurred in the basic Touring design. The front and rear fenders were reunited into a single element, and the moulded line which started from the front wheel arch ran without interruption down the side. At this same time there also appeared on some Touring coupes a translucent roof "Aerlux", which could be rendered opaque with an interior screen if required, another invention patented by this same body builder.

The 166 Inter coupe (019/S) shown at the Paris Show in October, 1949, was of this style. Borrani Rudge Record wire wheels and Englebert tires with white sidewalls were fitted to this Aerlux coupe, which was to forge a long list of competition honors at the hands of the Frenchman Jean Renaldo.

Several 166 Inters were given similar bodies, among them 019 S, 023 S, 025 S, 029 S, and 035 S.

At the end of 1950, Touring once again modified the design of their 166 Inter coupe by adopting, in imitation of the 166 Le Mans berlinetta presented earlier in the year by the same body builder, a "fastback" rear. The 166s numbered 047/S, 053/S, 057/S, 0073 S (?), 0075 S, 0077 S, and 0079 S were so bodied.

The second theme of Touring is visible on this 166 Inter coupe (019 S) shown at the 1949 Paris Salon, and which is seen here at Albi in 1952, one of the numerous races in which it was entered by Jean Renaldo. The same theme was repeated on 023 S, 025 S, 029 S, and 035 S.

At the 1950 Turin Show, the Touring coupe was shown with a fast-back rear derived, but with less success, from that of the 166 Le Mans berlinetta.

Thus were bodies 043 S, 047 S, 053 S, 057 S, 0073 S (?), 0077 S (?) and 0079 S, as well as 0075 S, which can be recognized here by the chrome bead which surmounts the grill.

Stabilimenti Farina proposed this lighter design for the 166 Inter, with a resemblance to the famous Cisitalia 202. The same theme was used on 009 S, 021 S, 031 S, 037 S, and 041 S (?).

The "Cabo Sport" wheels of "Carlo Borrani s.p.a. Milano" were a characteristic trait of the first street Ferraris. The rim is of polished light alloy, the disc stamped steel with perforations, and attachment was assured by a central Rudge-type nut.

While Carrozzeria Touring had the honor of being the first to body the street Ferraris, they did not have this honor for long. Nevertheless, it appears that they were the only ones to prepare bodies for the longest chassis.

Stabilimenti Industriali Giovanni Farina became, following chronological order, the second body builder for touring Ferraris. This firm was founded in 1905 by Giovanni Farina, and was one of the oldest body builders located in Turin. It was also a veritable nursery of talent. Among the designers that were to be heard from later can be cited Mario Boano, Giovanni Michelotti, and Frecesco Martinengo, without forgetting, of course, Battista "Pinin" Farina who developed his first designs at the shop of his elder brother before establishing his own business in 1930, Carrozzeria Pinin Farina.

The first Ferrari by Stabilimenti Farina (009/S) was a two-place fastback coupe, slightly lighter and more sporting in appearance than the Touring coupes. This very pure design, however, gave the impression of deja-vu, for it was in effect a very close copy of the marvelous design created in 1947 by Pinin Farina for the Cisitalia 202. This "sculpture in movement", shown at the Museum of Modern Art in New York, was considered the most significant example of the renaissance of Italian coachwork, so it is not surprising that it started a fashion. The 166 Inter of Stabilimenti Farina was only the first pleasant demonstration of the trend. There were produced, always with detail variations, at least five similar examples: 009/S, 021/S, 031/S, 037/S, and 041/S.

A competition sidelight occurred at the Monza circuit on May 29, 1949, at the Coppa Inter-Europa. This first Italian race confined to touring vehicles can be considered the beginning of the "Gran Turismo" races wherein Ferrari quickly established absolute superiority. At Monza that year, the three Ferrari 166s entered, with three different body styles, disputed the first three places from beginning to end. It was eventually Count Bruno Sterzi who won at more than 130 km/h (80 mph) with his Touring-bodied coupe, ahead of Gianpiero Bianchetti in his 166 Allemano (003/S) and Franco Cornacchia, the important Ferrari agent in Milan, who drove a Stabilimenti Farina coupe.

Monza, May 29, 1949: In the Coppa Inter-Europa, the first of the races restricted to "Grand Touring" cars, three of the first five street Ferraris built competed for the victory. The win went to the Touring coupe (005 S) of Count Sterzi, ahead of the Allemano coupe (003 S) of G.P. Bianchetti and the Farina coupe (009 S) of Franco Cornacchia.

The second Ferrari bodied by Stabilimenti Farina was presented at the Geneva Salon at about the same time. For this first showing outside Italy, Ferrari, represented by Luigi Chinetti, displayed three complete cars and an engine. The latter was equipped with the new individual air filters for the three carburetors, a setup which would soon become available on the 166 Inters. Carrozzeria Touring was responsible for the bodies on the 166 MM Barchetta and the 2/3-place coupe displayed at Geneva, but it was Stabilimenti Farina who built the first Ferrari cabriolet. With the exception of the roof, this light-colored convertible was almost identical to the coupe, the only obvious differences are the flatter trunk, made necessary by the cabriolet top, and the elimination of the air scoop ususally found on the hood of the coupes. Like all

the 166 Inters that preceded it, the Farina cabriolet was equipped with Borrani Cabo Sport wheels whose Rudge hubs were covered by chrome hubcaps stamped with the Ferrari logo. This cabriolet (011/S) became the first of many owned by the famous Italian film director, Roberto Rossellini. Its design would be used, with very few differences, on the Simca 8 Sport as well.

In the Spring of 1949, on Viale Trento Trieste, in the same location which, before World War II, had housed Scuderia Ferrari, an Allemano coupe (003 S), a Touring coupe, and a Farina coupe await their owners between two 166 MM barchettas. The car carrying the number 624 is that which won the Mille Miglia with Biondetti and Salani.

The first Ferrari cabriolet (011 S) was built by Stabilimenti Farina and shown at the 1949 Geneva Salon. The lines will be seen again on the Simca Sport.

A single carburetor, a unique two-part air filter, and special covers unifying the ignition were characteristics of the first touring Ferraris. (Here is the engine of 011 S)

In the same style, and during the same year, Farina built a second 166 Inter cabriolet (033/S), recognizable by its black top and an air scoop in the middle of the hood. This vehicle was also equipped with two anti-fog lights, which necessitated a modification to the contour of the grill, and a rectangular grid pattern within the grill. The bumpers were lighter, but the rear of the body was made cumbersome by the squared-off rear wheel arches. This second Stabilimenti Farina cabriolet became the first Ferrari of another faithful Ferrarist, Doctor Wax of Genoa.

A third 166 Inter cabriolet was built in 1950 by this same Turinese coachbuilder located on Corso Tortona, but the style was completely different. The fenders were continuous, the grill was sharply inclined to the rear, the curved windshield was in one piece, and the wheels were Borrani Rudge Record chrome wire spoke. This "Stabilimenti Farina Special" (063/S) was shown at the Paris Salon in October, 1950, and then at Geneva in March, 1951, before being sold to the Swiss driver Emmanuel de Graffenried. It appears to have been one of the last Ferraris bodied by Stabilimenti Farina. Unfortunately, it was later transformed into a replica of the 166 Corsa.

Never two vehicles completely identical: The seond cabriolet by Stabilimenti Farina (probably 033 S) was not an exception to the rule of that period.

The third body builder, in chronological order, to exercise his talents on the Ferrari 166 Inter was Alfredo Vignale, whose establishment, founded in 1946, was one of the newest in Turin. An ex-superintendent at Stabilimenti Farina, Alfredo Vignale was a body building technician and the majority of the designs which he built were those of Giovanni Michelotti, a young stylist who became independent in 1949 after also beginning his career in the celebrated Farina firm on Corsa Tortona. The Vignale-Michelotti duo had a completely original technique.

One of the last creations of the old Turinese body builder, this 166 Inter cabriolet (0063 S) "Stabilimenti Farina Special" is seen here on the streets of Barcelona after being shown at the 1950 Paris Show.

This is the first Ferrari project by the brilliant partnership formed by the stylist Giovanni Michelotti and the body builder Alfredo Vignale.

Michelotti laid out the design at the scale of 1:1 and Vignale copied it directly onto the aluminum sheets which constituted the body panels. As opposed to other body builders, not one pattern nor one mold was used. The only instruments used were, in order, a wooden hammer and a tree stump, then a flat mallet and a sack of sand, and finally a flat hammer and an anvil! The panel thus formed was checked for fit against the vehicle, and if correct, attached in place with rivets and screws. Once assembled, the body was coated with a good layer of "gumite" before being passed along to the painter. This marvelous method, utilized in the Middle Ages for the making of armor, required substantial experience, a sure eye, and a good hand but gave the vehicles slight differences from one to the other, even when made to the same design. The results were often obviously asymmetrical, and as Giovanni Michelotti explained it "just as two human heads are never identical, so a single head is never completely symmetrical"

The first Michelotti design for a Ferrari by Vignale was entitled "Coupe Grand Sport". This four-window coupe, compact and low, was characterized by several original features, among them the crease that horizontally extended the wheel arches, the grill which slanted slightly towards the front, and the carburetor air intake formed by scooping out the front bodywork. This design was adapted, with variations, to several 166 Inters with short chassis, among them 039 S, 045 S, 051 S, 059 S, 0065 S, 0067 S, 0069 S, 0071 S, 0075 S, and 0077 S as well as one or two 166 Mille Miglias. (051 S, now, by the way, has a Vignale Cabriolet body.)

Although more moderate, the execution by Vignale did not lose its attractiveness. The most typical Michelotti details are the air intake for the carburetors and the decorative moulding of the sides.

The same theme was found—always with infinite variations—on 039 S, 0059 S, 0065 S, 0067 S, 0069 S, 0071 S, 0073 S(?), and on 0051 S recognizable here by the built-in fog lights which dictated the unusual contour of the grill. . .

. . . on 045 S, recognizable by its flat rear flanks . . .

. . . or later on this 166 MM driven by Floch at Rouen in 1953.

There were two other body builders to put their names on these first Ferraris, but it does not appear that they had any great influence. One example of classic sobriety was the two-place cabriolet presented by the Carrozzeria Bertone at the Turin Salon in April 1950. It was most easily recognized by the indented lower flanks, but also notable were the excellent proportions of the whole design and the carefully controlled decoration. This cabriolet remains, however, one of the very rare Ferraris bodied by this firm, which became one of the greatest names in Italian coachwork.

The "Ghia S.p.A." established in 1915 at Turin made its entry into the select circle of Ferrari body builders under the impetus of its principal stylist, Mario Boano, another former employee of Stablimenti Farina. The first Ghia/Boano Ferrari (probably 049/S) was built in 1950 and took the form of a fastback, two-place, four-window coupe with pure and sober lines that approximate the proportions of the Bertone cabriolet and the Michelotti-Vignale coupes. A peculiarity of Ghia during this period was the almost exclusive use of sheet steel, in contrast to the other body builders who generally worked in aluminum. The most striking original feature of the Ghia 166 Inter coupe was the design of the grill, with the top edge raised in the center to mark the end of the converging lines of the hood.

The days of the 166 Inter were numbered when the 195 Inter was introduced at the Brussels show in

Sober but unique—note the grooved lower body—this 166 Inter cabriolet, unveiled at the 1950 Turin Salon, remained for a long time the only Ferrari signed by Bertone, one of the future great names of Italian coachbuilding.

January, 1951. Carrozzeria Touring, who had bodied the first 166 Inter, likewise bodied 0079 S, a fastback coupe which seems to have been the last example of a model produced in about 38 examples over a span of more than two years.

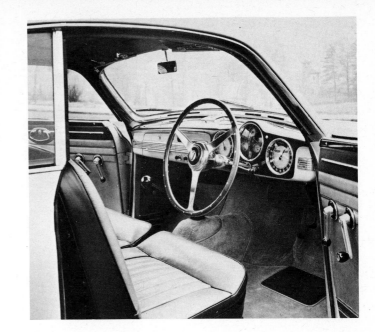

This two place coupe seemed to have been the only 166 Inter (probably 049S) by Carrozzeria Ghia with an interior decoration (above) very characteristic of this Turinese firm. The same design was used on several 195 and 212 Inters.

The 195 Inter
1951

(Left) The 195 Inter inspired from Michelotti and Vignale this black coupe, first shown at the Concours d'Elegance of Viareggio at the beginning of 1951. This theme will be repeated on several 195 Inters.

By the same authors, this coupe proposed a different rear. The decoration is perhaps a little heavy.

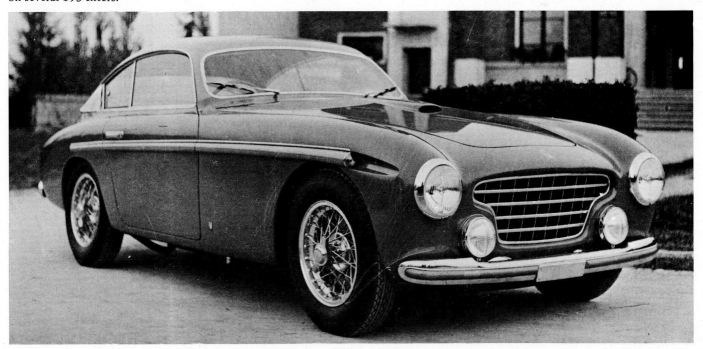

As with horse racing, where the knowledgeable know that racing improves the breed, so the most significant progress in automotive technology is born of the demands of racing and the severe testing which that constitutes. At the Ferrari factory, this policy has always been predominant, and the Type 195, which came along in 1951 to take the place of the 166 Inter, was another demonstration of that policy.

The 195 engine was in fact designed for competition, and it was that fact which allowed it to reach its full maturity. The increase in total engine displacement from 1995 cc to 2341 cc (giving 195 cc displacement per cylinder) was obtained by enlarging the bore from 60 to 65 mm, the other dimensions of the engine remaining identical to those of the 166. The power increase thus obtained was in the order of 20%, that is, about 170 hp instead of 140 hp on the sports version. The first race for the 195 Sport was undoubtedly the Targa Florio, in April, 1950. The first great success came in the same month, with the victory of Gianni Marzotto in the Mille Miglia, and the remainder of the 1950 season only served to confirm the quality of the 2.3 litre engine with victories by the same Gianni Marzotto in the Six Hours of Rome and Dolomite Cup, the win by Dorini Serafini at the Tour of Calabria, and the victories of Giovanni Bracco in several hillclimbs.

The touring version of the 2.3 litre, the Type 195 Inter, appeared in the second half of 1950, and in essence, it differed from the 166 whose place it took only by the new bore dimension of 65 mm. However, it should also be noted that the compression ratio was reduced from 8 to 7.5:1 by the new cylinder heads, and that a Weber 36 DCF carburetor replaced the 32 mm type on some examples. As in the past, the fitting of three double throat carburetors remained available as an option. With standard equipment the power was increased to 135 hp as against 115 hp, at the same speed of 6000 rpm.

For the remainder of the vehicle, the specifications of the 166 Inter are found to be almost completely duplicated. This was the case for the 5-speed gearbox, the drive shaft, and the rear axle. The majority of the 195 Inters seem to have used the 2.50 metre wheelbase chassis, and in that case, a two piece drive shaft. Suspension was likewise unchanged, with the standard transverse leaf spring at the front and two parallel leaf springs at the rear. As with the 166 Inter, the

shock absorbers were Houdaille lever-type hydraulic units. Finally, Borrani Rudge Record wire wheels, size 15 x 400, were generally used.

The first salon for the 195 Inter seems to have been the one at Brussels, in January, 1951, where Ferrari also announced the 212 (2.6 litre) and the 340 (4.1 litre), two models to be discussed later. A short time later Franco Cornacchia, the Ferrari dealer in Milan, won a first place award at the concours d'elegance of Viareggio with the 195 he entered, a black Vignale coupe.

Certain characteristic traits of the 166 Inter Vignale coupes were recognizable on the 195 design by Michelotti of Vignale, notably the grill inclined toward the front and the unusual air intake formed by hollowing out the front bodywork. But the roof, blending into the trunk on a slightly bent plane, was heavier, and this effect was reinforced by the curve which delineated the fender above the rear wheel arches. Several 195s received Vignale bodies similar to this, at least in most respects, among them probably 0083 S, 0091 S, 0095 S, 0097 S, 0103 S, 0119 S, and 0151 S. (0085 S presently has a Touring berlinetta body, No. 3465, and and 0117 S has been defined as a Vignale Cabriolet.) This design was to be seen again on several 212s. However 0115 S, with the rear fenders not quite so delineated, and with a smoother, truer "fastback" roof line, with a larger rear window, had a more agreeable appearance.

At the Geneva Show, in March, 1951, it was the French Ferrari agent, Luigi Chinetti, who represented the Ferrari marque. (Previously, he had won their first victory, in 1949, at the 24 Hours of Le Mans.) Among the five Ferraris shown on his stand was a 195 Inter coupe by Ghia which exactly reproduced the design already seen on a 166 Inter. Easily recognizable on this gray-colored fastback coupe were the pure, compact lines, as well as the double volume grill seen on the original. Several weeks later, at the Turin Show, the 195 Inter reappeared in the form of a Ghia two-place coupe. The design was again the same, but the distribution of the decorative chrome pieces changed: The three beads extending the grill onto the hood were missing, as were the engine compartment ventilation holes on the front fenders. The beads along the lower body were smaller, and two slim beads were fitted to the ends of the rear fenders, lengthening the combination signal/taillights. This

Still by the same authors, 0115 S had a lighter and more agreeable fast-back rear.

This design by Ghia, already seen on a 166 Inter, clothed several 195 Inters.

steel body would clothe a fairly large proportion of the two- and four-place 195 Inters, among them 0087 S, 0089 S, 0093 S, 0101 S, 0105 S, 0109 S, 0113 S, 0121 S, and 0133 S. A very similar style was to be adapted to several 212s.

At the same 1951 Turin Show, Carrozzeria Touring presented on their own stand a fastback coupe derived from the Le Mans berlinetta presented a year earlier, a design a little heavier than the one already seen on several 166 Inters the previous year. Several improvements, however, were made: the grill was more vertical, the bumpers were missing, and the vent windows were made of thermoformed perspex as on the sporting berlinettas. But, in spite of this, the body waistline remained too high, the two-piece windshield was out-of-date, and the two-tone paint scheme (a novelty on Ferraris) added nothing to the design. Indeed, it suf-

As usual, several variations of details can be noted on this Ghia coupe, which was shown at the 1951 Turin Show.

At the same 1951 Turin Show, Touring presented on its stand a new interpretation of the well-known theme, which was beginning to be a bit dated.

fered in comparison with the magnificent Alfa Romeo 1900 coupe by the same body builder exhibited nearby. These shortcomings appear, unfortunately, to have been noticed by the customers of Maranello, and it appears very unlikely that the Milanese body builder clothed many more than three 195 Inters, the only known examples being 0081 S, 0085 S, and 0123 S.

A similar Touring coupe, equipped with heavy bumpers and a 36 mm carburetor, was the object of a road test of 800 miles which was published in the May 4, 1951, issue of the British weekly **Autosport**. From a standing start, 105 km/h (on the speedometer) was attained in 10 seconds, and 126 km/h was reached in 13.2 seconds. 192 km/h (again according to the speedometer) was reached several times on the road from Rheims to Lyon. "This is a truly beautiful vehicle and is a first-class example of the modern Italian

Although probably earlier, this coupe was equipped with a transparent "Aerlux" roof, a feature patented by Touring.

specialist coachbuilder's art. Whilst possessing a superb road performance, it has the comfort and manners of a luxurious family saloon" was the judgement given to this same Ferrari with which Roy Clarkson was preparing to dispute the Tulip Rally and later the 1st Tour de France.

Another competitive sidelight occurred at Monza on April 15, where the 3rd edition of the Coppa Inter Europa, a two-hour race reserved for vehicles in the "International Gran Turismo" class. Four 195 Inters were entered, for Salvatore Ammendola, F. Munz, Franco Cornacchia, and Madame Piazza, but they were totally dominated by the new 212 of Luigi Villoresi.

The fourth, and probably last, body builder to set his signature on the 195 Inter seems to have been Ghia S.A., a Swiss firm located in Aigle, in the Canton of Valais. Despite its name, this company, which was also a dealer for the Ferrari marque, had no connection with Carrozzeria Ghia of Turin. To them can be credited three 195 Inters, whose designs were all the work of the prolific Giovanni Michelotti. Two of them, quite similar, bore a great resemblance to the coupes built by Vignale on the same chassis. Their roof line, however, was less extended toward the rear, their windshield was in two parts, and, on one of them, there appeared an original convex grill. A third Ferrari from the same duo of stylist/body builder, a two-tone coupe, was unusual in having an oval grill incorporating the two headlights. These three exercises, however, did not leave a lasting impression.

This creation by Ghia S.A. (Switzerland) from a design by Giovanni Michelotti was not disagreeable although it was not too successful.

Since it was introduced almost simultaneously with the 212, it should come as no surprise that the 195 had a very brief career. Despite this short production run it was still subject to the constant changes being introduced. Thus the last examples of the type were fitted with the new gearbox built for the 212.

In less than one year the production of the 195 probably did not exceed 25 examples, with serial numbers running between 0081 S and 0209/EL, although 0209/EL has been identified now as a 212. To this figure can also be added a number of 166 Inters which seem to have been subsequently bored out to 2340 cc, this probably being the case with 053 S, 0067 S, and 0079 S among other possibilities. Again, 067/S is now listed as a 212, but this could be the result of a further bore increase.

This other exercise by the same tandem suffers from the awkwardness of the decoration.

I·E
The 212 Inter
1951-1953

Continuing the policy of increasing engine displacement for the street Ferraris, and thereby increasing their power, the 212 Inter came along quite quickly as a replacement for the 195. Like the latter, and once again in accord with the principles originally stated at Maranello, the new specifications proposed for the 212 were created for the race track and were proven in competition. As a result, the 212 can be considered as the end result of experience gained in two different areas—with the 166 and 195 touring vehicles on the one hand, and with the 212 Export competition vehicles on the other.

The 212, like all the Ferraris which preceded it, took its designation from its single cylinder displacement, which measured about 212 cc. This was achieved by means of a new bore of 68 mm, while the stroke remained unchanged at 58.8 mm, giving a total displacement of 2562.51 cc. On the sportive "Export" version, the 2.6 litre engine equipped with three dual throat carburetors of either 32 or 36 mm was given a

(Left) A 212 Inter chassis before delivery to the body builder: Here 0157 E before being consigned to Vignale.

The exterior appearance of the V-12 engine was changed very little from the earlier version.

power rating of 160 or 165 hp at 7000 rpm. This engine was mounted in a chassis of 2.25 metre wheelbase, reinforced on some vehicles by a tubular superstructure, designated in Italian "tuboscocca".

The 212 Export first appeared in competition at the beginning of the 1951 racing season. Of course, it was usually beaten in the general classification by its new sibling, the 4.1 litre "America", but it won several significant victories such as the Tour of Sicily with Vittorio Marzotto, the Coppa Inter Europa with Luigi Villoresi, and the Coppa Toscana with Gianni Marzotto. This was only the beginning of a long career for the 212 Export in the hands of a large number of private entrants and drivers.

It is difficult to be precise about the specifications of the street version of the 212 as they seem to differ from one example to the other. To add to the confusion, the Export designation of the competition version was also given to some touring 212s. Such was the case with one of the very first examples shown, a two-tone Vignale coupe shown at the Turin Show in April, 1951. However, adherence to the specifications presented in the first catalog for the type, sent out at the end of 1951, reveals a number of notable differences between the 212 Inter and the sports version. The single 36 DCF carburetor was mounted on a heated manifold, and the compression ratio was reduced to 7.5:1. Under

these conditions the power was given as 150 hp at 6500 rpm. The 2.60 metre wheelbase chassis was very little different from that of the 195, while the four leaf springs shown at the rear appear to have been fitted to only a few touring vehicles. The five-speed transmission was connected to the differential by a two-piece driveshaft, and with a number of optional final drive ratios, the top speed was given as between 183 and 196 km/h.

The example shown in the same catalog was a fastback coupe designed by Ghia, which resembled the bodies which that body builder had previously fitted to several 166 and 195 Inter chassis. The grill, however, was redone in a more classical oval shape, and the windows had a lengthened contour. Ghia adapted this design to several 212 Inters, with only minimal variations—examples including 0149 E, 0153 E, 0155 E, 0169 E, and 0185 E. This same firm also built several examples of an awkward coupe (one being 0189 E) fitted with two rear seats on the 212 chassis (this being among their last designs).

Note that the Ghia design received several refinements on the 212 Inter shown at the Turin Salon in 1952.

A four-place coupe typical of the Ghia style.

Ghia seems to have been the only body builder to have pre-ferred cloth over leather in the interior finishing of the Ferraris.

Michelotti and Vignale were among the first to clothe the 212 Inter. From the beginning, their designs showed a close relationship with those they had built for the 166 and 195, such as the fastback coupe with the very long profile and unusual roof whose supportive posts were reduced to the minimum by a panoramic rear window which wrapped around almost to the side windows. The thick moulding of the sides, however, lacked a certain elegance.

But the famous Turinese duo did not take long to produce an impressive assortment of designs. There was, at the very beginning, a series of three roadsters (0076 E, 0090 E, and 0098 E) with spare and squattish lines which were probably built on the short (2.25 metre) chassis of the sports version. A cabriolet (0110 E) was built in the same period for the Portuguese ambassador to France, which repeated the same design but with more abundant chrome trim. The radiator grill consisted of a cross motif, and the sides received a chrome strip whose end emphasized the beginning of the rear fender. Another cabriolet (0106 E) utilized the same design and decorative pieces but in better proportions. These same proportions were also used on a third cabriolet which differed from the preceding only by the use of a more conventional and lighter radiator grill of rectangular egg-crate design. Finally, it is necessary to also include in this second wave of Michelotti-Vignale 212s a coupe which harmoniously combined the body of the cabriolets and a very elegant two-window hardtop roof line.

Built in a style that was once again different from the preceding was a two-tone coupe, notable for its grill with rectangular egg-crate texture and incorporating a central headlight. A sizeable ridge on the hood necessitated locating the traditional Ferrari badge off center to the right, and to restore the symmetry a second enamelled insignia, inscribed "212 Export, 12 V, cc 2560", was placed on the left. Very similar bodywork clothed 0111 ES, 0157 EL, and 0181 EL (in this last case, a 195 destined for the actress Anna Magnani).

The design of the burgundy-colored coupe (0135 E) which was shown at the 1951 Paris Show was yet another new style. The rear fenders are marked by a slight projection above the wheel arches, and the most conspicuous details were the concave grill and the chrome trim which surrounds the hood lid and extended to the rear, as two slim strips, as far as the trunk. A very similar design clothed the two Vignale coupes (0131 E and 0161 E) with which Taruffi/Chinetti and Ascari/Villoresi captured the first two places in the Carrera Panamericana in November. Decoration on the hood had disappeared and the radiator grill was redesigned as a convex. An almost identical coupe (0146 E) was later built for the German enthusiast Kurt Zeller.

This coupe, shown at the 1951 Turin Salon, was one of the first 212 Inters by the Michelotti-Vignale tandem, and differed very little from the several 195 Inters of the same style.

In the same vein, the 212 Inter (0135 E) of the 1951 Paris Salon differed, however, by the grill and the chrome decor-decorations.

Another design by Michelotti and Vignale which was seen again, on a larger scale, on the Cunningham.

The same design certainly produced a better effect on these shorter and lower 212 Exports, which recall the 4.1 litre winner of the 1951 Mille Miglia with Villoresi.

The design also inspired several roadsters, which were particularyly attractive, on the 212 Export chassis.

Built to the order of the Portuguese ambassador to France, this cabriolet (0110 E) conserved the same proportions— and probably the short "Export" chassis—but the deçoration was too awkward.

This "Export" cabriolet (0106 E) represented a similar design, in proportions and nearly identical grill. (Above)

This cabriolet differed only by the rectangular texture of the grill. (Above right)

Still in the same vein was this agreeable two-place coupe.

While the theme remained the same, the principal variation here was the unification of the fenders. The two large gauges were standard equipment on the 212.

The third and last "official" body builder for the year 1951 was Touring, who shared with Vignale the responsibility for clothing the racing models from Maranello. This period saw, however, a considerable diminishing of the role of the Milanese body builder in the area of touring Ferraris. The only known examples are a few rare fastback coupes derived from the 1950 Le Mans Berlinetta, a design becoming a little out of date and which had already been seen on several 166 and 195 Inters. The most famous of these 212 Inters by Touring was certainly the "Aerlux" coupe (0143 E) which the racing driver Mike Hawthorn utilized for his personal transportation as well as for reconnoitering the route of the 1953 Mille Miglia.

This other Michelotti/Vignale theme from 1951 was to be used several times again, and notably on a 195 Inter destined for the actress Anna Magnani. The central ridge on the front body (above) dictated the use of two symmetrical badges.

Other than two creations by Ghia-Aigle and a single isolated effort by Abbott in England, Ghia, Vignale, and Touring bodied almost all of the first Ferrari 212 Inters. In 1952, this order of importance was somewhat upset by the great influence of a new design counselor on retainer at the factory. Carrozzeria Touring was the first to suffer the consequences, as much for the sports Ferraris (the great majority henceforth passing through Vignale's workshop), as for the street vehicles. In fact, there were few if any more than three 212 Inters to come from the shops at Milan—one or two coupes (such as 0215 EL) which represented the known design, and a curious barchetta to which we will return later.

Ghia likewise lost ground and their 212s became increasingly rare. Two cabriolets, noticeable for their windshields being a bit too high and for their partially covered rear wheels, obviously did not leave a lasting impression on the visitors to the 1952 Turin Show, where an example was on display. However, it was too bad that their two-window coupe (0213 EL) was not copied. This two-tone coupe combined the body of the 2 + 2 with a lighter roof line and a flatter trunk, and was a very agreeable design.

The adoption of a curved windshield was insufficient to rejuvenate the Touring design, which had persevered from 1948 despite several refinements.

Ghia also lost orders in 1952. This cabriolet shown at the 1952 Turin Salon undoubtable did nothing to help reverse the trend.

On the other hand, this elegant two-window coupe (0213 EL) does not lack appeal.

One of the last creations of Stablimenti Farina, before that firm went out of business, was shown at the 1952 Turin Show. It was in the form of a four-window coupe, and evoked in several details, memories of the 166 Inter Cabriolet presented at Paris in 1950. A vertical grill surmounted by a thick chrome "moustache" characterized this 212 Inter, the last Ferrari to be bodied by the great Turinese firm.

In 1951 and 1952, therefore, the majority of Ferraris had their bodies created by Carrozzeria Alfredo Vignale of Turin. For them, the stylist Michelotti and the body builder Vignale spared neither their imagination nor their skill. The inexhaustible variety of their creations was testimony to this, as much in the racing Ferraris as in the touring versions which interest us here. Several

On this attractive Vignale coupe of 1952, note the lengthened lines, the roof covered with vinyl, the 16" wheels, and the rectangular grill. The same theme was reutilized on 0211 EL but with a more oval grill and a squarer trunk.

Michelotti-Vignale coupes appeared at the beginning of 1952, and while they each differed one from the other in a number of details, they can be classified as in the same family, which constituted, in effect, the fourth style of Vignale 212. Their point in common is a rather rectilinear waist line, and on the sides, a moulded indentation which formed a right angle at the level of the door handle and swept down to the base of the rear wheel arch. Their detail treatments differed, however, on a number of points. One had a rectangular grill with square egg-crate texture and a roof covered with vinyl; on another (0211 EL), the roof had the same lines but was painted and the grill was distinctly oval. Finally, a third coupe was given a fastback roof, and its headlights were removed from the fenders and located in the grill.

The inspiration for this 195 or 212 coupe was similar. Note especially the different grill.

These two additional Vignale coupes presented quite well the common characteristics, but their decorations made them individualistic.

The fifth style of 212 Vignale was once again quite different. It was applied to several four-window coupes (such as 0217 EL) and had a rather massive appearance. The very oval grill had a rectangular egg-crate texture which soon became the trademark of all Ferraris. The raised contouring of the rear fenders reappeared, and a rather high waist line was underlined by a thick chrome trim piece, fortunately shorter than the wheelbase. Massive bumpers, looking a bit "American", were fitted as well.

Undoubtedly inspired by the 340 Mexicos, these designs, which were found on several 212 Inters in 1952, appear less successful to us.

Without doubt, several cabriolets could also be considered part of this fifth generation of Michelotti-Vignale 212s, some of them using the left-hand-drive chassis, which we will return to later. The most characteristic, 0227 EL, is recognizable by bumpers painted the same color as the body, and by its oval grill which re-utilized the cross motif seen in 1951.

It was at about this same time that there appeared what seems to have been the first Ferrari bodied by Pinin Farina, a two-place cabriolet of very classic lines. The grill was of generous dimensions, the fenders formed a single unit, and the top was particularly well integrated into the whole design. Its sole fault was perhaps the hood, made cumbersome by having two air scoops superimposed on it. Battista Farina, nicknamed "Pinin", and the youngest brother of the great

Giovanni Farina, thus made a quiet entry into the closed circle of Ferrari body builders, but his establishment on Corso Trapani, in Turin, would soon be exercising a greater and greater influence on the aesthetics of the vehicles from Maranello.

This same year of 1952 saw several technical innovations appear on the Ferrari 212 Inter. With new cylinder heads and three Weber 36 DCF/3 carburetors as standard equipment, the power was increased to 170 hp, at the same engine speed of 6500 rpm. The 2.60 metre wheelbase chassis was revised on several points, and the steering control underwent a profound alteration. At about this same time, the steering wheel, which earlier was always on the right side, was moved to the left side in the uniform fashion with few exceptions, this occurring after serial No. 0211. In a practice which also seemed to have been uniform, the suffix EL (Export Lungo) was replaced by the letters EU, which without doubt correspond to the designation Europa which was given on occasion to the 212.

In spite of a tentative thinning of the volume of the bumpers, this cabriolet (0227 EL) remained affected by the same heaviness.

The first Ferrari by Pinin Farina dated from this same year, 1952. The discrete design of this cabriolet does not fail, however, to be resounding!

In October, two 212s were shown with these new specifications at the Paris Salon. Ghia was responsible for the four-window coupe which resembled, particularly in the front where the headlights were located between the grill and the fenders, several creations made for the Chrysler Corporation by this body builder. But the two-tone paint scheme, which cuts the body in two, did not help to lighten the design. This last 212 by Ghia was destined for the Argentinian Chief of State, Juan Peron.

In comparison, the Pinin Farina cabriolet which was displayed beside it seemed to be very plain, especially since the upper air scoop had fortunately disappeared from the hood. In fact, this second Pinin Farina cabriolet (0235 EU) differed from the first only by the use of left hand drive and the fitting of slightly more prominent taillights. It became one of the many Ferraris owned by Roberto Rossellini, and he entered it in the first edition of the 1000 Kilometres of the Nurburgring in 1953. Vignolo and the rally driver Gatsonides, who replaced the famous director on the starting line after Rossellini was detained in Rome, adapted themselves quite well to the luxurious cabriolet and finished in ninth place.

At the 1952 Paris Salon, Ghia presented this coupe in a new style . . .

... but Pinin Farina presented a new cabriolet on
the same stand ...

. . . which only differed from the preceding by
the use of left-hand drive, generally maintained
on the 212 Inters.

At the first edition of the 1000 Kms. of the Nurburgring, a meritorious 9th place was earned by
Gastonides, Vignolo, and this elegant cabriolet
entered by Roberto Rossellini.

Meanwhile, Pinin Farina had modified the design of his 212 Inter coupe. Once again the sober lines of the two cabriolets were repeated, but the rear fenders were slightly projected and the grill, obviously pushed forward, appeared heavier. The roof of the two-place coupe had four windows and the very curved rear window was usually divided into three parts by the fitting of two ribs. The first example (0229 EL) was sold into the United States at the end of the year, and the first public presentation of the 212 Inter Pinin Farina coupe was at the Brussels Salon in January, 1953. Several detail refinements ultimately were made, the most important being the line of transition from the windshield to the roof, and the less prominent grill. Finally, some examples were given two supple-mentary seats in the rear, without any apparent external modifications.

In all, and in less than one year, more than 15 examples of the 212 Inter Pinin Farina coupe were produced. This was an important number of examples manufactured, and served to demonstrate the very rapid breakthrough of Pinin Farina in building bodies for the street Ferraris as well as the competition berlinettas and roadsters. In 1953, Vignale was forced to concede to the newcomer a sizeable portion of the body building for the Ferrari competition models, an area which Vignale held as a quasi-monopoly in 1952. Farina's impact was even greater with the touring Ferraris.

The first 212 Inter coupe by Pinin Farina appeared at the end of 1952. It was produced in a series of about 15 examples.

Several details were refined in the course of the
series, such as the unification of the windshield
and the roof, and the one-piece rear window, but
a certain standardization was born.

The sixth and last generation of the 212 Michelotti-Vignale designs made its appearance in March, 1953, at the Geneva Salon, in the form of an imposing red and black coupe with a strong relationship to the enormous 340 Mexicos created especially for the 1952 Carrera Panamericana. The waist line was once again higher than it was on the 212s of the preceding generation, which in turn reduced by the same amount the window area of the coupe, giving the appearance of an even more elongated roof line. As on the Mexico, the headlights were located between the fenders and the aggressive grill, which was strongly slanted towards the front. Beneath this grill of rectangular egg-crate texture, the bumper was reduced to a simple blade. Supplementary protection was provided on the point of the fenders and above the headlights by two horizontal buffers which were extended on the sides by two chromed strips. At the rear, a wrap-around bumper was located at the same height, duplicating the standard lower bumper. This style was, to say the least, flamboyant, and unfortunately it announced the end of the collaboration between Vignale and Ferrari. This last design was found on some seven 212 coupes— 0257 EU, 0267 EU, 0271 EU, 0273 EU (?), 0285 EU, 0287 EU, and 0289 EU, and one 250 Europa.

The last street Ferrari of Carrozzeria Touring Superleggera (0253 EU) also came during this period. It was probably built on special order from the Ford Motor Company, to whom it was sold at the end of 1952. This odd exercise consisted of adapting to the 212 chassis of 2.60 metre wheelbase the barchetta body style made famous by the 166 MMs of 1948. But the approximate 35 cm which had to be added between the doors and the rear wheels totally destroyed the agreeable proportions of the original design.

Michelotti and Vignale produced several coupes in this style—here and example (0267 EU) destined for a French client.

The career of the 212 Inter was ended by the "coming out", in October, 1953, of the 250 Europa and 375 America. It appears that the 2715 cc engine (Type 225), which successfully powered the Ferrari sports cars of 1952 and which gave birth in 1953 to the 250 MM, was not adapted in the usual manner to the 212s intended for touring. For these cars the succession will be directly from 2.6 litres to the 3 litre 250 Europa. Without doubt, however, there were some 212s which were enlarged to 2.7 litres and even to 3 litres. An example of this practice was shown in 0237 EU, a Vignale coupe similar in design to the 225 Sports, but which probably continued to use the chassis with 2.60 metre wheelbase. This car was used in several races by Franco Cornacchia as a 2.6 litre, then in 1954 it was raced by Bruno Moroni as a 3 litre.

The last 212 (0291 EU), a Pinin Farina coupe, brought the production total for this model to about 80 examples. Like the majority of the preceding Inters, their distribution was essentially European, if not to say Italian. The two new models which succeeded it took direct aim at a new horizon. It will be a new chapter in the Ferrari legend.

The same vehicle at the Concours d'Elegance of Enghien. The style, as flamboyant as Pinin Farina was sober, marked the end of the Vignale-Ferrari collaboration.

II
The Attraction of America
II·A
The 340 America
1951-1952

(Left) The "Long" V-12 engine designed by Ing. Aurelio Lampredi was used in touring versions for the first time in several 340 Americas.

This 340 America (0132 A) was given this slightly over-decorated coupe body by Michelotti and Vignale, which resembled a 212 Inter by the same authors

The consistent policy of having the Touring Ferraris profit from the lessons of the race track always prevailed at Maranello. We have already seen the proof of this several times, and the "civilized" use of the "Lampredi" V-12 engine provided a new demonstration. But, before considering the new type, it is necessary to pay a visit to the racing department at Maranello to learn the particulars of this engine.

At the end of the Grand Prix season of 1949, when it became evident that the supercharged 1500 cc V-12 engine was not going to end the supremacy of the Alfetta, it was decided to abandon the "1500 cc supercharged" formula in favor of the other authorized formula, that of 4500 cc normally aspirated. Because the physical dimensions of the "Colombo" V-12 block would not allow increasing the displacement to a sufficient size, it was deemed necessary to design a new V-12.

Engineer Aurelio Lampredi was put in charge of the project, and rather than being a complete innovation, the engine was, in fact, a derivation of the original Ferrari V-12. The principles did not change, but it had several notable differences. Undoubtably, the principal innovation was the dimensions. The spacing between the cylinder axis was increased from 90 mm to 108 mm, which allowed a considerable increase in the bore—up to 88 mm with the 4.9 litre 410 S of 1955. As a result the block gained 13 cm, its total length increasing from 94 to 107 cm. The other major innovation of the "long" block was the cylinder heads, which were not detachable and which had the cylinder liners screwed into them. This served to insure maximum sealing for the very high compression ratios which allowed the use of alcohol-mix fuels in the formula racing single seaters and in some of the sports/racing cars.

In April, 1950, a first version of the "long" engine was tested during the Mille Miglia in the sports barchettas of Villoresi and Ascari. At that time the displacement was 3.3 litres. It was raised to 4.1 litres in the Formula One monoposto of Ascari for the Swiss Grand Prix in July, and the goal of 4.5 litres was attained at the Italian Grand Prix in September, 1950.

Meanwhile, a 4.1 litre sports version had been announced and it was presented with the name 340 America, at the Paris Salon in October, 1950. A catalog published at the same time gave a summary description and revealed that the 4101.68 cc displacement was the result of a bore and stroke of 80 and 68 mm. With a compression ratio of 8.0:1 and three Weber dual throat 40 mm carburetors, the announced power was 220 hp at 6000 rpm. The five-speed synchronized gearbox was attached to the engine, with power transmitted through a single disc clutch, and the chassis continued the classical characteristics already revealed.

It appeared that the decision to sell a street version of the new 4.1 litre was made very soon, for in March, 1951, visitors to the Turin Salon saw, in the display of Carrozzeria Touring, a two-tone Ferrari coupe whose uniqueness was not so much the body style — a not very seductive adaption of the 166 Mille Miglia "Le Mans" with a rounded and cumbersome rear — but the suspected 4.1 litre displacement of the engine. It was almost completely overlooked, which was not surprising in that the 340 Americas were just beginning to compete. The differences between the sports and the touring versions could be explained minimally as better trim for the touring version and a dry sump lubrication system that seems to have been an exclusive feature of the sports version. (The habit of the men at Maranello, however, was to be always changing and perfecting their thoroughbreds, which does not make the task of the historian easy.)

This 340 America roadster (0140 A), with a style that leaned toward the 1952 Vignale touring roadsters, is, in our opinion, much more seductive.

These first street versions of the 340 America, which retained the right hand drive of the sports version, were also numbered in the same even numbered sequence. The Turin coupe was, without doubt, 0122 A and, after several body modifications, was sold to Belgium and became the first Ferrari of the very enthusiastic Blaton brothers, "Blary" and "Beurlys"

The second (or third) touring 340 America (0130 AL) was an awkward 2 + 2 coupe designed by Ghia, and was shown at the Paris Salon in October of the same year. It was, after the Pegaso 102, the most powerful vehicle shown. It had an "exemplary" career, for it was acquired by David Brown, then president of Aston Martin-Lagonda. (The Lagonda 4.5 litre V-12 appeared in 1954!)

Vignale also figured on the list of body builders for the 340 America, having to their credit at least one coupe (0132 A), but the design by Michelotti did not benefit by the excessive use of chrome trim. There followed a series of another four or five Ghia coupes recognizable by a fast-back roof line squatted at the rear behind a long, drawn-out hood. One of them

Ghia gave several 340 America chassis this 4-place body, which was adapted as well to several 212 Inters.

(0148 A) became the first Ferrari of Michel Paul-Cavallier, president of Pont-a-Mousson, who shortly thereafter became one of the few non-Italian members of the board of directors of Ferrari. The Argentine head of state, Juan Peron, also owned one of these Ghia coupes (0142 A). Yet another (0150 A), owned by the American Tony Parravano, acquired considerable fame in the hands of Jack MacAfee and Ernie MacAfee by finishing an excellent fifth in the Carrera Panamericana.

Of a total of 22 of the 340 Americas that were built, it seems that there were not more than eight street versions, as best as these latter types can be distinguished from the sports versions.

Also by Ghia, this 2-place fastback bodywork equipped at least three 340 Americas, among them the one with which Jack and Ernie MacAfee finished 5th in the 1952 Carrera Panamericana.

Galleria

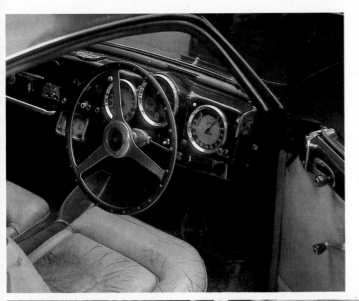

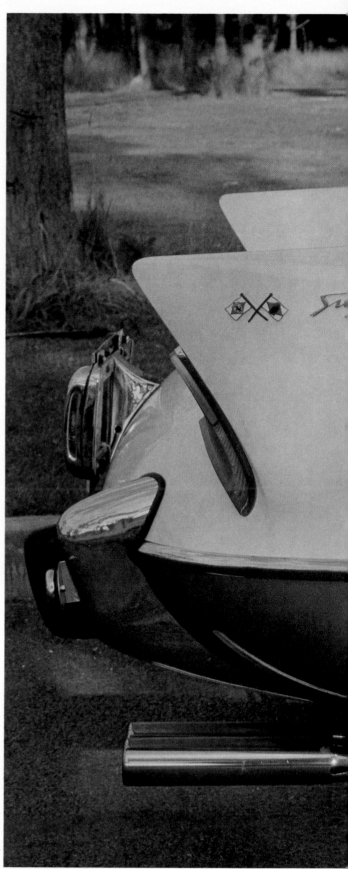

II·B
The 342 America
1952-1953

(Left) The 342 America mechanical unit, with its "long" engine characteristic of the Lampredi design. In comparison with the 340 America, note the different air filters and the new 4-speed gearbox.

This Pinin Farina 342 America cabriolet (0234 AL) was delivered to the King of Belgium in late 1952.

During the winter of 1952-1953, when the 340 America sports version was nearing the end of its career, a more civilized version of the 4.1 litre, the 342 America, came along to take the place of the street version of the 340 America. The 2.65 metre wheelbase chassis of the 342 retained the classic ladder design, but the front and rear tracks were increased. The major innovation was the transmission — a new four-speed synchronized gearbox coupled to the engine by a dry single disc clutch. The differential, as well, was redesigned and reinforced.

Being a purely touring vehicle, the 342 America was, therefore, quite different from the contemporary 4.1 litre sports versions. These cars, first the 340

On this 342 America coupe (0234 AL) with unusual door locks, note the lines of the Pinin Farina 212 Inter, but with the heavy grill pushed forward. This was a common trait of all the 342 Americas by the Turinese coachbuilder.

Mexico and then, in 1953, the 340 Mille Miglia, both with more powerful engines, were equipped with new chassis, retaining the five-speed gearbox and multi-disc clutch. Another distinctive feature of the 342 America was the left hand drive, with the sports versions retaining the right hand drive. At the same time, several innovations found on the 342 America chassis, notably the idea of a reinforced rear axle, were fitted to the sports version.

With a cataloged rating of 200 hp at 6000 rpm, the "long" 4.1 litre V-12 gained in flexibility but lost slightly in power. The accent was on luxury, and the 342 America became both fast and comfortable.

Left-hand drive was standard, as on the last 212 Inters, but note the different location of the two gauges.

In the same vein was this Pinin Farina coupe (0242 AL). It was, however, made awkward by the air scoops superimposed on the hood. Another example (0246 AL) differed only by having a rectangular rear window.

Shown at the New York Show, the last 342 America (0248 AL) hid a 4.5 litre engine. Undoubtedly it announced the 375 America.

For the bodywork, Pinin Farina appeared to have enjoyed an almost complete monopoly. After several 212 Inters, the Turinese body builder, who was still just starting out with Ferrari, was charged with bodying five of the six 342 Americas built, Vignale having apparently built only one cabriolet (0232 AL). The five examples, consisting of two cabriolets and three coupes, were all of the same style, having a slightly compact silhouette but with a front made heavy by a voluminous vertical and protruding grill. In addition, the double air scoops on the hoods of four of these cars did not improve their appearance.

The 342 America had a very brief production run with the six examples apparently being built in a span of less than four months, between October, 1952 and January, 1953. Their serial numbers were spread between 0232 AL and 0248 AL, the suffix AL signifying America "Lungo" in reference to the long wheelbase chassis.

It should be noted in passing that two obviously sportive vehicles, a Pinin Farina berlinetta (0236) and a Vignale spyder (0238), were built in this same period. They should probably be considered as the last of the 340 America sports versions even though they are sometimes referred to as 342 Americas.

The last 342 America (0248 AL) was shown at the New York International Motor Show, in January, 1953. The fact that this Pinin Farina cabriolet was fitted with an engine not of 4.1 litres but instead, 4.5 litres, was undoubtably a harbinger of the future. The power of the luxurious America was to be increased, and this would be the mission of the 375 America.

Model Data

342 AMERICA

S/N	Body Style	First Owner	Last Known Owner
0232 AL	Vignale cabriolet	O. Wild (CH)	N. Snart (USA)
0234 AL	PF cabriolet	King Leopold (B)	(USA)
0240 AL	PF coupe	Comm. Monti (I)	Andersson (S)
0242 AL	PF coupe		C. Tillitson (USA)
0246 AL	PF coupe	Geneva Salon 1953	W. Peters (USA)
0248 AL	PF cabriolet	New York Show 1953	A.H. Meyer (USA)

II·C
The 375 America
1953-1955

Ferrari
375 AMERICA
4 Litres 500 · 240 km/h
Coupé P. FARINA

(Left) The 375 America was revealed at the Paris Salon in October, 1953, in the form of this imposing light blue and gray Pinin Farina coupe.

Of the dozen examples produced from 1953 to 1955, at least seven repeated this design—with, of course, numerous variations . . .

To replace the 212 Inter, which had been quite successful, and the 342 America, which had a very limited production, Ferrari focused on two models for 1953. These were to have very different objectives although they shared a number of common elements. In fact, the 250 Europa and the 375 America were almost identical, the only difference being their engine displacements and, therefore, their performance. Their respective designations serve to sufficiently explain the differences: 3 litres for the 250 made especially to the European roads and the 4.5 litres (375 cc per single cylinder) for the 375 undoubtedly intended to be at an advantage on the American highways.

The two models were revealed to the public at the same time, on the occasion of the 1953 Paris Auto Show, traditionally held in the Grand Palace during the first two weeks of October. The 250 Europa will

be discussed later, the 375 America being the model which interests us here. The journalist John Bolster, writing in **Autosport**, referred to the car in this manner: "Of the continental high performance cars, none was more desirable than the new 4.5 Ferrari. This magnificent machine appeared with a Pinin Farina occasional four hard-top, in light blue and gray. As would be expected, the driving position was just about perfect, and the short central gear lever was ideally situated." The design of the coupe was reminiscent of the one created at the end of 1952 by the same Turinese body builder for the sportive 250 Mille Miglia, with proportions fitted to a chassis with a wheelbase of 2800 mm, the longest that was ever used on a Ferrari.

In order to accommodate this sizeable increase in length, the traditional "Ladder" chassis used previously was replaced by a new design, enlarged and reinforced by a larger network of stronger tubing, following the example of the contemporary sports/racing versions. The suspension, however, avoided innovations. Still being used were the Houdaille lever shocks and the transverse leaf spring at the front.

The long Lampredi V-12 engine, increased to 4522 cc displacement by a bore of 84 mm, was rated at 300 hp at 6300 rpm with a compression ratio of 8:1 and three 40 mm dual-throat Weber carburetors. By comparison, the 375 MM was rated at 340 hp at 7000 rpm with the same engine but had a compression ratio of 9:1 and three Weber four-barrel carbure-

tors. The 375 America engine was a civilized version of a sports/racing engine, which in turn was itself a derivation of the V-12 Formula One engine of 1950, the ancestor of the Lampredi V-12.

A new four-speed gearbox, fully synchronized, with direct drive in fourth gear, was connected to the engine by a dry multi-disc clutch. Three optional rear axle ratios listed in the catalog allowed maximum speeds from 232 to 250 km/h.

The competitive forays for this imposing Ferrari, with a more luxurious than sporting image, have not to our knowledge been previously detailed. With one example (0317 AL), however, Jacques Swaters and Alois de Mencik, its owner, won the over two litre class in the 1954 Geneva Rally, narrowly missing the overall victory. Among other owners of 375 Americas were the Italian director Roberto Rossellini and the French watchmaker Fred Lip, two faithful European Ferraristi who seem to have appreciated the type as much as the Americans — traditional advocates of large displacement engines — for whom the type was originally intended.

. . . the most important being the location of the steering wheel and the treatment of the roof line.

Jacques Swaters and Alois de Mencick narrowly missed an overall victory in the 1954 Geneva Rally with 0317 AL. Here it is shown at the start of a speed event on the Rheims circuit.

Vignale presented this bright yellow coupe (0327 AL), which did not want for air vents, at the 1954 Turin Salon. Except for a few details, this design was the same as that which had already been shown at the New York Show on a 250 Europa (see p. 119).

The production of the 375 America did not seem to have exceeded ten to twelve examples, whose serial numbers are found from 0293 to 0355 AL. The suffix designated the type (America) and the L (Lungo) made reference to the long chassis. Pinin Farina claimed nine examples, there being nine coupes similar, except for a few details, to the one shown at the 1953 Paris Salon. The most notable differences concerned the treatment of the "greenhouse", which included a wrap-around rear window and single side windows on some examples, or a normal rear window and rear quarter windows on others.

More variable than the equipment and the decoration was the range of available colors, a large selection made even larger by the use of metallic paints. In general, the colors most often used were sober, even somber, as befitted these vehicles with a great deal of "class". While the competition oriented cars of Maranello almost always bore colors that were bright and flashy, like the famous "rosso chiaro", the touring vehicles coming from Pinin Farina were generally discrete, with grays, blues, and very dark blue-grays. A second color was often used on the roof, and sometimes for the lower body although this was an unusual exception. Today one sees touring Ferraris of this type or from this period repainted bright red, to make them more "Ferrari" or more "racey". Whether or not this makes them more "Ferrari" is certainly a matter of taste.

The years 1953 and 1954 accented to a great degree the rapprochement between the manufacturer of Maranello and the body builder of 107 Corso Trapani. It appeared that Vignale did not body more than two or three 375 Americas. One of them was shown at the 1954 Turin Show in the form of a canary yellow coupe made rather awkward by a profusion of air vents of all types. The other was a cabriolet (0353 AL) for which Giovanni Michelotti produced an original and pleasant design, but the wrap-around windshield and reversed windshield pillar — obvious concessions to the American sytle — did not meet with universal acceptance.

Another 375 America by the same coachbuilder. This cabriolet (0353 AL) had an "American" windshield typical of the period.

With the 375 MM berlinetta (0456 AM) shown at the 1954
Paris Salon, Pinin Farina successfully created one of the most
significant exercises of automotive body design.

One of the most beautiful results of the young collaboration between Ferrari and Pinin Farina was certainly the 375 Mille Miglia berlinetta (0456 AM) shown at the 1954 Paris Show. Writing in the magazine **Autosport**, John Bolster was positively lyrical, but he interpreted quite well the impressions felt by all the visitors: "This poem is not merely the most beautiful car at the Salon; it is, in my opinion, the loveliest machine that has ever been exhibited at any motor show." Built for Ingrid Bergman who, however, never took delivery, this incontestable masterpiece is considered here even though it used the chassis of the sports version, the 375 MM. It marked the beginning of a completely new direction in the area of aerodynamics, and was a reservoir of almost inexhaustible ideas for the Turinese body builder. Among the innovations which became, sooner or later, the accepted style were the retractable headlights, the dynamic air intake for the carburetors, and the bare grill located very low which dictated a plunging hood line. This latter became a characteristic trait of the Pinin Farina Ferraris, the sports versions at first and then, rather quickly, the touring examples. The idea was also soon adopted by the majority of the manufacturers of sports/racing cars. In a way, it was the end of the radiator grill the last survivor of the very unaerodynamic blocks of the pre-war period.

Another revolution in this unique berlinetta was the treatment of the roof line and rear deck. The rear window was, in effect, set into the roof, between two sail panels which extended all the way to the rear in two parallel fins, this entire ensemble lifting upward to provide a large trunk opening. This design was to be used on a number of Pinin Farina Ferrari bodies, and the 308 GTB/GTS and the 512 BB of 1979 are continuing evidence of this.

In a different genre, the cabriolet (0488 AM) built in late
1954 for the King of Belgium was another masterpiece to be
added to the ledger of Pinin Farina.

On a different theme, the cabriolet built at the end of 1954 for the former King of Belgium on a special chassis with a 4.9 litre 375 Plus engine (0488 AM) was another masterly successful example of balance, finesse, and sober elegance. The streamlined covered headlights, the large oval mouth, and the irreproachable union of lines and masses gave a feeling of unfailing refinement all the way to the rear. These lines were to be found again on the magnificent 410 Sport of 1955 and, even later still, on the famous 250 GT Spyder Californias. At Pinin Farina, this admirable cabriolet had the nickname "the special which never grows old" ("la fuoriserie che non invecchia"). Twenty-five years later, it still qualifies as not being a day out of date.

Before leaving for the coachbuilder, 0488 AM was tested "in chassis" on the roads near Maranello. Note the shorter chassis and the 375 Plus engine with ignition by magnetos.

At the Turin Salon, in March, 1955, Ghia presented their own interpretation of the 375 America, a two-place, two-window coupe whose lines lacked neither aggressiveness nor originality, but which were not enhanced by the excessive decorations nor by another concession to the American style a three-tone paint job.

At the same 1955 show, Pinin Farina presented on their own stand a 375 America (0355 AL) specially bodied to the order of Giovanni Agnelli, the future president of Fiat. This two-place coupe was fitted with the inset rear window characteristic of the "Bergman" 375 MM but the design was somewhat unbalanced by a square front and a vertical grill!

Ghia displayed this slightly awkward 375 America (0347 AL) at the 1955 Turin Salon.

The last 375 America was this strange berlinetta (0355 AL) built by Pinin Farina to a special order, and displayed at the 1955 Turin Salon.

The blunt front and the finned rear did not make a very harmonious ensemble.

See the 375 America Model Data on Page 121.

Destined to replace the 212 Inter, the 3 litre 250 Europa was the twin sister of the 375 América and it deviated in a number of ways from the trail blazed by the 2.6 litre which preceded it. With the exception of the engine displacement, the Europa was actually identical to the America which was introduced at the same time. In the interest of uniformity, the chassis, engine design, and gearbox were the same on the two models. Even the Pinin Farina bodies, which clothed the great majority of the Europas and Americas, were identical, or very similar, as we will see later.

Undoubtably, it was the desire for uniformity which led to the abandonment of the "short" V-12 which powered the 212 (in 2.6 litre version) and continued, in the 3 litre version, to power the sportive 250 Mille Miglia. It was replaced by a "Lampredi" V-12 reduced to 3 litres, which allowed it to be fitted without modifications into the chassis that was common to the two new models. This engine was actually descended from the 250 S "experimental" which won the 1952 Mille Miglia with Giovanni Bracco. With a bore equal to the stroke (68 mm), it was one of the very rare strictly "square" engines in the history of Maranello.

With three 36 mm Weber dual-throat carburetors (in place of the 40 mm carburetors on the 4.5 litre engine, this being the only visible difference between the two engines), the 250 (Type 103) was rated at 200 to 220 hp, depending upon the catalog consulted. The maximum speed quoted varied between 180 and 217 km/h, depending on the rear axle ratio chosen from among the three available. The decreased power dictated the use of shorter ratios than those of the 375. There does not exist, however, a detailed test of this vehicle which would confirm or deny these figures, nor is there any knowledge of it having a competitive career. Several witnesses of those bygone days agree in the remembrance of the type as having its charms, but being too heavy for easy handling.

(Left) The new reinforced chassis with 2800 metre wheelbase was common to both the 250 Europa and the 375 America.

Only the size of the carburetors permitted external differentiation between the "long" 3 litre and the 375 America engine.

At the 1953 Paris Salon, the 250 Europa which shared the stand of the Franch importer, Autoval, with the 375 America, was an imposing Vignale coupe. Giovanni Michelotti was evidently the designer, for it somewhat resembled the aggressive 340 Mexico coupes of the 1952 Carrera Panamericana and even more closely resembled several 212 Inters built late in the year. But a very high waist line, a window area reduced by the same proportion, and a profusion of chrome regrettably dulled the appearance of this vehicle. The Michelotti-Vignale duo also created a 250 Europa two-window coupe with a panoramic rear window that was similar, except for the location of the headlights,

to the 375 America shown at the 1955 Turin Salon. This was one of their last orders for a customer of Maranello.

The total production for this model was about 21 examples, built in less than one year, from September, 1953 to July, 1954. Of this number, Pinin Farina was responsible for at least 16 coupes and one cabriolet. The coupes, usually four-place, are similar to those built for the 375 America, with the two styles of greenhouse and the personalized variations of detail, paint schemes, and chrome accessories. Unique for the type was the cabriolet "Ariowitch" (0311 EU), named for its first owner, which was shown at the New York Show in January, 1954. It was the one and only 250 Europa Cabriolet constructed.

Finally, it should be noted that the vast majority of the 250 Europas which survive today are refugees in America.

Before the end of 1954, a new 3 litre V-12, the 250 Gran Turismo, took the place of the Europa, and this model met with great success from the very beginning of its production.

The 250 Europa was unveiled at the 1953 Paris Salon with this body by Vignale, which was even less successful than the body design used on the last 212 Inters by Vignale.

At the 1954 New York Show, Luigi Chinetti displayed "in bulk" his single-seater 1953 Indianapolis 500 car, a 375 MM Pinin Farina Spyder, a 225 Sport Vignale Berlinetta, and in their midst, a 250 Europa Vignale Coupe. The same design was adapted to several other Ferraris in 1954.

At the same 1954 New York Show, Pinin Farina presented this special cabriolet (0311 EU), which was the only 250 Europa convertible made.

At least 15 of the approximately 22 250 Europas were clothed by Pinin Farina with these bodies, similar to those of the 375 America, with the principal variation being the treatment of the roof line.

Model Data

375 AMERICA (AL)—250 EUROPA (EU)

S/N	Body Style	First Owner	Last Known Owner
0293 AL	Pinin Farina coupe	H. Keck (USA)	H. Keck (USA)
0299 EU (?)	Pinin Farina coupe	R. Rossellini (I)	
0301 EU	Vignale coupe	Paris Salon 1953 (?)	
0303AL	Pinin Farina coupe	Bruxelles Salon 1954	J. Morley (GB)
0305 EU	Pinin Farina coupe	Magnolfi	
0307 AL	Pinin Farina coupe	F. Lip (F)	H. Raab (USA)
0309 EU	Pinin Farina coupe		E. Waterman (USA)
0311 EU	Pinin Farina cabriolet	Ariowitch (USA)	B. Shadlun (USA)
0313 EU	Vignale coupe	New York Show 1954	L. Renick (USA)
0315 AL(?)	Pinin Farina coupe		B. Shadlun (USA)
0317 AL	Pinin Farina coupe	A. de Mencik (B)	A. de Mencik (B)
0319 AL	Pinin Farina coupe	Carpenter (USA)	E. Waterman (USA)
0321 EU	Pinin Farina coupe	F. Ferrario (I)	J. Lombardi (USA)
0323 EU	Pinin Farina coupe (1)	Stockholm Show 1954	
0325 EU	Pinin Farina coupe	J. Murray	
0327 AL	Vignale coupe	Geneva Salon 1954 (?)	J. Marchetti (USA)
0329 AL	Pinin Farina coupe	Parravano (USA)	(USA)
0331 EU	Pinin Farina coupe	Count Somsky (CH)	J. Lombardi (USA)
0333 EU	Pinin Farina coupe (1)	Brinolf (S)	R. Tomson (S)
0335 EU	Pinin Farina coupe	Castillon du Peron (F)	G. Londi (USA)
0337 AL	Vignale coupe	Turin Salon 1954 (?)	B. Shadlun (USA)
0339 AL	Pinin Farina coupe	Cornacchia	D. Dethlefsen (USA)
0341 EU	Pinin Farina coupe	S. Bianchi	J. Hamm (CDN)
0343 EU	Pinin Farina coupe	Barge	J. Hall (USA)
0345 EU	Pinin Farina coupe	Stimson	R. Tarwacki (USA)
0347 AL	Ghia coupe ?		
0349 EU	Pinin Farina coupe		
0351 EU	Pinin Farina coupe	C. Brown (F)	S. Baker (USA)
0353 AL	Vignale cabriolet		W. Golomb (USA)
0355 AL	Pinin Farina special	Turin Salon 1955	E. Andrews (USA)

(1) Right Hand Drive

While the pace of production of the 250 GT, the new 3 litre that appeared at the end of 1954, continued to develop, a new Ferrari appeared in 1955 to take the place of the 375 America. The 410 Superamerica, as the car in question came to be called, represented important progress in the desgn of the engine, the chassis, and the body.

The "Lampredi" V-12, intensively tested in the Grand Prix single seaters (in 1951) and in the sports racers (up to 1954) was retained, but its displacement was increased to almost 5 litres (4962 cc) by the adoption of new cylinder liners giving a bore dimension of 88 mm. The rated power listed in the catalog was 340 hp at an engine speed of 6000 rpm. This engine (Type 126) was aimed, by the way, primarily at the American market, the traditional demander of large displacements, and remains (as of 1978) the largest to have ever powered a touring Ferrari.

In a similar fashion, the 2800 mm wheelbase chassis used for the 410 Superamerica also underwent an important revitalizing treatment, coming back to the solutions already in use on the 250 GT, especially in the area of the suspension. At the front, the coil springs replaced the single transverse leaf spring, and at the rear, the lever action shock absorbers were relocated beneath the side members of the new chassis

(Type 514). The front and rear tracks were increased by 130 mm. The four-speed synchronized transmission with direct drive in fourth gear was unchanged but the shift pattern was a bit unconventional in that, on the majority of these vehicles, first gear was found forward and to the right, and fourth was back and to the left. A range of optional rear axle ratios were available, from 9/33 to 9/28, and the announced maximum speed varied according to the ratio chosen — between 220 and 260 km/h at 6000 rpm. However, we have not been able to find a contemporary road test that would allow us to verify these figures.

(Left) The 410 Superamerica was unveiled "in chassis" at the 1955 Paris Salon. Note the new design of the chassis, which henceforth will pass above the rear axle.

Displayed along side two 250 GT 3 litre engines, the 410 SA engine showed its slightly greater length.

The chassis/engine ensemble had its world premier at the 1955 Paris Salon, but it was necessary to attend the Brussels Salon, in January, 1956, to view the completed vehicle. This 410 SA bodied by Pinin Farina was an altogether aggressive and refined design. The lines were similar to those created at about the same time for the 250 GT Boano (see page   ), with an almost rectilinear window sill line and a prominent oval grill. But the larger dimensions of the 410 SA gave it a more fluid and aggressive appearance. A discrete moulding shaped the contour of the rear fender and continued along the lower part of the body, pleasantly alleviating the side elevation, and the generous window area with the wrap-around rear window accentuated the refined elegance of this prestigous coupe.

The 410 Superamerica was without direct competition — it was alone in its class. Its price, of course,

The Pinin Farina body design was introduced at the Brussels Salon, in January, 1956. It was adapted to about sixteen vehicles, with numerous variations. Here is shown the 1956 Paris Salon car.

was quite high and was established "in accordance to specifications". At the New York Show, where a very similar blue-gray coupe was displayed several weeks after the Belgian show, the sum total of the bill came to $16,800. By way of comparison, the 250 GT coupe next to it was announced at $12,800.

From the end of 1955 to the end of 1956, the production total of the 410 SA was on the order of 14 examples, whose serial numbers (odd numbers only) were from 0423 SA to 0497 SA. About nine vehicles were bodied by Pinin Farina in a fashion similar to the coupe unveiled at Brussels.Similar, but not identical, because each was individually built and each differed one from the other in details, for example in the arrangement of the grill, the ventilation ports for the engine compartment, and even in the location of the body builder's emblems.

A functional and refined interior.

On this 410 Superamerica, being tested at Maranello during
the Winter of 1955-56, note the similarity between the Pinin
Farina design and that used by several European
constructors.

Although built as a series, the 410 Superamerica Pinin Farina coupes still presented variations. For instance the dark green coupe (0481 SA) of the watch manufacturer Fred Lip received a deflector typically used on more sporting Ferraris. Also note the absence of fender vents.

At least four vehicles received bodies that were truly special. The least surprising was certainly not the long red coupe (0473 SA) signed by Ghia. Mario Savonuzzi, then chief stylist at this Turinese carrozzeria, had created, several months earlier, the celebrated Chrysler "Gilda" whose styling was found for several years on American Chrysler production cars. The adaptation of this theme to the Superamerica was, to say the least, extraordinary.

For this 410 SA built by Ghia (0473 SA), the stylist Mario Savonuzzi resumed the theme originally created for the Chrysler dream cars, the "Gilda" and the "Dart". The American influence was effective to the extreme, and even the classic Nardi steering wheel was abandoned.

Carrozzeria Boano, newly established in Turin by Mario Boano and his son, Gian Paolo, both formerly with Ghia, seemed to be more attracted to Detroit than to Maranello. Their two 410 SAs, a coupe (0477 SA) and a cabriolet (0485 SA) were also sacrificed to the invading vogue of fins. In these two cases, the fins were created by an unusual concave moulding on the rear flanks. The divided design of the rear window on the coupe was a feature also found on the Czechoslovakian Tatra.

The new Carrozzeria Boano was more classical. This coupe (0477 SA), with its unusual two-part rear window, recaptured the style of the 250 GT cabriolet created some time earlier, a theme also adapted to a 410 SA cabriolet (0485 SA).

The most impressive, and the most special, of the 410 SAs was certainly the Superfast of Pinin Farina. Unveiled at the Paris Salon, in October, 1956, this impressive "dream car" (0483 SA) was certainly interesting for the styling exercise it represented, but perhaps it was even more interesting for the technical solutions not found on the other 410 SAs. Its 4.9 litre engine had the unique distinction of being equipped with an ignition system of 24 spark plugs, the supplementary row of plugs being fitted on the outer side of each cylinder bank, between the exhausts. This set-up was inaugurated in 1951 on the 375 Formula One car, and this 410 SA engine was probably one of those which served as an experiment for the 410 Sport. Two Scaglietti roadsters were actually equipped, at the end of 1955, with this competition derivation of the 410 SA which had, in addition, a dry sump lubrication system which was not used on the Superfast. The power of this engine, which also benefitted from the fitting of 42 mm carburetors, has never been revealed. It can, however, be estimate from those announced for the 410 SA and the 410 Sport, which were between 340 and 360 hp.

Another pecularity of the Superfast was its chassis, still a Type 514 but with a wheelbase of 260 cm, reduced by 20 cm from the Type 514 of the 410 SA. Otherwise there were no major differences, and the transaxle of the sports version was not adapted to the Superfast.

The uncontested star of the 1956 Paris Salon was the 410 Superfast (0483 SA) by Pinin Farina. Posing beside the car is the Spanish marquis and race driver "Fon" Portago; behind it (second person from the right), is Sergio Farina, the body builder.

Shown in the Pinin Farina shop, Superfast (0483 SA) displayed the compact lines which were adapted to a 410 SA chassis shortened by 20 cm. (below right)

Last but not least among the attractions of this genuine special was its bodywork, which marked an important stage in the history of Pinin Farina, to the extent that its influence was seen in the style of future years and future Ferraris. The body was cut by a low chrome strip, the effect of which was reinforced by the two-tone paint — white above, light blue below. The long oblong grill and the streamlined covered headlights were also an important change, inherited from the 290 MMs and 860 Monzas of 1956, and found later on a number of Ferraris, both sports and grand touring. The whole was a rather pure effect, even if the fins formed by the rear fenders were not to everyone's taste. Finally, the windshield was without posts, a final novelty similar to the "Vutotal" apparatus created by Labourdette in the 1930s.

After being displayed at the principal European salons, the Superfast was sold, as were most of the Pinin Farina specials, but not before it was deemed advisable to give it a windshield with conventional supports.

The oblong grill and covered, streamlined headlights established a school of design.

At the beginning of 1957, the 2.60 metre wheel-base chassis already used for the Superfast was adopted as standard for the 410 SA. Because of this, it became convenient to refer to these as "Series 2" even though the official designation, Type 514, did not seem to have been changed. The Pinin Farina design revealed at the 1956 Brussels Salon was not otherwise changed and only a close observation revealed that the 20 cm had been very discretely taken out of the length of the doors. The 410 SA coupe "Series 2" was produced in about seven examples during the year 1957 and the last one (0721 SA) was shown at the Turin Salon in November. As with the preceding series, they were all standard with some slight variations in the finishing details.

Beginning in 1957, the 410 SA adopted a chassis with 2.60 metre wheelbase. In this photograph of the 1957 Turin Salon car (0721 SA), it is noticeable that the 20 cm were taken up in the doors.

Another example of personalization: the special rear of this 410 SA "Series 2" (0713 SA).

At the 1957 Cannes Concours d'Elegance, this 410 Super-america coupe captured a first place, ahead of the English limousine pictured at its side. The two vehicles belonged to the same person, Mr. Norman. Can Pinin Farina be suspected of favoritism . . .

In addition to these seven Pinin Farina coupes, there were two truly special "Series 2" 410 SAs, notable chiefly for their bodywork. The 410 SA (0671 SA) bodied by Scaglietti to the order of Dr. Wax of Genoa was, in fact, completely original even though the design of its roof line bore a resemblance to that of the Superfast. The rounded lines and lowered grill also vaguely recalled the sportive creations of this Modenese body builder built for the Maranello marque, but the finish was perhaps pushed a bit too far. The stainless steel roof, the bumperette bumpers, the ventilation of the lower body, and the fins fitted to the rear contrast violently with the red body and the plastic silver and blue interior fittings and bucket seats. On opening the trunk, two 50 litre tanks were found fitted into the rear fenders.

The ideas in the Superfast were re-utilized by its creators in the "4.9 Superfast" (0719 SA) which left the workshops of Grugliasco in October, 1957. In contrast to the first Superfast, the engine used here was the 4.9 litre with single ignition equipped, however, with 42 mm Webers instead of the standard 40 mm. As for the design, it retained, happily, the better lines of the Paris Salon car of 1956. The chromed body belt gave way to a simple crease line and the fins were, thankfully, replaced by receding fenders which harmonized with the rear deck. On this rear deck there

appeared the inscription "Ferrari 4.9 Superfast". A simple wrap-around bumper replaced the vertical bumperettes at the rear although they were retained at the front, on either side of the grill. The car as a whole gained in lightness, in finesse, and seemed slightly more slim than the Superfast of 1956, although it was 12 cm shorter and 5 cm higher!

After having been shown by Pinin Farina at the 1957 Turin Salon, this magnificent creation was sold to Jan de Vroom, a Ferrari enthusiast (with a sympathetic name) who was also one of the principal figures in the North American Racing Team of Luigi Chinetti. Thanks to this fortunate and generous Ferrarist, **Sports Cars Illustrated** was able to publish in the September, 1958 issue, a very complete test of the 4.9 Superfast. It was, of course, a concert of praises. The main plaudits went to the lines, to the finishing, to the precise steering, to the flexibility of the engine, and, above all, to the acceleration, the most brilliant ever recorded by the American magazine, being 13.9 seconds for the standing start quarter mile.

Despite the abundance of chrome, the 410 SA "Series 2" (0671 SA) by Scaglietti still resembled the more sportive creations by this coachbuilder.

Presented at the 1957 Turin Salon, the 4.9 Superfast (0719
SA) synthesized with great success the innovations of the
1956 Superfast, and augured well for the future.

Among the fortunate owners of 410 Superamericas, the most famous were, without doubt, the Shah of Iran, the Emperor of Indochina Bao-Dai, and the faithful Maranello customer, French industrialist Fred Lip. Another Ferrarist of the first rank, Michel Paul-Cavallier, arranged a very special 4.9 litre Ferrari for his travels. In fact, his vehicle (0594 CM) was a true 410 Sport, with transaxle and dry dump but single ignition, which was bodied in 1956 by Scaglietti in the style of the contemporary 250 GT berlinettas.

Michel Paul-Cavallier, a Ferraristi of long standing, obtained this 4.9 litre Scaglietti berlinetta specially constructed for him using the chassis and engine of a 410 Sport.

Model Data

410 SUPERAMERICA
SERIES 1

S/N	Body Style	First Owner	Last Known Owner
0423 SA	Pinin Farina coupe		
0471 SA	Pinin Farina coupe		
0473 SA	Ghia coupe	R. Wilke (USA)	G. Wutke (USA)
0475 SA	Pinin Farina coupe	Carpenter	
0477 SA	Boano coupe		
0479 SA	Pinin Farina coupe		K. Thompson (GB)
0481 SA	Pinin Farina coupe	F. Lip (F) Paris Show 1956	J. Mastroianni (USA)
0483 SA	Pinin Farina Superfast	W. Doheny (USA)	P. Agg (GB)
0485 SA	Boano Cabriolet	Turin Show 1956	
0487 SA	Pinin Farina coupe		
0489 SA	Pinin Farina coupe	Fronteira	K. Franceschini (USA)
0491 SA	Pinin Farina coupe		
0493 SA	Pinin Farina coupe	Emp. Bao-Dai (F)	F. Violatti (I)
0495 SA	Pinin Farina coupe	P. Barilla (I)	T. Coady (USA)
0497 SA	Pinin Farina coupe		P. Sherman (USA)

410 SUPERAMERICA
SERIES 2

S/N	Body Style	First Owner	Last Known Owner
0499 SA	Pinin Farina coupe		
0501 SA	Pinin Farina coupe	F. Damman (B)	C. Kemp (USA)
0671 SA	Scaglietti coupe	Dr. Wax (I)	S. Sokol (USA)
0713 SA	Pinin Farina coupe	R. Wolfe (USA)	T. Churchill (USA)
0715 SA	Pinin Farina coupe	Morgan (USA)	C. DeBickero (USA)
0717 SA	Pinin Farina coupe	Paris Show 1957 (?)	K. Franceschini (USA)
0719 SA	P. Farina 4.9 Superfast	J. DeVroom (USA)	N. Silver (USA)
0721 SA	Pinin Farina coupe	Turin Show 1957	

II·F
The 410 Super America
Series III
1958-1959
Type 126A/514A

In October, 1958, the Paris Auto Show was once again an important event in the history of Ferrari as, of the three vehicles displayed on the stand of the importer, Cattaneo & Co. — a 250 GT Pinin Farina cabriolet, a 250 GT coupe, and a 410 Superamerica — two of them, the 250 GT coupe and the 410 Superamerica, were making their world debut. While the name was unchanged, the 410 Superamerica which interests us here had to be considered as a new model for it differed in a number of points from the 410 Superamerica produced between the end of 1956 and 1957. In order to easily distinguish between them we will continue to call them "Series 1", "Series 2", and "Series 3".

_____

(Left) Unveiled at the 1958 Paris Salon, the prototype of the 410 SA "Series 3" retained the short wheelbase and better lines of the 4.9 Superfast . . .

. . . even if the headlight covers were a bit bulbous and the fitting of bumpers was less successful.

The principal innovations in the Series 3 were found in the chassis and engine. For the latter, the success achieved in racing during 1957 with the V-12 Testa Rossa brought about a very complete redesign of the cylinder heads. The Lampredi long block was retained, undoubtable because it was the only one which could accommodate the large bore dimension, but the relocation of the spark plugs on the exterior of the V, above the exhaust manifolds, allowed a more efficient design of the combustion chambers and the power was notably increased. With three Weber 42 DCF carburetors and a 9:1 compression ratio, the power was rated at 360 hp at 7000 rpm for the engine, designated Type 126A.

In order to make use of this increase in performance, important modifications were made to the chassis. The diameter of the brake drums was increased to the same size as those used by the sports/racers before the adoption of disc brakes. As with the 410 Superamerica "Series 2", the chassis, approximating that of the 250 GT, used the 260 cm wheelbase. The track, however, remained wider by more than 10 cm.

This chassis had an official designation of Type 514A. Finally, a new four-speed gearbox had the common shift pattern, with first forward to the left, and fourth back and to the right.

The very beautiful two-tone body which clothed the 410 SA at the Paris Salon was signed by Pinin Farina and recalled in a number of ways the 4.9 Superfast of 1957. The upper structure repeated the design created in 1956 for the Superfast, but the windows which replaced the vented sail panels made it more attractive. On the sides, a discrete moulding connected the wheel arches, widening toward the rear, a detail that appeared on all the 410 Superamerica Series 3, as well as on several other designs by Pinin Farina in 1959. Unhappily, the front and rear lost some of their lightness, the headlight covers were a bit bulbous, and the rear was less sharp. On the other hand, the wider rim Rudge Borrani wire wheels gave an even stronger aggressiveness to this very beautiful vehicle.

For the Turin Salon, one month later, only the paint was changed.

The 410 SA shown at the Turin Salon several weeks later was identical except for the color, a dark green metallic. It was in all other respects identical, so it was unquestionably the same car, 1015 SA. (The car reportedly now has a Type 126 engine.) It is a pleasure to report that 1015 SA, as well as its two direct ancestors, the Superfast 0483 SA and the 4.9 Superfast 0719 SA, are all three today, in 1979, still in a perfect original state in the hands of their private owners, the first (0483 SA) in England and the other two in the United States. These three vehicles symbolize quite well the success of the Turinese coachbuilder, and in May, 1960, when SEFAC Ferrari was created, regrouping in a new corporation the expanded activities of Autocostruzioni Ferrari, it was not surprising to find Giovanni Baptista Farina on the list of the five directors. In 1959, Pinin Farina became Pininfarina, and had acquired a semi-monopoly on Ferrari coachwork. All the production vehicles owed their design to him, as well as the sports/racing

On the final version of the "Lampredi" 4.9 litre, the spark plugs were located on the outside of the V.

Testa Rossa. If, for reasons of organization, the building of certain models was conferred to other coachbuilders' workshops such as Ellena in Turin or Scaglietti and Fantuzzi in Modena, the fabrication of the most luxurious models always took place at Grugliasco itself. This was the case for the 410 SA Series 3 and it appears that no other coachbuilder clothed one of these vehicles.

The 410 SA Series 3 began appearing in January, 1959. It retained almost completely the characteristics and design of the prototype presented at Paris and Turin, the main difference being the sail panels which were no longer glass but metal panels with three vent-

ilation louvers as on the 4.9 Superfast of 1957. A vent window was mounted on each door, and the trimming of the side vent was redesigned. As was customary, each example had its own particular characteristics, the most notable being the headlight treatment, sometimes open, sometimes faired in under plexiglas bulbs as on the prototype. Their serial numbers ranged from 1015 SA to 1495 SA. Almost all were sold to the United States, where the magazine **Road & Track** was, to our knowledge, the only one to do a test of the car. In the issue dated December, 1962, the only complaints addressed to this vehicle, already three years old, were the optimism of the speedometer and the tendency of the clutch to slip, although it must be stated that the multiple disc original set-up had been replaced by a single disc, more practical for driving but less efficient in pure performance. Despite this, the standing start quarter mile was covered in 14.6 seconds and the maximum speed (at 6800 rpm) was recorded at more than 265 km/h.

The ten or twelve 410 SA "Series 3" produced in 1959 were, it appears, all bodied with this design by Pininfarina, which was very similar to that of the prototype.

The cockpit (here that of 1449 SA) was unusual because its dashboard was no longer covered with leather, but instead painted with black wrinkle-finish paint, a finish usually reserved for the strictly sportive Ferraris.

The principal variation known was the open headlights, applied to four or five of the last examples.

While the 12 to 15 410 SA Series 3s were all bodied in a very uniform manner, the one which was perhaps the last of the series served to console those who deplore monotony. This Ferrari, which was shown on the Pininfarina stand in November, 1959, at the Turin Salon, was in fact a truly different style, an astonishing assemblage of ancient and modern solutions. Very modern was the short wheelbase, undoubtably inspired by the all new 250 GT competition berlinetta. Also modern were the disc brakes which replaced the usual drums of the 410 SA. Finally the four headlights, mounted in two blocks of two, were very up-to-date. Anachronistic, on the other hand, were the "American" windshield from the early years of the 1950s, the transparent panel in the roof, and especially, the enormous, almost square, grill. Even after twenty years the execution can not be reproached but the aesthetics still seem strange, a sort of conflict between the aggressively round wheels and a brutally square silhouette.

There remains a question, however, concerning the true identity of this special Ferrari: is it a 410 SA or 400 SA? The question cannot be answered without knowing how many examples were built, the Maserati which received a very similar body being well known

It is not known for sure whether this strange creation, shown on the Pininfarina stand at the 1959 Turin Salon, was a 410 SA or a 400 SA, but the second solution seems to be the most probable.

and beyond our concern. If there was only one built, which seems the most likely, then the Turin Salon car was a 400 SA (1517 SA) and it had to undergo several modifications of details before being sold, in May, 1960, to Giovanni Agnelli. And that is a whole new story, as we will see in Chapter IV. But if, to the contrary, Pininfarina clothed two Ferraris with the same design, then that of the Turin Salon was truly a 410 SA.

While awaiting the solution to this enigma, the last legitimate 410 Superamerica was, until proven otherwise, 1495 SA, a "standard" Pininfarina coupe sold to New York at the end of 1959. And it is probably to this vehicle, still found today in America, which befell the honor of closing the era of the large Lampredi V-12. Ing. Aurelio Lampredi left Maranello in 1955, and the last extension of his work ceased to be produced after 1959. It was a final ending, but one that set a record. The 4953 cc of the 410 SA remains, in 1979, the largest displacement that was originally given to a touring Ferrari engine.

Model Data

410 SUPERAMERICA
SERIES 3

S/N	Body Style	First Owner	Last Known Owner
1015 SA	Pinin Farina coupe (1)	Paris & Turin Salons Day	E. Weschler (USA)
1265 SA	Pinin Farina coupe	Geneva Salon	
1285 SA	Pinin Farina coupe	Stalling	H. Sheronas (USA)
1305 SA	Pinin Farina coupe	Griffin	P. Van Gerbig (USA)
1311 SA	Pinin Farina coupe	Fulp	N. Silver (USA)
1315 (?)			
1323 SA	Pinin Farina coupe	Gill	H. Raab (USA)
1355 SA	Pinin Farina coupe	Murray	De Palma (USA)
1359 SA			K. Gerber (USA)
1373 (?)			
1387 SA	Pinin Farina coupe	(Nogara)	
1423 SA	Pinin Farina coupe (2)	Dulles	W. Dulles, Jr. (GB)
1449 SA	Pinin Farina coupe (2)	Fuller	
1477 SA	Pinin Farina coupe (2)	Ferrari California	W. Harrah (USA)
1495 SA	Pinin Farina coupe (2)	Chinetti Motors	D. Cummins (USA)

(1) prototype
(2) open headlamps

Specifications

"LAMPREDI" ENGINED STREET FERRARIS

Principal Characteristics

Model	342 America	375 America	250 Europa	410 SA (1 & 2)	410 SA (3)
Years	1952	1953-1954	1953-1954	1956-1957	1959
Bore x Stroke	80 x 68 mm	84 x 68 mm	68 x 68 mm	88 x 68 mm	88 x 68 mm
Single Cyl. Displ.	341.8 cc	376.8 cc	246.9 cc	413.6 cc	413.6 cc
Engine Displacement	4101.6 cc	4522.9 cc	2963.45 cc	4962.8 cc	4962.8 cc
Compression Ratio	8:1	8:1	8:1	8.5:1	9:1
Max. HP @ rpm	200 @ 5000	300 @ 6300	200 @ 6300	340 @ 6000	400 @ 6500
Carburettors	3 x 40 DCF	3 x 40 DCF	3 x 36 DCF	3 x 40 DCF	3 x 42 DCF
Gearbox	5-speed	4-speed	4-speed	4-speed	4-speed
Wheelbase (mm)	2650	2800	2800	2800 (1956) 2600 (1957)	2600
Track front/rear (mm)	1325/1320	1325/1320	1325/1320	1455/1450	1455/1450
Front Suspension*	TLS HS	TLS HS	TLS HS	ICS HS	ICS HS
Rear Suspension*	2 PLS HS	2 PLS HS	2 PLS HS	2 PLS HS	2 PLS HS
Tires Front	6.40 x 15	7.10 x 15	7.10 x 15	5.50 x 16	6.60 x 16
Tires Rear	6.40 x 15			6.50 x 16	

*TLS = Transverse Leaf Spring; ICS = Independent Coil Springs; PLS = Parallel Leaf Spring; HS = Houdaille Shock Absorbers

The year 1954 was a very important milestone in the history of Ferrari automobiles, for it was at that time that the 250 Granturismo was launched. In the approximately ten years of its career, the 250 GT—and it was under this appellation that it became best known—played a major role in the growth of the Maranello firm, and assured for it a truly world-wide reputation.

To illustrate the importance of the 250 GT, a few numbers are more appropriate than a lengthy discourse: Between 1949 and 1954, the production total for touring Ferraris approached 200 units, with about 35 being produced in the year 1954. By comparison, the production of the "sport" and "competition" Ferraris—single seaters not considered—came to about 250 units during the same period, with about 55 for the year 1954. In 1964, when the career of the 250 GT was ended, the annual production of gran turismo Ferraris was about 670 units. Thus in ten years Ferrari had multiplied by twenty its production of touring vehicles, and without doubt the success of the 250 GT was a primary factor in this increase.

The formula? It was simple, at least to explain, since it was typical of Ferrari: The 250 GT was born from racing experiences, it was constantly being perfected by the lessons of competition, and better yet, it was itself the origin of several of the most glorious thoroughbreds of the Scuderia, the Testa Rossa and the GTO being but two of many examples.

The 250 GT, therefore, had a long and captivating history, and is a major part of the Ferrari legend. We will not relate, however, the story of the "competition" models which has already been abundantly detailed by our friend Jess Pourret[1] and we will limit ourselves to the touring vehicles which constitute the subject of this book.

(Left) Ing. Ferrari and Frederico Giberti, one of his directors, pose alongside one of their 250 GTs, a 1956 Boano Coupe.

[1]Jess Pourret, The Ferrari Legend: The Competition 250 Berlinetta (Scarsdale, NY: John W. Barnes, Jr. Publishing, Inc., 1977)

III·A
The 250 GT Europa
1954-1955
Type 508/112

Because of its geographic location, but probably even more importantly because of its traditional place on the calendar, the Paris Automobile show was often judged by many manufacturers to be the most propitious occasion to introduce a new model. This was frequently the case for Ferrari as well, and new evidence of this was given in October, 1954, when the 250 Granturismo was unveiled in its world premier at the Grand Palace.[2]

This very latest Ferrari was not, however, the highlight of the show. That honor went, as we saw in the previous chapter, to one of its sisters, the masterly "Bergman" 375 MM by Pinin Farina. By comparison, the new 250 GT which concerns us here had the truly classical appearance. It resembled, externally at least, the 250 Europa which it was replacing. In fact, when viewed quickly, its bodywork appeared almost identical to that with which Pinin Farina had already clothed the majority of the 250 Europas and 375 Americas. Found on the ensemble were the same lines and the same details. The differences were subtle, but a closer examination revealed a profoundly altered general aspect. This was basically provided by a reduction of 20 cm in the wheelbase, which was reflected in a similar reduction in the overall length, and which gave to the new vehicle a more compact and slightly more harmonious silhouette. But if its appearance did not create a surprise, the 250 GT still constituted nothing less than a true innovation, primarily with its engine and chassis.

(Left) The first 250 Granturismo (0357 GT) being tested at Maranello shortly after its presentation at the 1954 Paris Salon.

The new 2.60 metre wheelbase chassis passed above the rear axle.

[2]For reasons which are not completely clear, the model continued for a while with the name 250 Europa, and this was notable in the catalog which accompanied its introduction. To avoid a great deal of confusion, we will call it the 250 GT, which very soon became its official name.

The 3 litre "square" version of the long Lampredi engine was abandoned, and from this time on it was the duty of a new derivation of the short V-12, designed in the beginning by Ing. Colombo, to power the 250. This family of engines had ceased to be used in street Ferraris after the cessation of production of the 212, but it had followed a fruitful career in racing. Adapted to the 250 MM in 1953, the 3 litre Colombo engine had gained many new competition successes, both with the official team drivers and with a number of private enthusiasts. Once again, Maranello put to use the experience of competition, and the first 250 GT engine (Type 112) was nothing more than a touring derivation of the 250 MM. It carried the same dimensions: A bore of 73 mm, a stroke of 58.8 mm (unchanged since the 166 of 1948, and a displacement of 2953 cc, which was only slightly less than 250 cc per cylinder and hence the designation of "250". The primary characteristics remained almost unchanged as well, the major difference being the nourishment by three dual-choke carburetors (36 DCF), instead of the four-barrel carburetors (36 IF4C) of the 250 MM, and the different cylinder heads.

Pinin Farina adapted the design created for the 375 America and 250 Europa to the 2.60 metre wheelbase. With several slight variations, it was fitted to about 27 of the 250 GT chassis.

The 250 GT, sometimes referred to by the name Europa GT,
gained a more compact silhouette...

. . . without reducing the interior space of this great touring
car. . .

The four-speed gearbox and multiple-disc dry clutch remained as descended from the 342 America, but in comparison to the chassis of the 250 Europa, the new chassis, which was designated Type 508, presented a different design. At the rear, the principal chassis sidemembers passed, from this point on, above the rear axle, but it was at the front that the most important innovation was made. There the front suspension had the traditional transverse leaf spring replaced by the more efficient coil springs. Finally, as already noted, the wheelbase was reduced from 2.80 metres to 2.60. These changes gave the new 250 notably improved road holding, while the interior space did not suffer from the 20 cm reduction allowed by the shorter engine, which was gained at the front of the chassis.

We have been unable to locate a road test of this model, which would allow a detailed comparison with its direct rival, the Mercedes 300 SL. But the good results acquired in competition by the 250 GT are strong arguments in its favor, and the competition versions which were derived from it in 1955 did not leave any chance for the 300 SL.

... which also made its mark on the circuit. Gendebien and Ringoir demonstrated this capability by being classed 3rd overall in the 1956 Tour de France with a two-year-old car.

Luigi Bazzi and Franco Gozzi with one of these coupes.

Alfredo Vignale (at left), the Princess de Rethy, and the
World Champion Nino Farina contemplate the "rough" of
what became the last Ferrari by Michelotti and Vignale.

The special coupe (0359 GT) of Michelotti and Vignale for
Princess de Rethy resembled, except for the overall length
and the closed bodywork, the 375 America cabriolet presented a short time earlier by the same team. (See page 109)

The 1954 Paris Salon car (0357 GT) represented the first example of a series which was more or less homogeneous, and which numbered about 36 vehicles all carrying the common designation 508/112. About 26 of these were bodied by Pinin Farina, with bodies made of sheet steel that were created a year earlier for the 250 Europa and 375 America. The last example of the series (0427 GT) was delivered shortly after being displayed at the Brussels Salon in January, 1956.

As was true with all Ferraris produced up to that time, this standardization was somewhat relative, with detail differences on most examples. The standardization was present, however, in many elements, for example, the treatment of the "greenhouse." All the 250 GTs were uniformly built with a panoramic rear window and an angled rear sail panel, while

on certain Europas and Americas of the same basic design true rear quarter windows eliminated the wrap-around. The 250 GT remains, however, outstanding because of its more harmonious profile and more compact silhouette. Today, 25 years later, the design is still found to be quite agreeable and very well suited for a touring vehicle with great class, even if the waist line of the body is a little high, thereby reducing the window area, in comparison with current aesthetic standards.

The 9 or 10 vehicles which comprised the remainder of the production received special bodies which were all, except one, the work of Pinin Farina. The last Ferrari by the Michelotti/Vignale tandem was a 250 GT (0359 GT) which was built at the end of 1954 for the Belgian royal family. Found on this two-tone coupe were most of the original themes applied a short time earlier to a 375 AM cabriolet (0353 AL): the "American" windshield with reversed pillars, the hot air outlets located high on the flanks, and the front bumper in two sections, on either side of the grill. At the rear, the two vehicles were very similar, but the 250 GT, made heavy by the addition of a roof, was less successful.

The Pinin Farina coupe shown at the 1955 Turin Salon differed from the "standard" coupe by the front signal lights and the grill.

Pinin Farina adapted the lines of the 250 and 375 MM to the
prototype for the 250 GT competition (0369 GT).

A new indication of the tightening of the bonds between Ferrari and Pinin Farina was furnished by the eight or nine examples of the 250 GT which were submitted by the grand coachbuilder of Turin, in addition to the "standard" vehicles which were literally a Pinin Farina exclusive. These specials have already been treated in detail by Jess Pourret, but we will briefly review them here because they prefigure in numerous ways the future direction of the touring 250 GT.

Four of them (0369, 0383, 0385, and 0415 GT) can be considered all at once as the last development of the 250 MM and the beginning of the 250 GT competition. They were, in fact, resolutely sporting vehicles. 0383 GT acquired an especially consistent list of honors, in Europe at first, and then in the United States, as a runner-up, and 0415 GT introduced to the racing world the Spanish Marquis Alfonso de Portago when, at Nassau in December, 1955, it won the first victory for the 250 GT competition. Their bodies recall very much those of the 250 MM berlinettas of 1953, or those of several 375 MM berlinettas built in the same period.

Three other 250 GTs received very similar bodies. Here is the one of Lena and Palanga (0383 GT) in the 1956 Tour de France.

Although made somewhat awkward by a bit too much chrome decoration, 0393 GT proposed a new design that became a style, with lines that were leaner, plus streamline headlights, and a row of parallel louvers on each sail panel. After having been shown at the 1955 Paris Salon, it was sold to the ex-Buggatist Andre Dubonnet.

The same frontal treatment, freed however of its excessive ornamentation, was also found on 0403 GT, whose rear re-utilized the very original design of the magnificent 375 MM "Bergman" created a year earlier. But, undoubtedly because it was less homogeneous, this new ensemble did not have the same allure as the original.

Despite some excesses, the Pinin Farina berlinetta at the
1955 Paris Salon (0393 GT) constituted a real innovation
and introduced the style of the 1957 competition berlinettas.

This other exercise (0403 GT) by Pinin Farina combined the
front of 0393 GT with the rear of the famous 375 MM
"Bergman" (See page 110-111).

With a more oval grill and rear fenders with more of a "fin", the special coupe by Pinin Farina (0407 GT) announced the 250 GT coupe for 1956.

The steering wheel and the abundant instrumentation of the dashboard are other peculiarities of the coupe (0407 GT) destined for Mr. Ferrario.

Very similar to the "standard" 250 GT, 0407 GT presented a larger oval grill and slightly protruding taillights, which portended the design of future touring 250 GTs.

Finally, the original design revealed at Paris on 0393 GT was refined for 0425 GT, most notably by reducing the amount of chrome and by making the upper edge of the rear fenders perfectly horizontal. The style of this vehicle, 0425 GT, shown at the 1956 Geneva Salon, was obviously the inspiration for future 250 GTs.

On a mechanical level, the early days of the 250 GT were also a time of an incessant search for perfection. Improvements were constantly being added, from one vehicle to the next, generally following the lessons learned on the "competition" vehicles which proved to be formidable competitors from their first outings. When applied to the luxurious touring vehicles, this experience proved to be very beneficial to the extent of making them shine in competition in their own right. For example, remember the 3rd place overall gained in the 1956 Tour de France by Olivier Gendebien, Michel Ringoir, and the "old" 250 GT coupe, 0357 GT, which was none other than the Paris Salon car of two years earlier!

The 1957 250 GT competition berlinettas derived the essence of their styling from this exercise by Pinin Farina, presented at the 1956 Geneva Salon.

III·B
The 250 GT Boano and Ellena 1956-1958

Even before the last 250 GT of the first series had been built and delivered, in January, 1956, a new series was being studied, and the first pre-production prototype (0429 GT) was being bodied at Pinin Farina by September, 1955.

The most striking innovation of this new car was the bodywork, the design of which gave it an appearance of greater length although neither the wheelbase (2.60 metre) nor the track were changed. The effect was probably due to the tauter lines, notably those of the fenders which started at the headlights (which were positioned higher than before) and stretched in an almost perfectly horizontal line for the length of the car before terminating with vertical taillights. The front was characterized by an ovalized grill of reduced volume in comparison to that of the preceding model. The locating of small fog lights at either end of the grill was made possible by recessing the traditional egg crate texture.

The rear received a very rectangular treatment, following the line of the fenders. This resulted in an appreciable increase in the usable volume of the luggage compartment, but also created a more massive general appearance which was less successful. Only the roof line remained somewhat similar to the preceding model, although the windshield was given a greater curvature.

A publicity brochure described the model as "the series-produced vehicle benefiting from the experiences of the race track." The lessons of competition were, in fact, present everywhere on the 250 GT engine, which continued its regular evolutionary development. At least two types of engines, sufficiently different to warrant distinct designations, the types 128B and 128C, were used in the 250 GT "Boano" and "Ellena" coupes. The basic dimensions were not changed, nor was the general architecture altered. However, the improvements, always discrete, were numerous. Among other refinements was the crankshaft, the main and rod journals being reinforced; and many other important components served to constantly rejuvenate the engine that was derived from the 250 S of 1952. When compared to the competition berlinettas whose production continued in parallel with the touring coupes, the engines for the coupes presented differences that were not always visible, but were important, such as the different camshafts and stages of tuning. A visible difference was the ignition, which on the coupes was furnished by a single distributor driven off the left camshaft.

In 1956 there appeared a new gearbox with Porsche synchronization. For these coupes, the shift lever was offset to the left of the console so that it was easier for the driver to reach. This dictated an unusual inversion of the shift pattern, giving the following scheme:

R		3		1
		4		2

Equally significant was the term "series-produced vehicle" contained in the brochure text which described these coupes. It revealed the new objectives, whose primary consequence was a complete reorganization of the bodywork segment.

(Left) Pinin Farina built several prototypes for the 1956/57 250 GT coupe. Here, in the courtyard at Maranello, is the car shown at the Geneva Salon in March, 1956.

The site which Pinin Farina occupied, Corso Trapani, was in effect, becoming too crowded, and a plot of six acres was acquired in the township of Grugliasco, on the outskirts of Turin. This location eventually came to have about 30,000 sq. metres of covered space, but was still under construction and not yet operational during the latter days of 1957. Therefore, Pinin Farina found it impossible to assure the "series production" of the bodywork which had been designed for the new Ferrari coupe. This task was consigned to the Carrozzeria Boano, a firm founded in Turin, on Via Collegno, by Mario-Felice Boano and Luciano Pollo after they left Ghia in 1953.

Before Boano began the series production, however, Pinin Farina finalized the design and refined its fabrication. This was accomplished by a pre-series of a half-dozen vehicles. One of them was shown at the Geneva Show in March, 1956, between a 250 GT Boano cabriolet, to which we will return in the following chapter, and a Pinin Farina 410 Superamerica coupe, of the same style as that unveiled at Brussels two months earlier. There existed a striking resemblance between the two latest creations by Pinin Farina, the 250 GT and the 410 SA already discussed in a previous chapter (see page 124). The advantage seemed, however, to slightly favor the latter. Undoubtedly the different proportions contributed to this, as well as the molded flanks of the 410 SA, which were an obvious improvement over the starkly bare sides of the new 250. Nevertheless, the refinements made to the "production" vehicles were minimal. The slight break of the line of the fenders, above the door handles, was eliminated and the fender line ran straight from the headlights to the taillights. Finally, the other deletions, affecting the Pinin Farina logo and several vertical bars in the grill, served to distinguish the "Boano" from the several Pinin Farina prototypes.

On the "production" coupes built by Boano, several changes can be seen.

In its January, 1958, issue, the American monthly **Sports Cars Illustrated** described as follows the new 250 GT, a standard Boano coupe on which they had conducted a very detailed test:

"The 250 GT, though, is no race car with touring coachwork. It is a designed-from-scratch high performance tourer that combines Ferrari's best competition chassis features with innumerable refinements that successfully tame the basic inner beast. It's a car that very feminine females have no difficulty handling. At the same time its recent victorious performances at Nurburgring and in the Tour de France suggest that it is today's fastest and most race-worthy production contender. On top of this, the new Ferrari is a luxury automobile in the grand manner. The design, detailing and execution of every part of its chassis and body reflect the builder's determination to put together a perfect machine. Finally, with a U.S. port of entry delivered price of $10,975 (for the Farina-bodied coupe we tested), the 250 GT is not only the best "road" Ferrari produced to date but also the least expensive."

The vehicle tested weighed 1,306 kg (2,880 lbs) with a full fuel tank (120 litres, 31.7 U.S. gallons) and the principal performance figures were as follows: 202.13 km/h (125.6 mph) for maximum speed (an average of runs in each direction, the best one-way run being 204.7 km/h or 127.2 mph); the standing start 1/4 mile (402.23 metres) was timed at 16.1 sec. with a final speed of 164.12 km/h, 102 mph). Finally, the fuel consumption varied between 17.8 and 25 litres per 100 km (9.4 and 13.2 mpg) depending on the style of driving employed.

The only flaw which stood out during the test concerned the reversed shift pattern. It is interesting to note that even the drum brakes were praised, as much for their power as for their resistance to fade, and it was interesting to learn that their total friction area

Jean Estager and the "Boano" in aluminum (0443 GT) with which he captured the G.T. category in the 1956 Alpine Rally.

of 2097 cm^2 (325 sq in) represented more than two times that normally given to heavy American production cars.

Although competition was primarily the domain of the berlinettas, several "Boano" coupes actually obtained competition successes that cannot be ignored. In June, 1957, on the Connecticut circuit of Lime Rock, Richie Ginther finished first, ahead of Walt Luftman, in the first "GT" race in the Eastern United States. For this grand premier the two Americans were driving "Boanos," the car of the winner being the one later used for the test by **Sports Cars Illustrated**.

The Italian Sergio Der Stephanian and a "Boano" coupe in the 1957 Mille Miglia.

Several coupes of this type also tackled the famous Mille Miglia. In 1956 Marenghi and Concari finished 33rd, and in 1957 Sergio Der Stephanian finished 14th in the GT category. Several of these coupes received bodies made entirely of aluminum. The best known was probably the one (0443 GT) with which Jean Estager captured the GT class in the 1956 Alpine Rally, and then a remarkable overall victory in the 1957 Acropolis Rally.

This 250 GT, which continues to be known under the name "Boano", can really be considered as the first Ferrari built in series. It gained, in addition, an appreciable success when in slightly more than one year of production, from debut in 1956 to spring of 1957, it was issued in almost 80 examples, whose chassis numbers ran between 0429 and 0675 GT. When compared with the number attained by the preceding models, this progress is particularly significant.

The rarity of special bodies was evidently a direct consequence of the newborn standardization. The

"one-off" creations were no longer so much the result of special orders from particular clients, but instead were more often actual studies being evaluated for future production. Such was precisely the case with the cabriolet (0461 GT) built by Boano which was shown at the 1956 Geneva Salon. It clearly represented a proposal by the body builder for a series of cabriolets which Ferrari intended to put into production in parallel with the coupes. We will return to it in the following chapter.

It appears that this era saw no more than two 250 GT specials, and the second was also created by Carrozzeria Boano. The precise reasons behind the construction of the bright red coupe (0531 GT) are not known, although it made a very complete tour of Italian concours d'elegance in 1957. Its general style was quite original, although it was not without some resemblance to the standard coupe. The front retained the same design but the oval grill was circled by a chrome ring, and carried in its center a ring surrounding a gold prancing horse. A double moulding ran along the sides, partially hiding the rear wheels, while the upper line made an "S" to rejoin the projecting edge of the rear fender. The rear fenders were similar in volume to those of the standard coupe, but they terminated in combination taillights that were larger. The roof line also retained the shape of the production coupe, but its appearance was transformed by a larger glass area achieved by the addition of two rear quarter windows.

This coupe was the last Ferrari signed by Boano. A short time later, in 1957, Mario-Felice Boano went to FIAT to take charge of creating a central styling office for the largest Italian automaker. He decided therefore to turn the works on Via Collegno over to his partner, Luciano Pollo, and his son-in-law, Ezio Ellena. The insignia was changed and the name of the firm became Carrozzeria Ellena. It was this new company which carried on with the body building for a small series of Ferrari 250 GT coupes.

This special 250 GT (0531 GT) retained the masses of the standard model, but produced a truly different effect.

The 1958 version of the 250 GT coupe was bodied at the works of Ellena (ex-Boano). It was characterized by a raised roof.

At about this same time, that is to say, during the summer of 1957, the 250 GT "Ellena" coupe was the object of several technical and aesthetic refinements. The ignition by a single distributor was made general, the brake friction area was increased to 2490 cm² (386 sq in), and a steering box made by ZF, with a worm gear, further improved the precise steering. Finally, a new method of locating the rear axle was used, which resulted from studies by Ing. Giotti Bizzarini. The drive shaft universal joints were modified, and the differential case was redesigned.

The refinements given to the body were for the essential purpose of improving its comfort and visibility. Therefore the roof was slightly raised, this being accomplished by using taller windshield, rear and door windows. Also, at this time. the vent windows were eliminated from the doors. The trunk also underwent some refinement, the spare tire being relocated under a floor panel and the usable space for luggage increasing accordingly. Finally, the rear was modified with a trunk lid which ended at a higher level, and henceforth the license plate was attached to the fixed rear panel, and not to the opening cover.

The first public showing of the 1958 250 GT took place at the Turin Salon, in November, 1957, but actually several examples had already been delivered before then. The production of the "Ellena" coupe lasted less than one year, and reached a number of about 50 examples, with chassis numbers between 0679 and 0889 GT. Although this number was less than the preceding series, it should not be interpreted as a decline for the 250 GT. For one thing, the period of production was shorter, and for another, a new series of 250 GT, the cabriolets, were put into production during the same period. Finally, several specials were not included in the number although they used the same base.

One of the specials, a coupe built by Pinin Farina for Prince Bernhard of Holland, was an exact replica of the 1957 Turin Salon 410 SA (0719 SA) already mentioned in Chapter II (see page 135). The two vehicles were being built simultaneously and only presented, other than the engine, of course, minimal differences, these being a single and darker color, and a different design for the fender vents on the 250 GT. As for the rest of the design, the harmonious low lines, the large grill flanked by two vertical bumperettes, and the covered headlamps, all were the same and just as admirable.

Another coupe (0751 GT) by the same bodybuilder, in January 25, 1958, Princess Liliana de Rethy, suffered by comparison. A certain heaviness occurred with the raised rear fenders and the voluminous chrome bumper which enveloped the rear skirt, following a design used on a cabriolet shown by Pinin Farina at Geneva some nine months earlier. Also the two additional bumperettes added under the grill were an unfortunate modification.

In 1958 several additional special coupes and cabriolets came from the new coachbuilding shops at Grugliasco, but in reality they were the prototypes for two new production 250 GTs. We will take them up in the two following chapters, which deal with these vehicles.

This 1957/58 250 GT chassis can be compared with that of 1954/55 (see page 151).

This sumptuous Pinin Farina coupe (0725 GT), destined for Prince Bernhard of Holland, only differed mechanically from the 4.9 Superfast built at the same time and shown at the 1957 Turin Salon (see page 135). (above)

Designed for Princess Liliana de Rethy, this other special Pinin Farina coupe (0751 GT) repeated several themes first shown nine months earlier on the first 250 GT spyder (see page 173). (below)

III·C
The 250 GT
Early Cabriolets
1957-1958
Type 508C/128C

(Left) With this imposing special cabriolet (0461 GT), unveiled at the 1956 Geneva Salon, Boano inaugurated the long dynasty of 250 GT convertibles. The same design was adapted to both a 410 SA coupe and a cabriolet.

Pinin Farina responded a year later with this very low, red, two-place spyder (0655 GT), shown at the 1957 Geneva Salon.

Repainted in dark green, this same spyder with the characteristic notched left door became the favorite mode of transportation of the race driver Peter Collins.

During the era of the 166 and 212 Inters, the vogue for convertible vehicles was such that a goodly number of Ferrari cabriolets were built by the principal body-builders. But this vogue seems to have completely evaporated following the advent of the 250 GT in 1954. It was the initiative of the young and dynamic Carrozzeria Boano, only two years old but already making its mark, which first gave a revival of interest to the combination of Ferrari + cabriolet.

The first 250 GT cabriolet (0461 GT) was, in fact, signed by Boano, and it was unveiled at the Geneva Salon in March, 1956, the same occasion that saw the introduction of the coupe from which it derived its mechanical base. In addition, it must be remembered that this coupe, designed by Pinin Farina, was built in a small production series by this same Carrozzeria Boano!

The coupe and the cabriolet which were presented side-by-side at Geneva were, however, of quite different styles. For the cabriolet, Boano extended the grill to almost the width of the automobile, and encased it on three sides by a unique bumper whose ends turned vertically, ending just under headlights set into the fenders. A similar bumper was adapted to the rear. Its vertical ends constituted the termination of the fenders. The roof and the windshield combined to create a harmonious roof line, but this unusual creation suffered from having a slightly top-heavy mass.

This cabriolet was shown at New York a few weeks after the Swiss salon, and Boano also displayed at the same time two 410 Superamericas bodied in the same style, the coupe and the cabriolet in Chapter II.

The first response from Pinin Farina came exactly one year later and it was unveiled at the Geneva Salon in March, 1957. It was more than a cabriolet, for it made its appearance as a true two-place spyder with a much more sportive aspect than the creation by Boano. In front, the heritage of the Superfast presented several months earlier was undeniably present in the profile, streamlined by the covered headlights, and in the large grill, low and thin, flanked by two vertical bumperettes which were the only "bumpers". The rear

was new, with fenders slightly projecting from the profile of the trunk, and terminating in a slightly oblique edge. Regretfully, the massive aspect of the bumper, which totally enclosed the rear skirt, a design which also appeared on the 250 GT special coupe of Princess de Rethy (see page 171), spoiled the style of the rear.

The most unusual detail of this very pretty car was probably the functional notch on the left door, for the elbow of the driver. Vignale had applied this design by Michelotti to several "sports" Ferraris in 1953, but here the contrast with the normal right door created a strange asymmetry that certainly drew attention. On the hood there was a generous air scoop which also did not pass unnoticed, and it extended even onto the top of the dashboard, carving out for itself a passageway under the windshield. The windshield itself was unusual, with its strong curvature and absence of a frame along the top edge. Finally, the top with metal frame disappeared completely, when folded, behind the backs of the two bucket seats.

After having excited the imaginations of the visitors to the Swiss salon, this "dream car" (0655 GT) was changed from its bright Italian red paint to a somber English green color, and became the property of Peter Collins. This brilliant driver for Scuderia Ferrari readily used this spyder for his travels, and he had it equipped himself, in England, with Dunlop disc brakes and wheels. This initiative was not ignored by Maranello, for these brakes were one day borrowed for testing on a Testa Rossa. A short time later, in 1959 for the "sports" Ferraris and a year later for the production vehicles, the traditional drum brakes were forgotten.

The second prototype by Pinin Farina was this strange exercise baptized "Spyder Competizione" (0663 GT).

Pinin Farina seemed to be more and more interested in the idea of an open Ferrari, and two months had not passed since the Geneva Salon before he displayed a new exercise on this theme, a curious mixture of "sport" and "touring" baptized the 250 GT Spyder Competizione. The design was still in the same vein as before, and only varied in the accessories. The windshield was replaced by a perspex racing screen that enveloped the driver's position. A streamlined headrest was fitted to the rear deck and the passenger's compartment was covered by a metal tonneau cover. Also in the "sports" theme, the latching of the hood was reinforced by two leather straps and two external catches, as on the competition roadsters and berlinettas. Finally, the massive rear bumper was replaced by two bumperettes similar to those protecting the front. This extraordinary vehicle (0663 GT) was sold to the Belgian driver Leon Dernier, known as "Elde," but it is not known if it ever had a racing career.

When, almost simultaneously, a third 250 GT Pinin Farina spyder made its appearance (0709 GT), it became obvious that a series of convertible Ferraris would soon be announced by Maranello. The basic lines of the "Spyder Competizione" were used again, but the curved windshield of the first prototype, reinforced by a complete frame, was fitted. Vent windows extended the windshield onto the doors, and the carburetor air intake was discretely reduced in scale. The rear received a simple wrap-around bumper. The name "cabriolet" was used here for the first time and it was retained for the coming series.

A third "speciale" (0709 GT) prefigured the definitive version except for some slight details, such as the vent windows on the doors.

Viewed from the front, the first three 250 GT convertibles
by Pinin Farina display the evolution which occurred with
the 250 GT cabriolet.

The fourth prototype (0705 GT) represented, practically, the final version, but the side vents were found on only a few versions and the gas cap door disappeared.

The cabriolet shown at the 1957 Paris Salon (0737 GT) presented unique "bananas" on the bumpers, through which the exhaust outlets passed.

A second cabriolet (0705 GT) appeared at about the same time with the definitive design. But the air vents located on the front flanks, similar to those on the 410 SA, were not uniformly fitted to all the following cabriolets, and the trap door in the right rear fender, covering the gas cap, disappeared. An unusual peculiarity of this beautiful red cabriolet, which was sold in Belgium, was the Borrani wire wheels whose spokes were not chrome but black! The hubs and knock-offs, as customary, were chrome and the rims were polished aluminum.

The first example of "production" (0729 GT) was delivered during the summer of 1957 to Mr. Oscar Olson, the sponsor of the Indianapolis-style racing single seater Olsonite Eagles. On this cabriolet the flanks were devoid of the air vents and two Marchal fog lights were mounted in front of the radiator grill. The approximately 22 to 24 examples which followed were all similar, and only an occassional rare example, such as the 1957 Paris Salon car (0737 GT), had the vents on the front fenders as seen on the fourth prototype.

These early cabriolets, bodied in steel by Pinin Farina, used almost intact the mechanical base of the 1956-1958 coupe (chassis 508C, engine 128C), often including a single distributor ignition and an offset shift lever.

The most frequent view of the 250 GT Pinin Farina Cabriolet.

The raised top did not detract from the appearance of this cabriolet (0789 GT), fitted with side vents. The disc brakes and the 15" wire wheels were later modifications.

During the summer of 1958, when a new 250 GT Pinin Farina coupe appeared, as well as a new, more sporty convertible, the 250 GT Spyder California, the front of the cabriolet was modified by adding a wrap-around bumper in place of the two bumperettes and, probably in the same concern for better protection, the fog lights were relocated behind the grill. A dozen cabriolets (0921 to 1439 GT) were built in this form, including a few right-hand drive versions, 0921 GT, for example. The last of the series (1475 GT) was delivered during the summer of 1959 with a changed body style which presaged a new generation of Pinin Farina cabriolets: the headlights were not covered and the profile of the rear fenders was becoming more rectangular.

As indicated on the generalized table following, this first series of 250 GT cabriolets was probably not issued in more than 40 examples. These elegant vehicles with low and harmonious lines live on as one of the most beautiful successes resulting from the Ferrari-Pinin Farina collaboration.

At the 1958 Paris Salon the 250 GT cabriolet was presented in its new configuration, with a one piece front bumper and fog lights placed behind the grill.

With more rectangular rear fenders and open headlights, the last example of this series of about 40 cabriolets introduced the style of the coming model, which first appeared in 1959.

Model Data

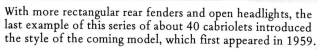

250 GT PININ FARINA CABRIOLETS
PROTOTYPES AND FIRST SERIES (1957-1959)

S/N	Year	First Owner	Last Known Owner
0655 GT	1957	Geneva Salon 1957/ Peter Collins	O. Zipper (USA)
0663 GT		Leon Dernier (B)	
0705 GT		Mr. Meert (B)	P. Schouwenburg (NL)
0709 GT		Prince S. Aga Khan	
0729 GT		Oscar Olson (USA)	G. Garrison (USA)
0735 GT		Frankfurt Show 1957 Munemann (D)	C. Crabbe (GB)
0737 GT		Paris Salon 1957/ Mr. Willard (F)	(F)
0759 GT		Turin Salon 1957	
0775 GT		George Arents (USA)	D. Rose (USA)
0777 GT		G. Fassio	D. Rose (USA)
0779 GT	1958	Mr. Hoffman (USA)	G. Makris (USA)
0783 GT		Porfirio Rubirosa (F)	
0789 GT		A. Fassio	Mr. Collizoli (I)

0791 GT		Parauto (I)	R. Donner (USA)
0795 GT		Mr. Deuppe (B)	K. Dedolph (USA)
0799 GT		Mr. Fabbri (I)	P. Bowers (USA)
0801 GT		Geneva Salon 1958/ DiStefano	H. Javetz (USA)
0809 GT		New York Show 1958/ Rifferts	N. Silver (USA)
0811 GT (1)		Ager Motors/ Lupini (ZA)	R. Van Zyl (ZA)
0813 GT		Mr. Norman	A. Andarko (USA)
0829 GT		Mr. Dupont	
0845 GT		Ferrari Rep. California	
0849 GT		Mr. Zacchirin (F)	Mr. Hennequin (F)
0873 GT		Chinetti Motors (USA)	R. Thompson (USA)
0913 GT		Mr. Lacloche	(USA)
0915 GT		Mr. Reggiani (I)	R. Stecker (USA)
0917 GT		Mr. Longhi (I)	E. Weschler (USA)
0921 GT (1)		I.S.C. Ltd. (HK)	A. Janson (S)
0961 GT		B. Rosenberg	
0963 GT		Count Volpi di Misurata (I)	J. Riff (USA)
0979 GT		Count Portanova (I)	
0981 GT		Paris Salon 1958	
1075 GT		London Show 1958	
1079 GT		Turin Salon 1958/ Mohamed Al Faisal	J. Clinard (USA)
1179 GT	1959	Garage Francorchamps (B)	J. Teagarden (USA)
1181 GT			
1193 GT		Sold In Italy	R. Lloyd (USA)
1211 GT		Sold in Italy	C. Steinberg (USA)
1439 GT			W. Denevi (USA)
1475 GT		Sold in Italy	H. Raab (USA)

(1) Right Hand Drive

The 250 GT
Pininfarina Coupe
1958-1960

At the end of 1957, while production of the 250 GT coupe with body by Ellena was still continuing, a new 250 GT coupe was being developed, and several proposals for the body were submitted by Pinin Farina during the winter. From the appearance of the first prototype (0843 GT), a great change obviously occured in the design. It was primarily due to a lowering of the waist line of the body so that the window area was able to be greatly increased. This resulted in an overall impression of greater length, while in actuality, this car was 6 cm (2.36 in) shorter than the Boano/Ellena coupes. At the front was the large rectangular grill that had been introduced several months earlier on the cabriolet. Above it were the headlights, which were also slightly recessed. When viewed in profile, the fenders had a horizontal line and, at the rear, terminated in two slanting ridges that were connected by a horizontal moulding which very successfully hid the cut for the trunk lid. Only the upper structure was still inspired by that of the Ellena coupe, with a generous wrap-around rear window. The encroachment of this window onto the sail panels dictated the roof supports being angled toward the rear.

On another prototype was found the same body, but the upper structure was transformed by a less important rear window which allowed the fitting of small supplementary windows on the sail panels. This special coupe (0853 GT) was sold to Prince Bertil of Sweden.

(Left) This special black coupe was very probably one of the first prototypes for the 250 GT Pininfarina coupe. Two similar examples (0841 and 0843 GT) were built and the two were later sold into France.

This other special (0853 GT) differed only by its roof line. It was delivered to Prince Bertil of Sweden.

The first pre-production prototype appeared a short time later. The kick-up marking the beginning of the rear fender had disappeared, as had the rear quarter windows, and the new rear window was characterized by four sharp angles.

The second, and probably last, pre-production prototype was a similar coupe but of a brighter color, officially introduced at a press conference held in Milan on June 25, 1958. Several months later it was found to be entered in the Concours d'Elegance at Antibes with a registration plate, Prova MO 58, which left no doubt about the identity of the entrant. This was probably the first time that a Ferrari was first entered into competition at a concours d'elegance.

Before the opening of the Paris Salon in October, 1958, production of the new 250 GT Pininfarina coupe had already begun. The bodies were being built in the new shops at Grugliasco, as were those of the cabriolet launched in 1957. In fact, it was at this time that both the new works of the Turinese coachbuilder became operational and that the insignia was changed from Pinin Farina to Pininfarina. The installations at Grugliasco obviously allowed for greater production, and being built there, in addition to the Ferrari coupes and cabriolets, were the bodies of many difuse models such as the Fiat 1100 and 1200 coupes and spyders, the Lancia B20 and B24, the Alfa Romeo Giulietta spyders, and even the Cadillac Brougham. This does not even take into consideration the Pininfarina designs put into production by the manufacturers themselves (Peugot, BMC, Lancia) or in the workshops

The first pre-production prototype already had the definitive lines.

of other body builders, as was the case with the Ferrari 250 GT berlinettas built under an agreement by Scaglietti, in Modena.

At the Grand Palais that year, the three Ferraris shown on the stand of the agent, Cattaneo and Co., were from Grugliasco. They were the prototypes of the new 410 SA (see page 138), the 250 GT cabriolet (see page 181), and the 250 GT coupe just then going into production. For its first salon, the coupe, shown in deep metallic gray with a black top, did not fail to attract some attention but the press remained skeptical of the usage of drum brakes as standard equip-

---

The second pre-production prototype was shown at Milan on June 25, 1958.

ment on this very rapid vehicle. The Aston Martin DB4 which was shown at the same time was equipped with four-wheel disc brakes, and even the elegant Facel Vega Excellence offered this equipment as an option.

At the London Motor Show several weeks later, the right-hand drive version of the new Pininfarina coupe was presented by a prestigious ambassador: Mike Hawthorn, who had captured for Ferrari the Driver's World Championship that year and whose family business, Tourist Trophy Garage, was also found to be the Ferrari agent for the British Isles. But the distribution of Ferraris in England was still modest, and it does not appear that the right-hand drive coupe was built in a great number of examples.

The cycle of European salons continued in November with the Turin exposition. As at Paris, a 250 GT coupe in metallic gray shared the Ferrari stand with the prototype of the 410 SA and a 250 GT cab-

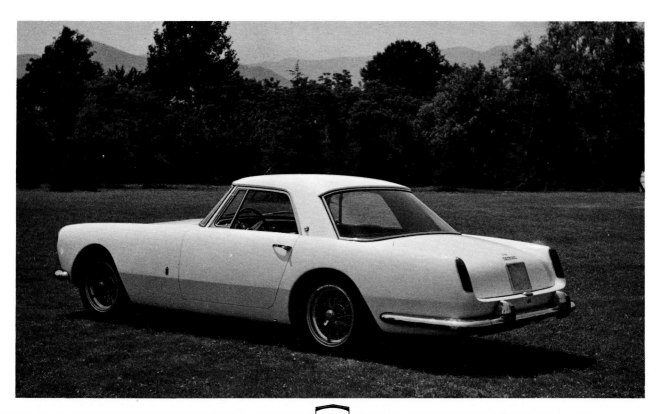

riolet. But on his own stand, Pininfarina presented a 250 GT coupe built to special order. The body was that of the production version, with the exception that the headlights were slightly recessed and streamlined under two perspex bubbles. Also different was a deep blue stripe, matching the color of the leather in the interior, running along the flanks of the car in contrast to the bright gray paint. Another change had the traditional Borrani rims painted the same shade of blue. Finally, this special coupe had fitted a transparent panel in the roof, with an interior screen which made it, if desired, opaque.

Paris, in October, 1958, was the first salon for the sober and classic 250 GT Pininfarina coupe. (top)

At the 1958 Turin Salon, Pininfarnia presented this special coupe, unusual with its covered headlights, its painted wheels, and its transparent roof. (bottom)

Another specially designed coupe was built by Pininfarina for Dr. Wax of Genoa. On this special the wraparound bumpers were replaced by vertical bumperettes similar to those of the "Spyder Competizione" (see page 174) while the skirts and rocker panels were covered by chrome panels and the little chrome horse was removed from the center of the grill and replaced by an enameled insignia on the front bodywork. In the interior, the dashboard was similar to that of the production coupe but a central console was added and, in place of the standard seats, two true bucket seats in red leather were fitted.

Another example of special finishing. This coupe was built in 1958 by Pininfarina for an old client of Maranello.

The cockpit was modified by a central console and bucket bucket seats.

But still the differences were more a question of special finishing rather than a truly new body design. A certain standardization came with the great increase in production of the 250 GT, and the only truly special body known to have been constructed on this base was the four-window coupe shown at the 1959 Geneva Salon. On this elegant metallic blue-green coupe (1187 GT) was found the more luminous roof line of the prototype for the 410 SA Series 3, as well as the moulding connecting the two wheel arches, and the hot air vents on the front fenders. Other than that, it was not much different from the normal coupe.

On the mechanical side, the 250 GT Pininfarina coupe retained the essentials of the layouts proven by the preceding models, layouts which in turn had been proven on the competition models. As a result, the first examples were found with the Type 128C engine, most with a single distributor, and the gearbox with offset lever and inverse shift pattern. The 128D engine was soon fitted and, later, the 128F with sparkplugs between the exhausts. This coincided with the adoption of a new gearbox, supplied with an electrically controlled overdrive, adding a fifth speed. Finally, beginning with the 1959 salons, most of the coupes were also equipped with disc brakes.

As with the preceding model, five rear axle ratios were available to choose (from 7/32 to 9/33) giving, at 7000 rpm, a catalogued maximum speed from 202 to 252 km/h (124 to 155 mph). The overdrive was available only with the lowest ratio, and the maximum speed was then given as about 260 km/h (160 mph).

One of the rare truly special bodies on this base, this 250 GT coupe (1187 GT), presented at the 1959 Geneva Salon, repeated the lines of the prototype of the 410 SA Series 3 (see page 138). Only the nose remained typically 250 GT.

The only test figures which were published were those obtained by **Road & Track** (June, 1960 issue) with a coupe with 128D engine, a four-speed gearbox without overdrive, a short rear axle ratio (7/32), and drum brakes. Among the figures given were the weight, which was 1370 kg (3014 lb) in driving form, and a time of 15.5 seconds for the standing start quarter mile, but the maximum speed was not measured. With the exception of the purchase price ($12,600), the admiration for the car was without reservation, even for the brakes, and it was summarized by this conclusion: "This is a car designed by enthusiasts for enthusiasts, and it shows."

The production of the 250 GT Pininfarina coupe continued for almost three years and totaled about 350 examples, whose serial numbers are between 0851 GT and 2081 GT. In these three years, the production at Maranello, racing cars excluded, was increased by 75% and it was without doubt the Pininfarina coupe which was the primary cause of the increase. At the end of 1960, the 250 GT/E, or 250 GT 2+2, firmly established this plan of increased production with an even greater success.

At the same time the sparkplugs were moved from the inside to the outside of the V.

Galleria

page 193-195:   The 250 GT Spyder California of 1960 to 1963 production is still, twenty years after, one of the most desirable Ferraris. The aesthetic reasons are obvious on this example (2891 GT) delivered in September, 1961 and maintained in a perfectly original condition.

Owner: Ado Vallaster (CH)

page 196:   Displayed at the 1961 London Show, this 250 GT Coupé (2821 GT) was a Pinin Farina one-off.

page 197:   The 250 GT 2+2 was a great success and still is a classic. Here is seen the 1963 prototype.

page 198-199:   Another classic of the Ferrari-Pininfarina style was the 250 GT "Lusso" berlinetta. On the left, the prototype, on the right, an "argento metallizzato" example (4433 GT) of the 1963 production.

Owner: Ado Vallaster (CH)

page 200:   The very original design of "Superfast II" in 1960, will be adapted to some thirty 400 Superamerica "Coupé Aerodinamicos."

page 201:   On the same 400 SA chassis, Pininfarina also produced some cabriolets.

page 202-203:   This other 400 Superamerica cabriolet (3309 SA) was presented successively at the 1962 Geneva and New York shows. Only the chrome decoration and the "rosso rubino metallizzato" paint differed.

Owner: Charles Robert (F)

page 204-205:   With its remarkable "greenhouse," the prototype "Superfast IV" was in fact a 1962 rebody of the 1960 "Superfast II."

page 206-207:   Contemporary of the 250 GT California Spyders, this unique 400 Superamerica (2311 SA) was specially executed in 1960 for Michel Paul-Cavallier, a director of the newly formed "Sefac."

Owner: A.J.M. VanDerLof (NL)

page 208:   A totally new 4 seater, 4 liter was born in 1964 with the 330 GT 2+2. Inherited from Superfast IV, the paired headlamps were bound to be commented upon.

III·E
The 250 GT
Spyder California
1958-1962

In the last days of 1957, in that same period during which the 250 GT Pininfarina cabriolet was being put into production in a small series (see chapter   ), there appeared the prototype for a new Ferrari convertible, the 250 GT Spyder California.[3] In all probability, the very existence of this spyder model was owed to the untiring enthusiast, Luigi Chinetti. He was the winner of the first post-World War II 24 Hours of Le Mans, thereby furnishing Ferrari with his first internationally famous victory, and subsequently Mr. Chinetti set up a Ferrari business in the United States. He soon inoculated the Americans with a Ferrari virus that became an incurable disease.

The coexistence of two 250 GT convertibles might, at first observation, seem questionable, but in fact the two vehicles were very different in both their intent and their characteristics. The Spyder California was more sporty than the Pininfarina cabriolet and, just as the cabriolet was directly derived from the coupe with which it shared a common mechanical base, so the spyder was itself closely inspired by the berlinettas which were primarily destined for competition. Like the berlinettas, moreover, it also owed its design to Pininfarina, but was bodied at Modena in the workshops of Scaglietti. For many years this firm exercised its talents primarily in the building of "sport" and "competition" models for Maranello.

The Spyder California was built in small numbers over a period of about four years, from 1959 through 1962, and its technical evolution closely followed that of the berlinettas, progress which also greatly benefitted, in a less direct manner, the other 250 GTs, the cabriolet and the coupe. This evolution can be schematically covered in five stages, although the continuing improvements and the numerous special orders gave individual differences to almost every example of the type.

The first stage was that of the prototype (0769 GT) which appeared in the last days of 1957. In both its mechanical aspects and its appearance, the car was nothing more nor less than a convertible version of the contemporary berlinetta. The engine was of the same type (128C) and the chassis (type 508C) had the same wheelbase of 2.60 (102 in) and the same specifications. For the body, the very pure lines of the 1957 berlinetta were recognizable, although the absence of a roof required a new windshield and a redesigned trunk lid. Also, the joining of the front and rear fenders was modified. The exterior dimensions remained the same as those of the berlinetta, but the weight of the spyder, whose body was usually made of steel with the exception of the doors and deck lids (in aluminum), was heavier by about 220lb. in full road trim. Despite this, lightness remained a primary objective in the conception of the Spyder California, and this undoubtedly explained the less luxurious finish it had in comparison to the coupes and cabriolets bodied by Pininfarina.

(Left) The prototype of the 250 GT Spyder California (0769 GT).

[3]This model has already been the object of an excellent and strongly detailed work by George M. Carrick, entitled The Spyder California, A Ferrari of Particular Distinction. Therefore the information given here is only a summation.

The relationship with the 1957 Series 2 berlinetta is evident both from the exterior. . . .

. . . and the interior, where the finish is more spartan than on
the Pininfarina cabriolets and coupes.

About seven examples of this style were built through the second quarter of 1958, but in the third quarter, important changes were introduced. The spyder received the engine with reinforced connecting rods and crankshaft (type 128D) and a new chassis (508D) which still retained, however, the 2.60 metre wheelbase. The bodywork was only changed in some small details, such as the rear shape of the wheel arches, and a few examples received uncovered "open" headlights. Between the end of 1958 and the end of 1959, this Spyder California "2nd Series" was produced in about 27 examples. Several vehicles of the type, fitted with competition engines and, on occasion, with bodies completely in aluminum, obtained good results in competition. The most notable success was probably the 9th place overall and GT class win of Richie Ginther and Howard Hively in the 12 Hours of Sebring, or perhaps even more notable was the 5th place overall of Bob Grossman and Fernand Tavano in the 1959 24 Hours of Le Mans with a spyder (1451 GT) entered by the North American Racing Team of Luigi Chinetti. The Scuderia Serenissima of young Count Volpi entered, on several occasions, a spyder that was characterized by a transparent air-scoop above the carburetors. This very fast car of Scarlatti, Serena, and Abate captured the GT class at the 12 Hours of Sebring in 1960, but was crashed by Gereni during the 1000 Km. of the Nurburgring several months later.

Beginning in 1959, several Spyder Californias were given open headlights. With a similar spyder, Richie Ginther and Howard Hively finished the 1959 12 Hours of Sebring in 12th place.

On this competition spyder (1451 GT), which placed 5th in the 1959 24 Hours of Le Mans, note the new, more pronounced, design for the wheel arches.

The rapid competition spyder of Scuderia Serenissima at the 1960 1000 Kms. of the Nurburgring.

In the last months of 1959, there appeared a third version of the Spyder California, with the outside plug V-12 engine, as developed from the lessons learned with the 250 Testa Rossa. Another important innovation at this time was the adoption of disc brakes. In appearance the bodywork was changed very little, but a subtle improvement of the rear fenders, which became less protuberant, was noted as well as a new rear deck which brought about a horizontal expanse between the new one-piece taillights, which were more angled. In a rather short period of time, between the end of 1959 and the first quarter of 1960, there were about 15 of this type Spyder California built.

The most important change took place at the Geneva Salon, in March, 1960. There, on the Ferrari stand, was found the complete, unified range of 250 GT models for the better part of 1960. This consisted of four cars: two bodied by Pininfarina, a coupe of the style introduced in 1958 and a cabriolet to which we will return later; and two bodied by Scaglietti, a berlinetta and the Spyder California derived from it. It was actually to the 250 GT berlinetta shown at the Paris Salon in October, 1959, that the new spyder traced its ancestry. While the coupe and cabriolet retained the 2.60 metre wheelbase, the two models whose bodies were designed by Pininfarina but built by Scaglietti shared a common chassis, type 539, whose principal innovation was a wheelbase reduced to 2.40 (94.5 in). This reduction was intended to improve the handling and to especially increase cornering speeds. The suspension remained classical Ferrari, with independent wheels and coil springs at the front, and a rigid rear axle with two parallel semi-elliptical leaf springs and four locating rods at the rear. The track was considerably wider, however, and another innova-

In 1960 the Spyder California adopted the short wheelbase chassis (type 539) of the new 250 GT berlinetta, but the design by Pininfarina remained the same.

tion was the abandonment of lever-type shock absorbers in favor of four adjustable telescopic units.

The 250 GT engine in this later version (type 168) was shared by the berlinetta and the new Spyder California. With new heads and larger valves it had gained 20 horsepower (40 horsepower in the competition versions which had, among other improvements, even larger TR valves, high lift camshafts, and connecting rods and pistons of lighter weight). Several of these short wheelbase Californias were equipped with the competition engine, notably in the case of the car (2015 GT) of Sturgiss and Schlesser at the 1960 24 Hours of Le Mans.

The bodywork, usually in steel, was changed very little and in spite of the difference of 20 cm (7.9 in) in the length of the wheelbase, it was often difficult to externally differentiate a short wheelbase Spyder California from the preceding model, unless they were side-by-side. The most sure method was probably to refer to the carburetor air scoop. On the long wheelbase models it formed a complete raised structure on the hood, while it was partially recessed into the hood of the newer model, which required a sort of trench on the forward part of the hood.

At the end of 1961 the Spyder California received, along with the berlinetta, several detail modifications to the chassis (type 539/61) and the engine (type 168/61), and its production continued until the end of 1962, as did the berlinetta. The last example (4167 GT) was sold to the United States in February, 1963.

In total, the production of the Spyder California passed, slightly, the 100 example mark, with about 47 long wheelbase and 57 short wheelbase examples. But this limited production has not stopped the type from being among the most desirable Ferraris ever produced.

The air scoop partially recessed into the hood permits rapid
identification of the short wheelbase Spyder California.

Specifications

SPYDER CALIFORNIA

	Type 128/508 (Long wheelbase)	Type 168/539 (Short wheelbase)
ENGINE	V 12 at 60°	V 12 at 60°
Displacement	73 × 58,8 mm	73 × 58,8 mm
	2 953,211 cm³	2 953,211 cm³
Compression ratio	128/C = 9,2 : 1	168 = 9,3 à 9,5 : 1
	128/D = 9,1 à 9,6 : 1	168/61 = 9,2 : 1
	128/DF = 9,2 à 9,4 : 1	
	128/F = 9,4 à 9,6 : 1	
Carburettors (3)	128/C&D = 36 DCL 3	168 = 40 DCL 6, 36 DCL
		168/61 = 40 DCL 6, 42 DCL 3
(Weber)	128/F = 40 DCL 6, 36 DCZ 3	ou 36 DCS
Power (catalog)	250 ch at 7 000 r.p.m.	280 ch at 7 000 r.p.m.
CHASSIS		
Wheelbase	2 600 mm	2 400 mm
Front track	1 354 mm	1 378 mm (1 354 mm)
Rsar track	1 349 mm	1 374 mm (1 349 mm)
Shock absorbers	Houdaille	GMF, Miletto, Koni
		Telescopics
Brakes	Disques (fin 1959)	Dunlop discs
Wheels	16 × 5,5	5,5 K × 400; 16 × 5,5 K
	5,5 × 400	15 × 5,5
		15 × 6
Tyres	Continental, Dunlop, Pirelli	Pirelli
	Englebert	
BODYWORK		
Length	4 400 mm	4 200 mm
Width	1 650 mm	1 720 mm
Height	1 400 mm	1 370 mm
Kerb weight (catalog)	1 000 à 1 075 kg	1 050 kg
Fuel tank capacity	90 l	90 to 100 l
	136 l (competition)	120 l (competition)

III·F
The 250 GT
Pininfarina Cabriolet
Series II
1959-1962

Even before the first Pininfarina cabriolet of the first series was delivered during summer, 1959, a new generation of 3 litre cabriolets was already being planned by Maranello and Grugliasco. The objective of this planning was to create a greater differentiation between the Spyder California and the Pininfarina cabriolet. As seen in the preceding chapter, the Spyder California evolved directly from the competition berlinettas. The cabriolet, which had always been closely related, at least on the mechanical plane, to the touring coupes, was aimed in the opposite direction, and the relationship with the coupes was accentuated

and the new cabriolet came to even more closely approximate the 250 GT Pininfarina coupe which had been in existence for a year.

The utilization of already proven solutions had the advantage, among others, of allowing a rapid realization. Therefore, when the Paris Salon was opened in October, 1959, the new version of the cabriolet was ready to be displayed. It demonstrated an obvious close relationship with the most recent version of the coupe, an example of which was displayed on the same stand, in both its mechanical specifications and its coachwork. The two Ferraris had the same engine type (128F) with outside sparkplugs, coil valve springs, ignition by two distributors, and the same gearbox with four forward speeds plus an electric overdrive. The two chassis were also of the same type (508F) and used the well-proven Houdaille lever-action shock absorbers as well as the new Dunlop disc brakes that had only recently been offered on the production Ferraris.

The 250 GT Pininfarina "Series 2" cabriolet shown at the 1959 Turin Salon several weeks after its introduction at Paris.

The top was of an agreeable design, and the hardtop which was offered as an option in 1960 repeated the same design with the addition of an amply curved rear window. This was, along with the hardtop offered for the California at the same time, the first instance of a removable hardtop being offered on a Ferrari convertible.

In its conception, design and finishing, the new cabriolet did not lack for elegance. Less sporty than the preceding model, and much less so than the Spyder California, it gained in both comfort and amenities for a touring use. It was well suited for its objectives. From this point onward, the two Ferrari convertibles followed their own separate and distinct careers.

The completely flat hood, identical to that used on the coupe, seems to have been used very rarely on the cabriolet.

As for the bodywork, the influence of the coupe was almost as great. The masses were the same, and the differences very subtle. The short and vertical nose and the long rear overhang of the coupe were adapted without apparent modification to the cabriolet. On the other hand, the kick-up that marked the beginning of the rear fender and the molded line which traversed the flanks between the tops of the wheel arches were two typical motifs which were borrowed from the old cabriolet. The longer rear served to increase both the usable volume of the trunk and the roominess of the cockpit, while the more vertical windshield allowed a top which gave the occupants more headroom. The side window area (the new cabriolet had the vent windows as on the coupe) was also increased. The result was an interior, where the layout was almost identical to that of the coupe, with slightly more space and comfort, still for only two people, in comparison with the first series of cabriolets.

Whether it had the top up, the top down, or the optional
hardtop in place, the 250 GT "Series 2" cabriolet, here the
example shown at the 1962 Geneva Salon, was certainly very elegant.

Another example of the new cabriolet was shown at the Turin Salon in November, 1959, and at that time the bi-monthly **Auto Italiana Sport** published the price in Lira for the various Ferrari models. At 5,800,000, the cabriolet was the most expensive 250 GT. The coupe, the spyder, and the berlinetta were all the same price at 5,500,000.

Production of the series did not really begin until 1960, and it continued until the end of 1962. To our knowledge the only really special body of the series was, oddly enough, a coupe (2821 GT) built by Pininfarina and shown at the 1961 London Show. The frontal aspect, as far back as the windshield, was identical to that of the cabriolet, but the roof line and the fastback rear were those of the Pininfarina 400 Superamerica from the same period (see chapter IV).

There was also constructed a "spyder speciale" with a hardtop (1737 GT), built in 1960 by Pininfarina for a Parisian client. But its mechanicals and its 2.40 metre wheelbase chassis were those of the competition berlinettas, and therefore not directly related with the cabriolets being considered. The bodywork of this vehicle was, moreover, directly derived from the 400 Superamerica cabriolet unveiled that same year at the Brussels Salon.

Otherwise, the only variations known to exist on the cabriolets concern finishing details, and it is often uncertain whether or not these details are original or later modifications. However, we can cite a few examples: a cabriolet delivered to the King of Morocco with a hardtop in brushed aluminum (1925 GT); the cabriolet given an award at the 1960 Concours d'Elegance of Rome (1817 GT) whose flanks were given vents similar to those of the 410 SA "Series 3" coupes; and the cabriolet with covered headlights presented that same year at the Concours d'Elegance of Rimini. And this doesn't cover the details of the many cabriolets modified "after the fact" by stylists, often non-professional, who were not always well inspired.

At the end of 1962, when production of the 250 GT Pininfarina cabriolet ended, the number produced in some two years was on the order of 200 examples, whose serial numbers were from 1537 to about 3803 GT. This represents a considerable increase when compared to the approximately 40 examples of the first cabriolet. It was necessary, however, to wait until the end of 1964 and the advent of the 275 GTS for the launching of a new generation of Ferrari convertibles.

One of the very rare specials of this series was the 250 GT Pininfarina coupe (2821 GT) which combined the front of the cabriolet with the roof and rear of the 400 Superamerica coupe.

The design of this 250 GT cabriolet speciale on a short
wheelbase competition chassis (1737 GT) was also found on
several 400 Superamericas.

The 250 GTE 2+2
1960-1963

During 1959 Ferrari and Pininfarina worked together in the greatest secrecy on the conception and realization of a four-place coupe. The idea actually involved a completely new orientation, for up until then all the Ferraris produced "in series" had been strictly two-place types. True, in the early years of the 1950s, some Ferraris had been made with occasional seats fitted behind the main seats, but these were special order or part of a small series. These arrangements were seen on several rare 212 Inter and 340 or 342 America coupes bodied, primarily, by Ghia, and a short time later on some 375 America and 250 Europa coupes by Pinin Farina. But at that time these rear seats were

usually squeezed into a very small space, and were usable only in an emergency and, for the comfort of the passenger, only for short periods of time.

Several questions had to be resolved for the new vehicle. Could a true Gran Turismo automobile be other than a two-place car? In the case of the 250 GT in particular, would it not be too daring to attempt to reconcile the problems for a staisfactory habitation for four people with the 2.60 metre wheelbase chassis and the lengthy 12-cylinder engine? Would not the basic nature of the ensemble be altered in appearance? Would not a grave imbalance be created that would injure both the vehicle's performance and its aesthetics? It would seem that these considerations would have been enough to discourage Ferrari and Pininfarina, and make the entire concept presumptuous and even useless. But suddenly, in 1960, the concept became reality and very quickly became a great success.

(Left) The first prototype of the 250 GT 2+2 was recognizable by its chromed headlight rims and its functional air vents located behind the rear windows.
Its dashboard was similar in many details to the definitive version.

The secret studies were well guarded, for at least two prototypes were built and tested without the press picking up even a rumor. Thus, the 250 GT 2+2 (two seats + two) created a true surprise when it first appeared in public on the occasion of the 24 Hours of Le Mans in June, 1960. There, one of the prototypes, probably the third, was put at the disposition of the Automobile Club de l'Ouest and was used as the Course Director's car. After watching its sisters, with the same famous 3 litre V-12 engine, capture the first two places in the general classification and the first four places in the GT class, the "future" 250 GT 2+2 returned to Paris where it was presented in detail to the press.

A great amount of careful planning had been done in order to adapt the 250 GT to its new vocation, with the chassis and the bodywork receiving most of the attention. So that sufficient interior room would be provided without lengthening the 2.60 metre wheelbase, the engine was moved 20 cm (8 in) forward in the chassis. This allowed the location of the two supplementary rear seats to be well forward of the rear axle. For this a new chassis was created (type 508E), with all the principle specifications of the preceding models (coupe and cabriolet), but in different dimensions as indicated in the following table:

	Coupe	2+2
Length	4395 mm	4700 mm
Width	1650	1710
Height	1397	1341
Wheelbase	2600	2600
Front Track	1354	1395
Rear Track	1349	1387

Most of the remaining equipment did not change. However, the Houdaille lever-action shock absorbers which were used on the prototype were replaced by the new telescopic units at the start of production.

The engine was similar to that which was already being used in the Pininfarina cabriolet and it was the latest version of the 250 GT, with cylinder heads derived from those of the Testa Rossa, carrying spark plugs on the outside, or exhaust side, and using coil valve springs. With its three Weber 40 DCL/6 carburetors, it supplied 240 horsepower at 7000 rpm.

Finally, the four-speed gearbox with electrically actuated overdrive on fourth gear was used, the same that was already being used in the cabriolet. It had been specified that the overdrive would only be supplied with the shorter of the two proposed rear axle ratios, but actually all of the cars were equipped with the overdrive.

The famous Turinese coachbuilder was found to be more than equal to the delicate design task required, and he succeeded in giving this four-place vehicle the traditional allure of the Ferrari Gran Turismos. As a result of studies conducted in a wind tunnel, the lines given to the 2+2 remain a great classic of the genre. The fender line, starting at the prominent headlights, was rectilinear all the way to the rear, ending in a slightly less than vertical line which comprised the taillights. A discreet short crease on the flanks served to lighten the appearance. The windshield was sharply inclined, and the roof line, which was kept very horizontal to allow maximum headroom for the rear passengers, was subtly balanced by the more plunging line of the side windows. The rectangular, slightly curved, rear window was marked by a distinct break in the

roof line, and blended with the trunk in a very open and almost flat angle.

As for the interior, the original concept of a four-place vehicle was very carefully respected, and the rear seats provided two true supplementary places for occupants of average height.

On the second prototype, fitted with "Snap" exhaust extractors, the trunk lid acquired its definitive contour and the front fender blinker lights made their appearance. (right)

While it was the first example shown to the public, the "pace car" for the 24 Hours of Le Mans in 1960 was probably the 3rd prototype built. (middle)

The side vents in the front fenders made their appearance with this prototype, which was used for the illustration of the first sales brochure. (bottom)

Several prototypes were built before the October, 1960, Paris Salon where the 250 GTE 2+2 was shown for the first time. As was indicated above, two prototypes were probably built before this vehicle made its debut at Le Mans, although they were not shown before then. The first was recognizable by its headlights encircled by traditional chrome rings and by two sets of cockpit ventilation air outlets located on the sail panels.

The second prototype differed in several details. Blinker lights visible from the side of the vehicle had become mandatory in Italy at the beginning of 1960, and these were located on the sides of the front fenders, just above the end of the front bumper on this example. The headlights were recessed into the tip of the fenders and the upper contour of the trunk lid was modified to incorporate the lid covering the fuel tank filler. Finally, this second prototype was recognizable by the "Snap" exhaust extractors mounted on the four tailpipes as on the competition berlinettas. The Le Mans vehicle had a similar appearance, except for the exhausts, and it was only on later examples that the engine compartment vents appeared in the front fenders, at first cut into the actual body, and later on, panels that were set into the body. This then was the appearance of the 2+2 (2043 GT) shown at the Paris Salon, with a remodeled dashboard and a new central console as well.

The success was immediate and the first production examples, on which the side blinker lights were oval and remounted at the same height as the moulding which runs along the sides, began to appear at the start of 1961. Production of the two-place Pininfarina coupe ceased at the same time.

The range of 250 GTs available in 1961 consisted of four models: the Pininfarina cabriolet, the Spyder California, the berlinetta in two versions (competition and touring), and the 2+2. The following numbers, while they are only estimates, seem to clearly attest to the success achieved by the new 250 GT with four seats. Of some 400 of the 250 GTs produced in 1961, a 22% increase over 1960, the respective share for each model was about 6% for the spyder, 11% for the cabriolet, 15% for the berlinettas, and 68% for the 2+2.

One of the first tests of the new Ferrari GT was that published by **Moteurs** in its issue of the 1st quarter of 1961. On the road circuit at Montlhery, Alain Bertaut recorded a best lap of 4 min 31.4 seconds at an average speed of 121.786 km/h, (75 mph), the best time he had ever recorded on the circuit with a GT vehicle. The only reservation which he expressed was as follows: "The behavior of the car, under the extreme circumstances imposed while posting a 'fast lap' of the Montlhery circuit, was astonishing if one takes into account the weight.

"But it was very obvious that the moving of the engine forward in the chassis has had a slightly perceptible influence on the handling. This remained exceptional, but the under-steering characteristic was found to be accentuated, and so to take the curves quickly required an abrupt movement of the steering wheel, breaking the rear wheels loose into a lateral slide, and then controlling the slippage with the accelerator and the steering wheel."

(Left) Several details were revised before the first salon, at Paris in October, 1960.

The production 250 GT 2+2 of 1961/1962 had still other slight revisions.

Production was accelerated in 1962, and during that year some important modifications were made. At the 1963 Geneva Salon, the "new series" 250 GT 2+2 appeared with changes in both aesthetics and mechanics. The fog lights were removed from the ends of the grill and instead were fitted into the bodywork on either side of the grill, and the more traditional chromed headlight rims reappeared, as on the first prototype. At the rear, the slightly lengthened fenders terminated in a more vertical line and the six taillights were regrouped into two combination units. In the interior were found new seats and a redesigned dashboard that allowed the placing of two air vent outlets. The rear suspension received the addition of coil springs incorporated with the shock absorbers, and the Borrani wire wheels were made a little wider. New cylin-der heads allowed larger valves and a slightly higher compression ratio.

At the end of 1963 the 250 GT 2+2 was replaced by the 330 America which, temporarily, held a four litre engine in the same bodywork. This 330 America was, in fact, an intermediary version before the 330 GT 2+2 was introduced in January, 1964. It only had a brief career and we will return to it in the following chapter.

The total production for the 250 GT 2+2 was about 950 examples, with serial numbers between 2043 GT and 4961 GT, an absolute record which did not remain unbeaten for long. Without any doubt the formula for a four-place GT was confirmed as a success, and with Ferrari and Pininfarina the theme still had some good days ahead of it.

At the end of 1962 the disposition of the front and rear
lights was redesigned.

The "spoiler" tried in 1962 was not retained but the offset of the rims was slightly increased.

In 1965 Fantuzzi built, for Luigi Chinetti, this cabriolet with
a "basket-handle" similar to that used on the sports/racing
Ferraris also built by this Modenese coachbuilder. It used the
chassis of a 250 GT/E.

The 250 GT
Berlinetta Lusso
1962-1964
Type 168U/539U

Since the production of the 250 GT Pininfarina coupe had stopped when the 250 GT 2+2 was introduced, the 250 GT "Lusso" berlinetta (type 168-539) bodied by Scaglietti was the only closed two-place vehicle available in the range of Ferrari three litres. This magnificent vehicle[4] was, however, of only limited production probably due to the fact that it was closely related to the competition version and therefore it had a level of comfort and finishing that was barely justifiable for a touring vehicle. In some two years of production there were probably no more than 80 examples built. But before its production ended, in the later days of 1962, Ferrari and, as usual, Pininfarina, had designed a new two-place berlinetta to take its place, and the emphasis was squarely on providing greater comfort for the occupants.

[4]See again the book The Ferrari Legend: The Competition 250 GT Berlinetta by Jess Pourret which treats this model in detail. Also, The Berlinetta Lusso, by Kurt H. Miska has a full history.

(Left) One of the first prototypes for the 1963 Pininfarina berlinetta (probably 4053 GT) before its presentation.

Pininfarina created an historic precedent with this truncated rear.

Several prototypes were undoubtedly built, but the first to make an appearance was the one (probably 4053 GT) which was displayed at the Paris Salon in October, 1962. The success was instantaneous, and the design with which Pininfarina had adorned this metallic pearl-gray Ferrari was certainly attractive. The very low lines gave a sleek effect that was accomplished by graceful curves free of any superfluous decoration, and the result was extraordinary. Pininfarina had obviously left the "cubist" period with which we associate most of his earlier designs from the 250 GT and the 410 SA coupes which first appeared in 1956 through the 2+2 of 1960.

The frontal treatment evoked memories of the 1960-1962 berlinetta, but with a more gracefully curved and more prominent grill, and with a greater projection of the headlights. The new, unfettered design had an even more aggressive aspect, and this effect was emphasized by the new three-piece bumper, a horizontal blade under the grill and two bumperettes under the lights. Placed slightly low, but distinctively pushed forward, the headlights gave origin to the fender line, which continued in a curve that stretched as far as the doors. The line of the rear fenders began at the windshield posts and joined with the trunk panel, all in an abrupt ending (the only sharp break on the entire car), forming an almost imperceptible aerodynamic spoiler above a truncated rear panel, all in accord with the aerodynamic theories of Dr. Kamm. This design had been introduced in 1961 by Ferrari on the sports roadsters, and reappeared in 1962 on the 250 GTO berlinetta before being adapted by Pininfarina to this touring berlinetta which thus found itself a pioneer of this new aerodynamic vogue. On the new berlinetta, the concave rear panel was underlined by a thin bumper which wrapped around and extended for some distance onto the rear fenders.

The strongly inclined and curved windshield along

Battista Pininfarina (at right) came in person to the 1962 Paris Salon to present the prototype of the new 250 GT.

with the side and rear quarter windows which extended to a point gave the roof a vary flowing line, which then blended into the rear deck in a particularly harmonious curve. The large glass area was completed by a vast rear window which was separated from the rear quarter windows only by two very thin roof supports. The convex flanks, lightened by their perfect contour, did not require any corrective artifices, and the classic 15" Borrani wheels with chrome spokes and polished alloy rims admirably completed this veritable rolling sculpture.

While the short wheelbase (2.40 metres) of the berlinettas and spyders was retained, a new chassis (type 539/U), in which the engine was located several centimetres further forward, allowed a much more roomy and comfortable interior. Two true bucket seats were fitted and the one gave an excellent driving position. Behind them was a large plateau reserved for luggage, with two leather straps to hold it in place. Finally, the dashboard was unique in that it was completely covered by anti-reflective black leather, with the two large diameter instruments, speedometer and tacho-

On this special berlinetta (4335 GT), built at Grugliasco at the beginning of 1963 for the personal use of Battista Pininfarina, note the streamlined hood bulge, the absence of a vent window on the right, the 400 SA-type door handles and, at the rear, the more accentuated spoiler.

The 168/U engine remained the final road version of the famous 250 GT.

The fog lights recessed into the body on either side of the grill became standard shortly after the beginning of production.

meter, located in the center but angled toward the driver for better visibility. The five additional gauges, of smaller diameter, were located directly in front of the driver.

Although the chassis design was derived from that of the GTO, the chassis actually carried the accessories of the preceding 250 GTs, and the only contribution of the GTO was the new layout for locating the rear axle, two Watts linkages binding the differential case to the chassis.

The engine (type 168/U) used the block common to all the 250 GTs of the period, and the rest of the engine was in some cases related to the "Lusso" berlinettas of 1960-1962 (valves, crankshaft, camshafts), and in some cases to the 2+2 (rods, pistons, cylinder heads). With three Weber 36 DCS carburetors and a compression ratio of 9.2 or 9.3 to 1, it was rated, depending upon the source consulted, at either 240 or 250 horsepower at an engine speed of 7500 rpm.

The only fuss caused by this alluring Ferrari seems to have been its name: 250 GT Pininfarina Berlinetta 1963; Scaglietti Berlinetta unificata; type 168/U-539/U; or even 250 GT/L were, with more or less ap-

peal, some of its official designations. However, it passed into posterity under the completely semi-offical designation of "Berlinetta Lusso" (luxury), probably due to the inscription "250 GT/L" which appeared on the data plate.

A new prototype appeared at the Turin Salon in November. Except for its color, it only differed from the preceding prototype by details of its finishing, among which were the false grill decorating the hood bulge, and the door handles. Production started immediately, and the first examples were delivered before the end of 1962. Scaglietti, who was charged with the body building, made few changes to the prototypes. The modifications seen at Turin were retained, and the only other changes were two fog lights recessed into the body on either side of the grill and, at the rear, two flatter taillights replacing the four conical elements of the prototype. A little later, wider Borrani wire wheels (15 x 6 1/2" in place of the 15 x 6") became standard equipment, while the same Pirelli Cinturato 185 x 15 tires were retained. This was the manner in which the berlinetta shown at the Geneva Salon, in March, 1963, was equipped.

The centrally located main gauges were an individuality of that berlinetta.

The bodies, built at Scaglietti's shops, were reunited with their chassis at Maranello.

A definitely valid judgement of the "Berlinetta Lusso" was delivered by Count Giovanni Lurani, in **Auto Italiana Sport**, after a marathon test through Milan, the Monte Cenis Pass, Lyon, Tours, Le Mans (for the 24 Hours, of course), Orleans, Bale, Lucerne, the St. Gothard Pass, Lugano, and Milan. The title "The Best in the World" very well summarized this test, which concluded with the following observation: "The 250 GT berlinetta 'designed by Pininfarina' thoroughly confirmed its right to be considered as the most exceptional high performance sports car in existence today. It showed the excellence of its mechanical base, refined from an incomparable competition tradition, and a remarkably brilliant aesthetic conception which bore the signature of the greatest body builder in the world."

Some basic performance figures were obtained, using two berlinettas, one equipped with the "standard" rear axle (8 x 32) and the other with the "optional" ratio (9 x 34). With the first, the maximum speed was 230 km/h (142 mph) at 7500 rpm, and the standing start 1000 metres was covered in 26.2 seconds. With the second, the car used on the trip, the

Pininfarina's personal berlinetta (433 GT) was rebodied a short time later, but its new appearance was not unveiled until October, 1964, at the London Show.

figures were changed respectively to 243.5 km/h (mph) (still at 7500 rpm) and 17.4 seconds. The only reservations expressed concerned a slight lack of watertightness for the floorboard, and the type of gearbox fitted. Count Lurani regretted that a five-speed box, like that used on the GTO, had not been specified, particularly on the model with the long rear axle ratio. Several owners of "Lussos" have expressed a similar comment, being a bit perturbed by a first gear that was too high. One such owner unhesitatingly installed, as a replacement, a five-speed gearbox from a 1966 330 GT, and found with usage that the problem was effectively corrected.

Other than some individual modifications, the "Lusso," which, like the 2+2, was also produced in a right-hand drive version, followed its career without notable change. And, there were relatively few attempts by individuals to give it special bodies. Who, after all, could have improved upon it other than the masters of Grugliasco themselves? The only two true specials known, this excluding vehicles more or less "customized," were both due to Pininfarina and were even one and the same vehicle (4335 GT). The first version, which is often taken for the first prototype of the "Lusso", was built at the beginning of 1963 (thus well after the Paris Salon prototype) and was characterized by a slimmer hood bulge that lacked the

grill, by the absence of a vent window on the left door, by the recessed door handles, and by a slightly more accentuated spoiler on the rear. As for the interior, the dashboard was more conventional, with the speedometer and the tachometer located in front of the driver while the other gauges were located on a central console. This metallic gray car only appeared in photographs used in several advertisements for Pininfarina, who owned it. In the same year, 1963, its front was radically transformed, still by Pininfarina,

with a small oval grill, covered headlights, and a two-piece bumper. These three traits were typical of the 400 Superamerica Pininfarina coupes to which we will return in the following chapter. It was only shown once in public, at the London Show in October, 1964, and served as a beautiful final chapter to the career of the "Berlinetta Lusso." A new berlinetta, the 275 GT, would soon be presented as a replacement for the 250 GT.

The front resembled that of the 400 SA by the same body builder. . .

. . . the rear with its more pronounced spoiler was changed only by the addition of the inscriptions.

The career of the "Lusso" came to a close at the end of 1964. The last one built (5955 GT) was probably the 350th, a production number that only the 2+2 could beat. With the end of the "Lusso" came an end to the prestigious dynasty of the 250 GT.

In ten years, the 250 GT was built in about 2500 examples. Few constructors of high performance and great luxury cars were able to attain such production numbers.

In the 1964 Tour de France, the Swiss team of Muller and Walter showed that the "Berlinetta Lusso" could also honorably comport itself in competition, although that had never been an objective seen by its designers.

IV
Power and Luxury
IV·A
The 400 Super America
1959-1964

While the 250 GT in its various forms assured Maranello a constantly increasing production, the limited production of the Superamerica continued without interruption to satisfy the fastidiousness of a few perfectionists who demanded even more performance, comfort, and refinement, and who wanted even more of an image of prestige and exclusivity than could be provided by the "standard" Ferrari. Perhaps the confidential manner of the construction and sale of these special cars was the reason that the transition from the 410 to 400 Superamerica seemed to have passed almost unnoticed by most observers. But this 400 was an entirely new Superamerica.

The long engine and fixed cylinder heads conceived for the 4.5 litre Grand Prix engine in 1950, and used on the Americas and Superamericas through the 410, was completely abandoned. The 400 Superamerica engine (type 163) was a new derivative of the 125, the first V-12 Ferrari engine that had been designed in 1946 by the engineer Giocchino Colombo. It retained, in effect, the general architecture of that first engine, the detachable cylinder heads, the 90 mm distance between each cylinder bore center, etc., and the external dimensions as well. It also bore the latest refinements of the 250 GT such as the spark plugs on the outside of the V and the coil valve springs. While retaining the original block size, the technicians at Maranello successfully increased the bore to 77 mm, while a new crankshaft permitted the lengthening of the stroke from 58.8 to 71 mm. The single cylinder displacement thus obtained was 330.62 cc, for a total displacement of 3967 cc. It should be noted in passing that for the first time in the history of touring Ferraris the designation "400" did not reflect the single cylinder displacement, but instead about 1/10th of the total displacement. Some observers have wanted to read in this number the horsepower of the engine, but in reality this was about 340 horsepower at 7000 rpm. The compression ratio was 8.8:1, and the carburetion was generally provided by three Weber 42 DCN units. Occasionally, however, the 400 SA was fitted with Solex carburetors, and also occasionally, with larger dimension Webers.

Another important innovation was the gearbox, which remained in the front position, but which had an electrically actuated overdrive added, giving a fifth speed that was over-multiplied. It was joined to the engine via a single-disc dry plate clutch.

The chassis was also shortened by comparison with the last 410 SA, and the maximum wheelbase was 2.42 metres. As on the 250 GT of the same era, the lever-action shock absorbers were replaced by Koni telescopic units and Dunlop disc brakes were mounted on all four wheels.

The official presentation of the 400 Superamerica occured at the Brussels Salon in January, 1960. The newest member of the family of top-of-the-line touring Ferraris was shown there as a two-place cabriolet (1611 SA). It was designed by Pininfarina and resembled in numerous ways the 250 GT cabriolet created in 1957, as well as the cabriolet which came later, in 1959. The most notable affinity was the profile of the fenders and the molding which ran along the flanks between the wheel arches. But the approximately 20 cm reduction in the wheelbase, slightly perceptible in the length of the front, and the shortening of the false threshold at the rear, gave the new 4 litre cabriolet a more stocky aspect. Also notable was the different treatment of the nose, with its upright headlights, low and slender grill, and large air scoop on the hood, all three characteristics being common traits of the last series of 410 SA coupes.

The numbers circulated at that time credited the new Superamerica with three Weber 46 DCF/3 carburetors, a compression ratio of 9:1, and a power rating in the vicinity of that given to the preceding 5 litre, or about 400 horsepower. As we have seen above, this last figure was probably somewhat optimistic.

The cabriolet seen at the 1960 Brussels Salon was not, however, the first 400 Superamerica. That honor

(Left) The first 400 Superamerica was this startling Pininfarina coupe (1517 SA). It is very likely that it was in reality only a retouched version of the coupe shown at the 1959 Turin Salon. (See page 144).

went, at least by its earlier serial number (1517 SA), to the special Pininfarina coupe which was delivered at the end of May to Giovanni Agnelli, the future President of Fiat. This coupe, easily recognized by its almost rectangular grill, its "panoramic" windshield, and its roof with a transparent panel, was actually only a touched-up version of the coupe which had been shown at the Turin Salon in 1959, under the designation 410 Superamerica. The most visible changes were the grill, whose dimensions were slightly reduced, a new one-piece front bumper, an air scoop located further forward on the hood, the disappearance of the air vents above the former two-piece bumper, and the removal of the enamelled insignia of the marque. However, there was good reason to believe, as we have seen in Chapter II, that Pininfarina built these two consecutive exercises on one and the same chassis, 1517 SA, the first 400 Superamerica.

Several weeks after the Brussels Salon, the same cabriolet was shown at the New York Show and sold off the stand. In total, in a little more than one year, six examples were built, all to the same design, but with many variations in finishing and decoration. Some were even given a hard top characterized by rear quarter windows embracing the contour of the windows on the doors and an almost flat rear window. Finally, also part of the series was the very similar cabriolet (1737 GT) which was built to special order during this same period, but on the chassis of a 250 GT short wheelbase competition (see page 225).

This cabriolet (1611 SA) was shown successively at the Brussels Salon and the New York Show in early 1960. It was the first of a series of six very similar 400 Superamericas.

The same theme was seen again, with different decoration and a special hard top, on the yellow cabriolet (2407 SA) which was shown at the 1961 Geneva Salon.

The sixth and last example (3309 SA) was shown at the 1962 Geneva salon, with yet different decoration and covered headlights.

A completely new Pininfarina style appeared at the 1960
Turin Salon with the Superfast II (2207 SA).

While the design of these cabriolet bodies had nothing to offer that was very new, exactly the opposite was true of the Superfast II which was unveiled on the Pininfarina stand at the Turin Salon in November, 1960. This experimental creation by the great Turinese coachbuilder was actually quite remarkable for the completely new style which it proposed. Born in a wind tunnel, this harmonious design resembled the profile of an airplane wing. The leading edge was, in fact, the nose of the car, in the middle of which was the air intake for the radiator, an ellipse of very reduced dimensions resembling that of several sports Ferraris. The trailing edge was represented by the rear deck, streamlined to a point, upon which converged the curves of the roof. The graceful curve of the hood, devoid of all harshness, was particularly remarkable, as was the shape of the windshield, whose posts, very noticeably curved inward, reinforced the effect. Undoubtably to further purify the lines of the front, the headlights were located under lids actuated by electrical commands, and which disappeared completely into the bodywork of the nose. At the rear the joining of the various curved elements was no less pure.

This marvelous two-place coupe can certainly be considered as one of the most significant examples of the art of coach building.

In the winter of 1960, the Superfast II received several modifications, among which were an air intake on the hood, vent windows, and the removal of the rear wheel skirts.

As with 1517 SA, a persistent falsehood has tried to make this Superfast II a 410 Superamerica whose chassis had been shortened. However, it is unlikely that the voluminous 4.9 litre engine could have been housed under the hood. It was in reality a true 400 Superamerica (2207 SA) which underwent several aesthetic revisions before being sold, as will be seen below.

The first revisions were made during the 1960-1961 winter. The hood received a large air scoop for the carburetors, the side windows had front vent windows added and the skirts, which partially masked the rear wheels, disappeared. It was in this form that the first 400 Superamerica coupe was shown, at the 1961 Geneva Salon, with several additional modifications. The principal change was in the frontal treatment, with the headlights no longer retractable, but instead streamlined under clear covers in a more conventional manner at the beginning of the front fenders. Thirteen examples of this style were produced up to the summer of 1962. As always, variations differentiated between these great luxury coupes, whose sale price was much greater than that of the 250 GT. The door handles were sometimes recessed, sometimes projecting, the skirts for the rear wheels were not always fitted, and the finish of the interior differed from one vehicle to another. Certain examples were even equipped with uncovered headlights and, at the same time, some samples had a radiator air intake that was larger and similar to that used on the cabriolets.

The "Coupe Special Aerodinamica" which was derived from Superfast II, was shown at the 1961 Geneva Salon. It was built in thirteen examples that were personalized in details for the customer.

The principle variations concerned the rear wheel skirts and, above all, the uncovered headlights which dictated a different design for the nose.

A test of one of these rare coupes was published by **Road & Track** in June, 1963 and it was interesting for a number of reasons. Owned by William Harrah, the famous collector who was later the Ferrari distributor for the Western United States, the 400 Superamerica tested had been made the object of very important mechanical modifications by his shop. Displacement was increased to 4590 cc by a bore enlarged from 77 to almost 83 mm. With Forgedtrue pistons, Testa Rossa camshafts with 10 mm lift, reworked cylinder heads, and three 46 mm Webers in place of the 40 mm Solex carburetors originally fitted, the power was increased to 420 horsepower at 7500 rpm. While not exceeding 7500 rpm, the speeds attained in each gear were 58.5 mph in first, 83.7 mph in second, 115.3 mph in third, and 179.6 mph in fourth with the overdrive.

The principle innovation of the Superfast III (probably 3361 SA) shown at the 1962 Geneva Salon was its much more open greenhouse.

For the standing start quarter mile it was timed in 15.8 seconds. When its exact weight is taken into account which was 3710 pounds as tested, the power of the extraordinary vehicle can be better appreciated.

At the Geneva Salon, in March, 1962, Pininfarina presented a new experimental project on the base of the 400 Superamerica, the Superfast III. This spectacular bright metallic green coupe (probably 3361 SA) proposed several new and original design solutions, while still retaining the essential lines of Superfast II and the limited series of coupes which followed it. The most striking change, and perhaps the most agreeable, concerned the greenhouse. Its volume remained the same, but the rear roof support posts were reduced to a minimum and the rear window descended further down onto the rear deck. This permitted a much greater window area, and a design that was even more elegant. On the nose, which retained the retractable headlights, the radiator air intake could be completely closed by a shutter which was thermostatically controlled. Finally, a ventilation duct for the rear wheel well appeared on the lower rear fender, and the moulding which extended from the front wheel arch was stretched to about the middle of the door.

Another innovation of the Superfast III, an air intake for the radiator that was thermostatically opened and closed.

The luxurious and functional interior of a 400 Superamerica. Here is that of the Superfast III.

Superfast IV followed immediately. This dark green coupe recreated, with several similar details, the large glass pavilion of Superfast III, but its frontal aspect was profoundly modified by the two pairs of headlights which were located, without covers, at the front of each fender. This newer design lost, with these modifications, a part of its harmony.

In all probability, Superfast IV was built on the same chassis (2207 SA) as Superfast II, which would explain the regretable disappearance of the latter. Superfast IV was sold in August, 1962, apparently without ever having been shown, and it can be found today in the United States.

Probably built in 1962 on the chassis of Superfast II (2207 SA), the Superfast IV repeated in numerous details the upper structure of Superfast III but the front with four headlights was less successful.

At about this same time the chassis of the Superamerica was appreciably lengthened in order to give more interior space. The wheelbase thus became 2.60 metres, as with the last 410 Superamericas. This additional room created behind the seats remained, however, strictly for luggage, and a four-place example of the 400 Superamerica coupe is not known. The overall design of the whole was retained, but the additional 18 cm (7 in) was visible, especially in the distance between the door and the rear wheel well.

Several changes also occurred in the finishing details. The carburetor air intake disappeared, replaced by a simple elongated hood bulge, the partial covers for the rear wheels seem to have been completely abandoned, and several examples received the ventilation duct on the rear fenders, as seen on Superfast III and IV. Finally, the uncovered headlights remained catalogued as an option, and several examples were so equipped. Between its introduction, at the London Show in October, 1962, and the demise of the 400 Superamerica, at the end of 1963, the long wheelbase coupe was produced in about 19 examples.

The cabriolet body also remained available on the new long chassis. Again, the design of the first series was retained, but it appeared somewhat unbalanced by the additional length of the rear, and its production did not exceed four examples.

Several 400 Superamericas received truly special bodies. One was a spyder with right-hand drive built for Michel Paul-Cavallier, President of Pont a Mousson and a director of SEFAC Ferrari. This 400 Superamerica (2311 SA) repeated almost completely the design of the 250 GT Spyder California. The front was a little larger but the additional 2 cm (0.8 in) in the wheelbase were imperceptible. It is not impossible, by the way, that another spyder of the same type was built.

One of the two 400 SA of 2.42 metre wheelbase that were bodied by Scaglietti was this right-hand drive spyder (2311 SA) which followed the design created by Pininfarina for the 250 GT Spyder California.

At the end of 1962 the wheelbase of the 400 Superamerica was increased from 2.42 to 2.60 metres. As a result the design of the Coupé Aerodinamico underwent several subtle modifications.

It was built in about 19 examples, always personalized by some details. Here the ventilation ducts for the rear brakes. . . .

. . . here the open headlights and the shape of the radiator air intake. . .

... or here, on one of the last examples, which was shown at the 1963 Frankfurt Salon, the larger blister on the hood. (above)

The design of the "Coupé Aerodinamico" was applied to several 250 GT berlinettas with 2.40 metre wheelbase. On the first (2429 GT), the theme was faithfully respected.

Another special was the Pininfarina 2+2 coupe (2257 SA) that was especially created for the patron himself with all the outward appearances of the 250 GT 2+2 coupe. Very likely this vehicle served as a study for the 330 GT which will be discussed shortly. Discovered later in the United States was a Superamerica (3097 SA) given a body similar to that of the 1963 250 GT "Berlinetta Lusso." It appears very probable, however, that his was not the body originally mounted. In each of these instances, note that although the designs were by Pininfarina they were not really new designs. This was also the case with 3673 SA, built at the end of 1962, combining the 400 SA engine with the body of the 1961/62 Scaglietti berlinetta.

In actuality, Pininfarina had particularly good success with the design of the 400 Superamerica coupe, and this probably explains the relative uniformity of the series. The style, which was sometimes designated "aerodinamico" was, in addition, adapted to several 250 GT specials. There was the magnificent coupe, 2163 GT, built for Prince Bernhard of Holland, on the chassis of a 1960 Berlinetta, a competition berlinetta (2429 GT) with an all aluminum body built in 1961 for a Parisian client, one or two 250 GT coupes with 2.60 metre wheelbases, one of which (2821 GT) was shown at the 1961 London Show (see page 224), and even the very special berlinetta, 2643 GT, one of the first prototypes of the GTO.

At this point it would be easy to digress to the competition applications of the 400 SA engine, although this is beyond the scope of this book. But

Built for the Prince of Holland, this 250 GT (2613 GT) differed in several points, notably by the open headlights and the deeper rear window.

briefly, it was utilized, with Testa Rossa specifications, in several experimental berlinettas and, above all, in the TRI 330 LM which won the 1962 24 Hours of Le Mans. In 1963 it was used in the competition 330 LM berlinettas, and in the first mid-engine prototypes.

In the early days of 1964, while the last 400 Superamericas were being delivered, its direct descendant, the 330 GT, had already begun its active career, but its objectives were quite different. These last Superamericas were only, and one is tempted to say voluntarily, built in about 48 examples. This was both very few and very many. Many in comparision with the preceding Superamerica or in comparison with its most direct contemporary rival, the Maserati 5000, but few in comparison to the production figures attained by the 330 GT. This is another story, however, and the true replacement for the 400 Superamerica was the 500 Superfast. This will be covered after the 330 GT.

The third (2463 GT) was even more different and it served as a prototype for the "GTO."

Model Data

400 SUPERAMERICA   SERIES 1–SHORT CHASSIS

S/N	Body Style	First Owner	Last Known Owner
1517 SA	PF coupe Special	Turin Salon 1959 G. Agnelli (I)	G. Ranney (USA)
1611 SA	Pinin Farina cabriolet	Brussels/N.Y. Shows 1960 G. Arents (USA)	R. Spangler (USA)
1885 SA	Pinin Farina cabriolet	Mouzino	
1945 SA	Pinin Farina cabriolet	Horten	(USA)
2207 SA	Pinin Farina Superfast 2	Turin Salon 1960	P. Sanders (USA)
2257 SA	Pinin Farina Superfast 4 Pinin Farina coupe 2+2	N. de Nora (I)	
2311 SA	Scaglietti Spyder	M Paul-Cavallier (F)	D Van Der Lof (NL)
2331 SA	Pinin Farina cabriolet	Comm. Gosce (I)	P. Swartzel (USA)
2373 SA	PF coupe Aerodinamico	Geneva Salon 1961	A. Aberman (USA)
2407 SA	Pinin Farina cabriolet	O. de Nora (I)	G. Garrison (USA)
2631 SA	PF coupe Aerodinamico	E. Rivetti	W. Nelson (USA)
2809 SA	PF coupe Aerodinamico	Count Volpi (I)	
2841 SA	PF coupe Aerodinamico	Count Somsky (CH)	W.B. Leface (USA)
2861 SA	PF coupe Aerodinamico	Paris Salon 1961	
2879 SA	PF coupe Aerodinamico	Turin Salon 1961	(USA)
2893 SA	PF coupe Aerodinamico	Benelli (I)	G. Ranney (USA)
3097 SA	PF coupe Special		Forney Museum (USA)
3221 SA	PF coupe Aerodinamico	M. Charpentier (F)	
3309 SA	Pinin Farina cabriolet	Geneva Salon 1962	Ch. Robert (F)
3361 SA	Pinin Farina Superfast 3 (?)	Geneva Salon 1962	
3513 SA	PF coupe Aerodinamico	A. Lauro (I)	
3559 SA	PF coupe Aerodinamico	C. Marshall (USA)	M. Kerr (USA)
3621 SA	PG coupe Aerodinamico	M. Colombo	B. Batagol (AUS)
3673 SA	Scaglietti Berlinetta	FIMA (I)	S. Halpern (USA)
3747 SA	PF coupe Aerodinamico	(USA)	E. Marandola (USA)

Model Data

S/N	Body Style	First Owner	Last Known Owner
	400 SUPERAMERICA	SERIES 2—LONG CHASSIS	
3931 SA	PF coupe Aerodinamico	London Show 1962	
3949 SA	PF coupe Aerodinamico	Turin Salon 1962 E. Goldschmidt (USA)	A.Goldschmidt (USA)
4031 SA	PF coupe Aerodinamico		S. Markowitz (USA)
4059 SA	PF coupe Aerodinamico	M. Franzozi (B)	B. Shadlun (USA)
4109 SA	PF coupe Aerodinamico	M. Alessio (I)	
4111 SA	PF coupe Aerodinamico	Geneva Salon 1963 G. Filipinetti (RSM)	H.K. Edgeley (GB)
4113 SA	PF coupe Aerodinamico	C. Faina (I)	
4241 SA	Pinin Farina cabriolet	Henry (F)	(F)
4251 SA	PF coupe Aerodinamico	Bolt (USA)	R. Taylor (USA)
4271 SA	PF coupe Aerodinamico	Riva	
4729 SA	PF coupe Aerodinamico	Mereghetti (I)	E. Saadi (USA)
4423 SA	Pinin Farina cabriolet	Maggiore (I)	
4443 SA	PF coupe Aerodinamico	Count Chandon (F)	Thepenier (F)
4465 SA	PF coupe Aerodinamico		
4651 SA	PF coupe Aerodinamico	Horath	Nardi (USA)
4679 SA	PF coupe Aerodinamico	W. David	
4781 SA	Pinin Farina cabriolet	Shapiro (USA)	(USA)
5021 SA	PF coupe Aerodinamico	Turin Salon 1963	(USA)
5029 SA	PF coupe Aerodinamico	Maggiore (I)	
5093 SA	Pinin Farina cabriolet	Bloomingdale (USA)	
5115 SA	PF coupe Aerodinamico	Rockefeller (USA)	(USA)
5131 SA	PF coupe Aerodinamico	Reiss (D)	P. Street (USA)
5139 SA	PF coupe Aerodinamico	Rolando (I)	

IV·B
The 330 America
& 330 GT 2+2

The very first four-place, four litre Ferrari was probably born during the winter of 1960-1961, being, as we have already seen, the 400 Superamerica special (2257 SA) built at that time for Mr. Ferrari himself. That creation was nothing more than the installation of the new four litre engine in the almost new 250 GT 2+2. The 400 Superamerica had been in service for barely a year, and the Pininfarina 2+2 coupe was just going into production. Two years later, the 2+2 had gained a great deal of success, and the four litre engine had been completely tested, at first in a touring version with the 400 Superamerica, and then, in a competition version on various racing Ferraris. All these elements were then reunited for the production of a more powerful, but already proven, 2+2 coupe.

The first examples came along to quietly replace the 250 GT 2+2 in the last months of 1963. This new type, the 330 America, retained in effect the Pininfarina body of the 250 GT 2+2, and there was no external differentiation from the three litre other than an "America" insignia on the trunk of some examples. A transitional model, this 330 America had an extremely brief career, only a few weeks, and it does not appear to have been produced in more than fifty

(Left) The 330 GT was already in production before it was officially unveiled, at Maranello, on 11 January 1964. A new wing of the factory was inaugurated at the same time.

Externally, nothing differentiated the transitional 330 America from the last Pininfarina 250 GT 2+2s.

examples, between the serial numbers of 4953 and 5125.

The 330 GT 2+2 coupe was officially presented during the traditional first-of-the-year Ferrari Press Conference, on January 11, 1964. Several examples had already been produced and were present there to face the verdict of the journalists.

In all respects, the 330 GT was a new Ferrari. The engine (type 209) appeared to be somewhat remodeled in comparison with that of the 400 SA (type 163), although it retained the same bore and stroke dimensions (77 x 71 mm), and therefore the same total displacement (3967.40 cc). In order to improve the circulation of the water in the block, the engine was lengthened, with the distances between the cylinder bore centers increased from 90 to 94 mm. This also allowed a better positioning of the spark plugs, but required a complete revamping of the production machinery. Also new was the water pump, still driven by a belt, which necessitated a new timing case, and a 40 amp alternator replaced the outmoded generator.

The power was notably increased, even if the officially announced figure of 300 horsepower at 6600 rpm seems somewhat less than reality. In order to make effective use of the more than 25% increase in power, the internal parts of the transmission were reinforced to some extent, and the Laycock overdrive was modified so that it automatically disengaged when fourth gear was disengaged.

The chassis retained the traditional architecture of electrically welded oval-section tubes, and the engine, as usual, was mounted at four points. But the wheelbase of 2.65 metres gained 5 cm (2 in) over those of the 250 GT 2+2 and late 400 Superamerica, and the suspension was modified in several ways, most notably by the adoption of Koni adjustable shock absorbers. Finally, the disc brakes, still made by Dunlop, were redesigned for better efficiency in wet conditions, and the front and rear brake circuits were totally independent, each having its own servo, its own master cylinder, and its own fluid reservoir.

In its aesthetic appearance, the 330 GT brought about a change of style that was no less radical. The lines were somewhat more bare and the curves were more gentle, but at the front the adoption of four headlights, grouped two by two as on Superfast IV, was a concession to the fashions of the day and was met with mixed reviews. The bulbous rear was also somewhat bulky. On the other hand, the interior was improved, with increased comfort especially for the rear passengers who were given 10 cm (4 in) additional leg room. Finally, on the dashboard there appeared new anti-reflective circular visors around the speedometer and tachometer. These black plastic cylinders remained characteristic of Ferrari dashboards for a number of years.

The 330 GT 2+2 coupe's aesthetic design perhaps lost part of the aggressive and cat-like character typical of Pininfarina Ferraris, a character which had been retained on the first 2+2, but the performance and the pleasure of its use did not suffer, which was well and good.

The starker lines were one of the most pleasant characteristics of the entirely new 2+2 coupe. Several differences in details can be noted on this prototype when compared with the first production examples.

The first public showing of the 330 GT occurred at the Brussels Salon immediately after the press conference at Maranello, and production followed immediately, continuing without major change up to the middle of 1965. At that time several radical modifications were introduced. The overdrive was completely abandoned in favor of a new five-speed, fully synchronized gearbox. With the same rear axle ratio (8x34) (4.25 to 1), the maximum speed remained at 152 mph at 6400 rpm, but the lower gears had been noticeably lengthened. Following the practice that was becoming standard (after being first introduced on the single-seat Formula 1 cars) was the fitting of new wheel rims of cast light alloy, while the traditional Borrani wire wheels were now available only as an option. Finally, continuing the search for greater comfort, power steering and air conditioning eventually became available upon demand.

Several styling revisions were made at the same time. In addition to the new wheels, the most significant change in appearance concerned the frontal treatment,

In 1965 numerous important mechanical modifications were introduced. Several aesthetic changes in Pininfarina's design occurred at the same time, notably a more classical front with two headlights.

which was cleaned up by the removal of the two supplementary lights. Of somewhat less importance was the new design for the engine compartment vents, located on the front fenders, and the overriders which were added to the bumpers.

A later important modification concerned the mounting of the engine to the chassis. By reducing from four to two the number of mounting points, the transmission of noise and vibration into the interior was reduced. Also, thanks to this new design of the engine block, suspended accelerator, clutch, and brake pedals were fitted, which were more agreeable in usage. These modifications were a direct result of the introduction of the newer 330 GTC, presented at the 1966 Geneva Salon.

The career of the 330 GT was terminated at the end of 1967 by the unveiling, at the Paris Salon, of the 365 GT 2+2. In four years the 330 GT had been built in about 1000 examples, thereby confirming the success of the 2+2 formula initiated seven years earlier by Ferrari.

Alloy wheels replaced the traditional Borrani wire wheels; however, these latter remained available as an option.

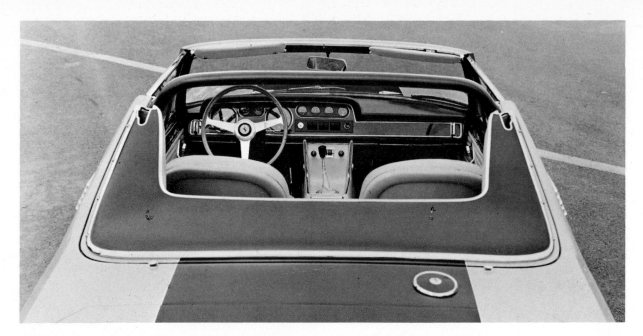

Built in 1967 by Michelotti on order from Luigi Chinetti, this yellow and black cabriolet was more unusual than it was pleasing.

After several years, there was a very sharp decline in the demand for special bodywork, and it appeared that there were built only three specials on the base of the 330 GT. Curiously, they were all three commissioned by the United States importer, Luigi Chinetti. The first was a cabriolet (6109) signed by Giovanni Michelotti and recognizable especially by the protective arch above the occupants. The design deviated completely from that of a normal 330 GT, but the decoration was perhaps a little too heavy, especially the ornamental cut of bright yellow and matte black paint. The second was a coupe by the same author with a similar design. The third was a three-door station wagon done by Vignale. Here also the Pininfarina design for the production 2+2 was completely abandoned. Of special interest were the headlights, artfully concealed behind two groups of horizontal strips, with the same decoration being used to conceal the taillights. The agreeable proportions of this original design were, however, flawed by several superfluous decorative details, such as the treatment of the arch which cut the roof into two segments. Shown at the 1968 Turin Salon, this special 330 (7963) was the last Ferrari by Alfredo Vignale. The talented body builder disappeared in 1969 in a merger with Ghia, shortly before these two names were regrouped under the banner of Ford.

Vignale also attempted a special 330 GT with this station wagon (7963   ) with slightly over-done lines, which was shown at the Turin Salon in 1968.

Galleria

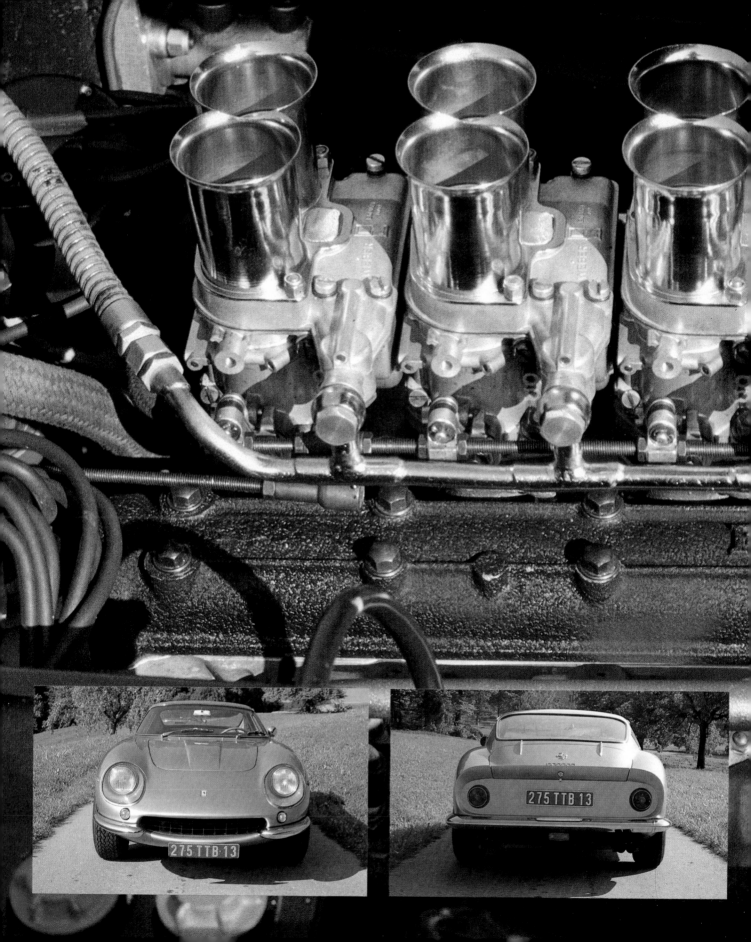

IV·C
The 500 Superfast
1964-1966

Two months did not elapse between the delivery of the last 400 Superamerica, at the end of January, 1964, and the presentation of the 500 Superfast, which was introduced to continue the tradition of a top-of-the-line, prestigious, touring Ferrari. The premier occurred on the Pininfarina stand at the Geneva Salon, in March, 1964. The long metallic blue coupe which was unveiled there showed an uncontestable family resemblance with the preceding 400 Superamerica coupes, but it concealed mechanical solutions that were unique to it.

In effect, the essential lines and aesthetic style of the "aerodinamico" coupes were retained, but the flanks were devoid of the mouldings. At the front the headlights remained in the same position, but they were no longer streamlined under transparent covers. The rear did not terminate in a point, as on the 400 SA, but instead ended in a truncated vertical panel which gave the rear deck a decidedly less steep angle.

Finally, as on the 330 GT born a few months earlier, the Borrani wire wheels, fitted with 205 x 15 tires, were appreciably larger than those of the Superamerica.

The Superfast also had a V-12 engine that was unique to it, a "long" block in which was found a distance of 108 mm between the cylinder bore centers, a spacing that was typical of the "Lampredi" V-12 of 1950. This was, however, the only common point between these two engines, the new 5 litre (type 208) being given, of course, removable cylinder heads as with the "Colombo" designed V-12. With a bore of 88 mm and a stroke of 68 mm, its total displacement was exactly 4961.57 cc which, rounded off to 5 litres, gave the type its "500" designation, following the same system which had given the last Superamerica the designation of "400." With a compression ratio of 8.8 or 9 to 1 and three Weber 40 DCZ/6 carburetors, it was rated at 400 horsepower at 6500 rpm.

(Left) Presented at the 1964 Geneva Salon as a replacement for the 400 Superamerica, the 500 Superfast can perhaps be considered as the Ferrari "Royale."

As for the remainder of the car, it consisted of the same particulars as the 330 GT, notably the four-speed with electrically operated overdrive gearbox. The chassis, with 2.65 metre wheelbase, was also similar, with the same suspension and the dual brake circuits.

The bodies, built with very particular care at the shops of Pininfarina, were almost all identical. However, the large, practical bulge on the hood of the prototype shown at the 1964 Geneva Salon was replaced on subsequent vehicles by a slightly higher, but extremely smooth hood. There can also be noted several variations with regard to taillights and door handles.

The 500 Superfast was produced in two limited series. As indicated on the list at the end of this section, the first series comprised about 25 vehicles.

The second series appeared during the summer of 1966, with several modifications following the changes which had occurred in the 330 GT. These were, basically, the adoption of the new five-speed fully synchronized gearbox and the disappearance of the overdrive. Also, as on the 330 GT, the new suspended pedals were adapted to the 500 Superfast. Finally, for ventilating the engine compartment, a new panel of three outlets on each fender replaced the panel of eleven louvers. This was the only external difference allowing recognition of the Series II, which was produced in a dozen examples, at the rate of about one a month.

With the 500 Superfast, the refinement, the finish, the comfort, and the immense power which seemed a paradox with such luxury, Ferrari and Pininfarina had, without question, created quite well the Ferrari "Royale."

On the 2.65 metre wheelbase chassis of the 330 GT, Pininfarina created a design that was remarkable as much for its elegance as for its aerodynamic qualities.

A first series of about 24 500 Superfasts were constructed in this form, with several variations from the Geneva Salon prototype.

The second series, about a dozen examples, incorporated several technical modifications. These "Series II" 500 Superfasts were easily distinguished by the new design of the engine compartment vents.

Model Data

500 SUPERFAST
SERIES 1

S/N	Delivery Date	First Owner	Last Known Owner
5951 SF	4 Mar 1964	Prototype/Geneva Salon 1964/Autobecker (D)	
5977 SF	16 Jun 1964	Simons	A. Vallaster (CH)
5979 SF	8 Jul 1964	Zaffaroni (USA)	T. Perkins (USA)
5981 SF	1 Aug 1964	Turin Salon 1964 (I)	N. Soprano (USA)
5983 SF	9 Dec 1964	Brussels Salon 1964	
5985 SF	23 Dec 1964	Chicago Show 1965	
5989 SF	12 Jan 1965	Porta (USA)	R. Taylor (USA)
6033 SF	26 Jan 1965	Reiss (D)	J. Marchetti (USA)
6039 SF	25 Feb 1965	Geneva Salon 1965	O. Chandler (USA)
6041 SF	16 Mar 1965	New York Show 1965	R. Jacoby (USA)
6043 SF	31 Mar 1965	Hanson	
6049 SF	16 Apr 1965	Prince S. Aga Khan (F)	
6267 SF(2)	6 Aug 1965	Prince Bernhard (NL)	(USA)
6303 SF	23 Apr 1965	Livanos (GR)	R. McEntyre (USA)
6305 SF	14 May 1965	Mouzino	B. McMullen (USA)
6307 SF	29 May 1965		N. Silver (USA)
6309 SF	15 Jul 1965	Sachs	
6345 SF (1)	1 Oct 1965	London Show 1965/ R. Wilkins (GB)	Destroyed
6351 SF (1)	28 Nov 1965	Hood (GB)	
6605 SF	8 Jun 1965	Shah of Iran	
6615 SF	21 Sep 1965	(D)	P. Schwartz (USA)
6659 SF (1)	4 Sep 1965	E. Miller (GB)	E. Miller (GB)

Model Data

S/N	Delivery Date	First Owner	Last Known Owner
6661 SF (1)	9 Jun 1965	J. Durlacher (GB)	I. Halbert (GB)
6673 SF (1)	22 Jul 1965	Hyams (GB)	K. Bradshaw (GB)
6679 SF (1)	30 Sep 1965	Peter Sellers (GB)	G.V.K. Burton (GB)

(1) Right Hand Drive
(2) 330 GT with Superfast Body.

500 SUPERFAST
SERIES 2

S/N	Delivery Date	First Owner	Last Known Owner
7817 SF	11 Nov 1965	(USA)	
7975 SF	27 Nov 1965	Shah of Iran	H.K. Edgeley (GB)
8019 SF	22 Dec 1965	Brussels Salon 1966	G. Nickel (USA)
8083 SF	10 Dec 1965	Bailard	B. Pessin (USA)
8253 SF	20 Jan 1966	Friden (USA)	M. Fitz-Gerald (USA)
8273 SF	31 Jan 1966	Knowles	H. Holzer (USA)
8299 SF	8 Feb 1966	New York Show 1966	
8459 SF (1)	1 Mar 1966	J. Durlacher (GB)	
8565 SF	2 Apr 1966	J. von Neumann (USA)	
8739 SF	30 Apr 1966	Battendar (USA)	H. Desormeau (USA)
8817 SF	30 Jun 1966		J. Winter (USA)
8897 SF (1)	1 Aug 1966	Col. R.J. Hoare (GB)	J.G. Crowther (GB)

(1) Right Hand Drive

IV B
The 365 California
1966-1967

For *Ferraristi*, the greatest novelty of the 1966 Geneva Salon was the 330 GTC, a two-place coupe which will be covered in Chapter VI. Our interest here is the 365 California which was unveiled at the same time. This very luxurious cabriolet only had its name in common with the three litre spyder of 1958, being in effect the direct successor of the 500 Superfast. While it was destined to be produced in a very limited number, it nevertheless presented several new ideas which would be found on later production vehicles from Maranello.

Its engine was derived from the single-cam V-12 which was used during the 1966 racing season in the 365Ps of the semi-official racing teams. It retained that engine's principle dimensions, notably the bore (81 mm), the stroke (71 mm) and the total displacement of 4390 cc. With a compression ratio of 8.8 to 1, this new engine was rated at 320 horsepower at 6600 rpm. It was coupled with a five-speed gearbox similar to that which had equipped the 500 Superfast, and continued to equip the 330 GT 2+2. The chassis, with a 2.65 metre wheelbase, was also common to these

(Left) The prototype of the 365 California cabriolet was unveiled at the 1966 Geneva Salon. For this very refined cabriolet, destined to replace the 500 Superfast (and using the same 2.65 metre wheelbase), Pininfarina conceived a harmonious design which was seen again, in part, on the 330 GTC Speciale at the 1967 Brussels Salon.

The angular lines of the rear formed an astonishing contrast with the all curving lines of the front.

three models. Finally, power steering and wire wheels were standard, the alloy wheels similar to those of the 330 GT being available as an option.

The design, created and built by Pininfarina for this cabriolet, did not lack originality. The very well-formed and slender lines were highlighted by a discrete crease running the length of the vehicle. Another characteristic trait of the design was the long side scoop on which was mounted the door handle. This original layout had been introduced on a prototype Dino shown at the 1965 Paris Salon. It will be found again on other Dinos, as will be seen in Chapter VII.

The front and rear of the 365 California were related to those of the 500 Superfast, but the headlights were now covered and the fog lights retracted into the nose, recalling the headlights of Superfast II and III. At the rear was a vertical, truncated panel with, however, a contour and taillight treatment that was different from the 500 Superfast; this even varied from one California to another. Finally, note the astonishing black and while leather interior on this metallic blue cabriolet.

Several months elapsed between the presentation of the prototype at Geneva and the delivery of the first 365 California, but the rhythm of production of the 500 Superfast, about one vehicle per month, was then maintained.

The last California was delivered in July, 1967, a short time before the presentation, at the Paris Salon, of an all-new 2+2 coupe, the 365 GT, which considerably increased the diffusion of the 4.4 litre engine. The same engine also served in the 365 GTC and the 365 GTS spyder, but these Ferraris, which had much greater production figures, will be covered later in Chapter VII.

Certain details varied from one example to another, as can be seen here on the example (8347) of the Marquise de Cuevas. The registration number referred to the North America Racing Team of Luigi Chinetti.

The 365 California, which was produced in about 13 examples in 1966 and 1967, used a chassis with 2.65 metre wheelbase, as on the 330 GT and the 500 Superfast. The 4.4 litre engine, on the other hand, was new.

Model Data

365 CALIFORNIA

S/N	Delivery Date	Original Owner	Last Known Owner
8347	26 Jul 1966	Geneva Salon 1966 D. Fabbri (I)	
9127	10 Oct 1966	Mis de Cuevas (USA)	
9447	19 Dec 1966	Turin Salon 1966	S. Drummy (USA)
9615	30 Jan 1967	(E)	
9631	13 Feb 1967	Geneva Salon 1967	G. Garrison (USA)
9801	22 Mar 1967	New York Show 1967	A. Rabinof (USA)
9849	4 Apr 1967	B. Bickel (USA)	S. Nichols (USA)
9889	11 Apr 1967	M. Joffolini	
9935	19 Apr 1967	M. Jenksbury (USA)	
9985 (1)			A.M. Rind (GB)
10077	29 May 1967	(USA)	
10155	23 Jun 1967	(D)	M. Lampe (USA)
10327	27 Jul 1967	(USA)	VIP Toy Store
10369 (1)			Destroyed

(1) Right Hand Drive

300

It was once again the Paris Salon, in October, 1964, that was chosen by Ferrari for the introduction of a new series, a berlinetta and a spyder, the 275 GTB and and 275 GTS, with a common chassis and engine. The GTB will be taken up first, which was destined to be produced in greater numbers. It was truly in the evolutionary line from the preceding Ferrari berlinettas, although it was more sportive than the 250 GT "Lusso" which it replaced, and the most recent developments in the competition Ferraris were reflected in numerous areas of the GTB.

The design created by Pininfarina for the 275 GTB recaptured with great success the better elements of the styling of the "GTO" 62 and 64, as well as, at the rear, the styling of the GT "Lusso" of 1963. Note also that the famous Borrani wire wheels were abandoned in favor of cast light alloy wheels whose design was directly inspired by the wheels of the 156 Formula 1 of 1963.

The engine, officially designated as Type 213, was the latest incarnation of the V-12 that had been born in 1947. The stroke remained at 58.8 mm, but the bore was increased to 77 mm, giving a single cylinder displacement of about 275 cc and a total displacement of exactly 3285.7 cc. It thus directly inherited the lessons learned with the competition spyders and berlinettas, the 275P and 250M. With a compression ratio of 9.2:1 and three Weber 40 mm dual-choke carburetors, it was rated at 280 horsepower at 7600 rpm. The fitting of six Weber 40 DCN/3 carburetors was offered as an option on the berlinetta, giving about 20 additional horsepower. It is interesting to note that between the 125 of 1947 and the 275 of 1964, that is to say in an 18 year career, the V-12 engine initially conceived by the engineer Giacchino Colombo had gained more than 140% in specific power.

But the most important innovations on this new Gran Turismo berlinetta were found in the chassis and gearbox. An independent rear suspension appeared for the first time on a touring Ferrari, showing once

again the direct influence of the sports/racing Ferraris, with engines centrally located this time, which had been developed with great success by Maranello during the preceding two racing seasons. As at the front, this suspension consisted of unequal length A-arms, combined with a coaxial unit of adjustable tubular shock absorbers and coil springs attached to the A-arm. Another innovation on this touring Ferrari was the five-speed rear-mounted gearbox, allowing a better distribution of masses. Ferrari had already utilized this arrangement on the single seat formula racing cars, and then on the sports/racing cars, as far back as the early '50s. In this instance, the clutch remained coupled to the engine, and a very slender drive shaft was held in place only by a central support with a roller bearing.

Gear selection was effected by an extremely rigid lever, and an exposed gate removed any doubt as to which gear was selected.

As for the rest, the classic chassis of welded tubes was utilized, and a wheelbase of 2.4 metres, typical of Ferrari berlinettas since the end of 1959, was used. Finally, the traditional Borrani wire wheels were replaced by 14 inch wheels cast in light alloy, which recreated the design used on the 156 Formula 1 of 1963. The wire wheels remained available if the owner desired them, however.

The body, designed by Pininfarina and built by Scaglietti at Modena, was the perfect envelope for this powerful berlinetta. The long, plunging hood, the small radiator air intake, the streamlined covered headlights,

the short, truncated rear, and the steeply inclined and sharply curved windshield were all reminiscent of the 250 GTO 64, and the plunging fastback roof line harmonized well with this overall ensemble. Despite this, some observers deplored the slightly deficient height of the windows in relation to the whole design. "It is regrettable that the body of the 275 GTB was dulled by dreary traditionalism, which gave the new model a resemblance to an out-dated vehicle," noted l' **Auto-Journal** after the Salon. But on the other hand, other observers thought that the aesthetic classicism was a major virtue of the GTB. The future would prove them correct, for the styling of the 275 GTB remained a model for the kind, as much for its character as for its originality.

On these frontal views, the prototype (light color) and the production GTB, the one shown at the 1964 Paris Salon, (darker car) displayed several differences, notably the air intake added to the hood of the production version.

Production began just after the Salon, with several examples being delivered before the end of 1964, and it continued without major changes up to the end of 1965.

Jose Rosinski concluded in these words the test of one of these GTBs, published by **Sport-Auto** in July, 1965: "The 275 GTB is, therefore, a superlatively vigorous, very agile and quick automobile. The road holding, while precise and sportive, has some inconveniences along with its improvements. Its comfort, the quality of its finish, the original lines of its bodywork all justify its exceptionally high price, for it is an exceptional automobile. It is a thoroughbred, with luxury devoid of excess, and a fiery temperament. . . ."

The standing start quarter mile was timed in 13.8 seconds, and the mile in 24.8 seconds. A top speed of 148 mph was attained at an engine speed of 7100 rpm. The only reservations expressed concerned the road holding under certain circumstances: "On the road circuit at Monthlery, we were able to fully appraise the road holding of the 275 GTB. The vehicle is very slightly sensitive to roll, and is characterized by a slight tendency to spin, a tendency which is always perfectly controllable and which can be noticeably tamed by using "racing" tires. It is practically impossible to spin the wheels, thanks to the excellent efficiency of the independent rear suspension. The steering is extremely direct and reacts instantly to the smallest corrections by the driver. In 'competition driving' on a circuit where one knows every little bump this is not very troublesome. On the other hand, when traveling fast on the highway it is necessary to be always attentive, and absolutely avoid excessive or abrupt movements of the steering wheel. Because the suspension picks up the little undulations and changes in the pavement, and because these reactions are transmitted to the steering, one is constantly 'at work.' Due to this the GTB is slightly tiring to drive at a fast pace, especially if the pavement is irregular in the correct line."

Several 275 GTB "competition" were sold with this configuration. Note the vent louvers behind the rear wheel well, the external fuel filler on the right sail panel, the bulge in the hood, and the recessed, covered, additional driving lights.

Ferrari also built a few very special GTBs, probably not more than two or three, whose homologation in the GT category was only approved, however, before the 24 Hours of Le Mans. Here one of them is seen at the start of its first race, the Targa Florio of 1965.

In one year the 275 GTB was probably produced in about 250 examples, and this included numerous vehicles bodied entirely in aluminum. Some were used with success in competition by their owners, and notable among these were the Italians Benelli, Billotti, Conti, Rondanini, Gallo, Failli, and Maglione, the Swiss S. Zwimpfer, who captured the Swiss Championship in 1966, and the Portuguese A. de Brito.

At the Frankfurt Salon, in September 1965, Pininfarina presented a new interpretation of the GTB. The headlight covers were devoid of their rims, a bulge appeared on the hood above the carburetors, and the vent window was missing from the driver's side. More important even were external hinges for the trunk lid in order to increase the amount of space available for luggage.

This show car was to remain a one-off and at the Paris Salon, one month later, a new version of the 275 GTB was even further modified. The frontal treatment was totally revamped. In order to eliminate a certain tendency of the nose to lift at high speed, and to improve the steadiness of the bow in the same conditions, the nose was lengthened and lowered, and the radiator air intake was reduced to an ellipse of minimal dimensions. At the rear were found the external trunk hinges and also, a noticeably enlarged window to improve the visibility.

At the Brussels Salon, in January 1966, was displayed the final version of the 1966 GTB which differed externally by a new design of the wheels, without radial fins, directly inspired by those of the prototype P2s of the 1965 racing season.

On the mechanical plane the most important innovation concerned the transmission. In order to eliminate the problems of poor alignment between the engine and the gearbox, the drive shaft was henceforth contained in a tube which assured the rigidity of the engine/gearbox assembly. This important modification was, moreover, adapted to a large number of GTBs of the first series.

The 275 GTB "Series 2" had a somewhat brief career, but it was nevertheless produced in some 200 examples before the series was ended during the winter of 1966. The serial numbers (always odd) were comprised between 7800 and 9000.

Several GTBs, more or less modified, were used in competition by their owners, but this role was more precisely that of the 275 GTB Competition, or 275 GTB/C, which appeared in the spring of 1966. While it retained the appearance of the 275 GTB "Series 2," the 275 GTB/C was a profoundly different automobile, so much so that it was really more than a "competition" development of the 275 GTB.

The differences were quite radical in comparison with the production vehicles. The search for greater power was most visible in some of the components of the engine, these being the high lift camshafts, 250 LM valves, reinforced pistons, a special crankshaft, and new Weber 40 DFI 3 carburetors. At the same time, a strong campaign was waged against excess weight. Very light alloys were used in the building of many of the mechanical pieces, as well as the chassis. The aluminum of the bodywork was thinner than usual, and with the exception of the windshield, all windows were of plexiglas. The only obvious difference was the larger wheels, usually Borrani wire wheels, and the wheel wells which were slightly flared to accommodate them. Finally, for better lubrication during intensive use, a dry sump engine lubrication system with separate oil reservoir was adopted, as in all the sportive creations by Maranello at this time.

A dozen examples were built and sold between May and August, 1966, with serial numbers 9007, 9015, 9027, 9035, 9041, 9051, 9057, 9063, 9067, 9073, 9079, and finally 9085, which in fact ended the 275 GTB series and announced a new 3.3 litre berlinetta, the 275 GTB/4.

This special 275 GTB, built by Pininfarina, was shown at the Frankfurt Salon in 1965. It presented several innovations and announced a new version of the 3.3 litre berlinetta.

The 275 GTB "Series 2" appeared at the 1965 Paris Salon with some important modifications, in both mechanical specifications and appearance. As for the aesthetics, note the larger rear window and the new profile of the front.

The purity of the Pininfarina design can be appreciated from
all angles.

A Ferrari in the snow. The special GTB of Pianta and Lippi during the 1966 Monte Carlo Rallye. It did not finish but retains to this day the honor of being the only Ferrari to have been entered in that event.

By finishing 8th in the general classifications and 1st in the GT class at the 1966 24 Hours of Le Mans, Roy Pike and Piers Courage with the 275 GTB/C (09035) of Maranello Concessionaires, achieved one of the most significant results for this model.

V·B
The 275 GTB/4
& NART Spyder
1966-1968

The 275 GTB/4, the first touring Ferrari to be powered by a four overhead camshaft engine, was first presented at the Paris Salon in October, 1966. This was two years almost to the day after the introduction of the 275 GTB, which was itself the first touring Ferrari with independent rear suspension. In both instances, Maranello furnished new proof of the benefits which competition cars can give to the Gran Turismo vehicles.

Although by its external appearance the new 3.3 litre berlinetta was very similar to the last version of the 275 GTB, that which had been shown at the Brussels Salon in January of the same year, its mechanical architecture was quite radically changed. Its engine, with four overhead camshafts (Type 226) was directly derived from the 3.3 and 4 litre engines which equipped the 275 and 330 P2 prototypes of the 1965 racing season, engines which were in turn derivatives of the 3.5, 3.8, and 4.1 litre engines of the 290, 315, and 335 sports/racers of the 1957 season. Thus, while the Type 226 engine retained the same dimensions, it differed in a number of areas from the 275 GTB (Type 213). Especially revised were the cylinder heads, each fitted with two camshafts which acted directly on the valves without the intermediary of rocker arms. Another change was the adoption of a system of lubrication by dry sump, as on the 275 GTB/C. The separate oil reservoir increased the quantity of useable oil from 10 litres (2.6 gal) to more than 16 litres (4.2 gal).

The announced power output for this new engine was 300 horsepower at 8000 rpm, a number that was less important than the gain in torque and in flexibility. An imposing battery of six Weber 40 DCN 17 carburetors played an important role in achieving that effect.

(Left) Nothing externally differentiated the 275 GTB/4 from the preceding 275 GTB other than a slight bulge in the hood.

Note in the interior the dashboard no longer covered with wood.

The chassis (Type 596) was equally revised and, as on the 330 GTC presented at the beginning of the year, the engine, the drive shaft tube, and the trans-axle were a rigid assembly mounted at four points.

Aesthetically, the design by Pininfarina, a design that had been judged a bit too conservative by some, was carried over intact from the 275 GTB. A raised center section on the hood was one fairly accurate way to distinguish at first glance the new "four-cam" from the 275 GTB of 1966.

An interesting opinion of the 275 GTB/4 was that given by Jean Pierre Beltoise to the readers of l' Auto-Journal (January 19, 1967): "It is, first and foremost, a serious and comfortable gran turismo, but it retains the lineage of a race car in the response of the engine and the quality of the handling. The 275 GTB/4 is one of the greatest automobiles created in our times."

His only reservations concerned the synchronization of first and second gears, the forward visibility, the lighting, and the balance of the brakes, which he judged was a bit too strong on the front.

On the other hand, one can only remain in awe of his judgement of the GTB/4 on the autoroute one Sunday afternoon: "I covered, in complete safety and the greatest comfort, without having to once use the brakes hard and while carrying on a normal conversation with my passenger, the 75 km (46 miles) which separate the Porte d'Orleans from Nemours in a little less than 23 minutes, that is to say, at an average of more than 195 km/h (121 mph), which is remarkable enough without noting that I had to stop for the toll gates."

It appeared that the 275 GTB/C did not have a true counterpart in the GTB/4 series, but several GTB/4s did gain important competition successes in the hands of their owners, particularly in Italy, with L. Nocca, L. Ravizza, P. Barbetti, and "FFI." It also seemed that some examples obtained, at the works itself, special treatment. This was, for example, the case of 09413/GT-4A which, in addition to its special designation, received among other modifications, special pistons, an aluminum body, an external fuel filler, and Borrani wire wheels. It is not known how many similar examples were built.

The major innovation was truly the four overhead camshaft engine, with six double-choke carburetors and dry sump lubrication (Type 226).

While it was not, perhaps, completely official, the NART spyder constituted a very interesting variation on the theme of the GTB/4. It was the direct inspiration of the dynamic and inventive Luigi Chinetti, who probably wanted to offer a more sporty spyder, now that the GTS had been "civilized" by the adoption of the 4 litre engine. There were built, therefore, at Maranello, a limited series of spyders on the base of the 275 GTB/4, and Scaglietti successfully perfected this spyder which retained the lines of the berlinetta. As a form of baptism, the first example (09437) was entered in the 12 Hours of Sebring early in 1967 where it finished in 17th place, driven by Pinky Rollo and the journalist Denise McCluggage. The same spyder was shortly thereafter tested by **Road & Track** (September, 1967) under the title "The Most Satisfying Sports Car in the World."

That test, one of the few to have been published on the 3.3 litre 4-cam, achieved a top speed of 250 km/h (155 mph), with the standard rear axle ratio of 9/32 (3.55 to 1), and the standing start quarter mile was covered in 14.7 seconds.

This magnificent spyder, which was not part of the official Ferrari production, was sold exclusively by the American importer, and it seems that there were not more than 9 examples made.

The career of the 275 GTB/4 was very short. The progressive closing of the American market to vehicles which did not conform to the new rules concerning safety and exhaust emissions played an important role in determining the life span of the 275 GTB/4, as well as other Ferraris. By 1970 the entire production line-up of Ferrari had been entirely renovated. It was the 4.4 litre "Daytona" which became the true replacement for the 3.3 litre berlinetta, even though it was not yet ready when production of the latter ended, in the spring of 1968. In one-and-a-half years the 4-cam berlinetta was produced in about 280 examples, the first known carried the serial number 09233 GT, and the last, 11069 GT.

The NART Spyder, an idea by Luigi Chinetti, that was fantastically executed by Scaglietti.

Visibly inspired by the GTB, the Nembo Spyder of NEri and
M. BOnacini (Carrozzeria Autocorse, Modena) in reality utilized the chassis of a 250 GT. Built in the first quarter of
1966, it was, moreover, earlier than the NART spyder.

V·C
The 365 GTB/4
& 365 GTS/4 Daytona
1968-1973

The idea for a four-cam berlinetta even more powerful than the 275 GTB/4 was born in 1967, at a time when the 3.3 litre engine was just being introduced to the market. The vehicle in question was to be quite different and also would be able to satisfy the new American regulations, so the gestation period was quite lengthy. Between the conception of the project and the building of the definitive prototype on one hand, and then between the official presentation of this prototype and the first deliveries to customers on the other hand, no less than two years had slipped by.

As it was presented in its world premiere at the Paris Salon of 1968, the 365 GTB/4 still had some differences from the final definitive version, the first examples of which were not delivered for another year.

The first known prototype appeared during the winter of 1967, and its bodywork already indicated the lines of the definitive model, although the front part remained directly inspired by the style of the 275 GTB. Much more interesting in this prototype, however, was the V-12 engine which was being tested at that time. It was a 4 litre with four overhead camshafts, three valves per cylinder, dual ignition, and flat, Heron-type cylinder heads with the combustion chamber being formed in the pistons. This engine, however interesting (Type 243), was not retained. The chosen engine (Type 251) was a more conventional 4.4 litre with hemispherical combustion chambers in the cylinder heads and single ignition. In general it retained the architecture of the preceding four-cam, but all of its components were new. In order to accommodate the sizeable increase in displacement, the block was lengthened. The bore and the stroke (81 x 71 mm) were identical to those of the Type 245 engine which

was already in use in the 365 GT 2+2, GTC, and GTS but once again the common pieces were extremely rare. As with the 275 GTB/4, the engine lubrication system of the new 4.4 litre was a dry sump system, and the campacity of the oil reservoir was 14 litres. The compression ratio was 8.8:1 and, with six Weber 40 DCN 20 carburetors, the power was rated at 352 horsepower at 7500 rpm, and the torque rated at 44 kgm at 318 lb/ft) 5500 rpm.

The chassis, of welded oval section tubes, was well within the tradition of the gran turismo Ferraris, and the ensemble consisting of the engine and the five-speed transaxle linked by a rigid drive shaft tube, was mounted to the chassis at four points, two on the engine and two on the transaxle. The 2.40 metre wheelbase was also retained but the front and rear tracks were appreciably increased. The diameter of the brake discs was slightly reduced, but this was compensated for by an improved internal ventilation system. Finally, the wheels of cast light alloy, 7½" wide and 15" in diameter, were of a new five pointed star design inherited directly from the Formula 1 Ferraris. Also notable at this time was the appearance of Michelin as a supplier of tires for the gran turismo Ferraris.

To clothe the 365 GTB/4, Pininfarina created a classical design which admirably continued the traditional lines of the berlinettas from Maranello, being both aggressive and functional at the same time. While retaining the same general balance, with a long hood and a cockpit huddled at the rear, the design did not lack for innovations, among which were the band of perspex which wrapped around the front and screened the headlights and the turn signals, the large glass area extended by rear quarter windows, and the harmonious joining of the roof line to the rear fender line. Several sharp edges appeared, most notably on the front fenders, in contrast to the curves prevalent on the 275 GTB. Finally, the grill lost its oval shape in order to be integrated into the design of the front.

Only the prototype body was actually built by Pininfarina. As with the preceding berlinettas it was Scaglietti who actually built the bodies in steel (with the opening parts in aluminum) for the production examples.

It was, however, the Pininfarina-built prototype which was shown at the first public presentation of the 365 GTB/4. The occasion was once again provided

The V-12 engine of 4.4 litres displacement and with four overhead camshafts was rated at 352 horsepower at 7500 rpm. The air filter for the six carburetors was of a different design on the production versions.

by the Paris Salon, in October, 1968. The car was an immediate success and the press immediately adopted the nickname "Daytona" for this new Ferrari, in honor of the triumph of the red cars at the American 24-hour race the preceding year.

There were a few purists who reproached Ferrari for not producing a gran turismo with a mid-engine, as Lamborghini had done with the Miura. Jose Rosinski was one such critic, writing for the readers of **Sport-Auto**. In **Virage**, Pierre Dieudonné gave an opposing opinion: "The test bank of Ferrari is racing, thus the new 365 GTB/4 is not as avant-garde as it could have been if built as an answer to the Miura, but is instead a synthesis of practicality giving an automobile of the most refined form." **Road & Track** perhaps stated the final argument in titling its test of the car: "The fastest, and best, GT is not necessarily the most exotic." The future would prove them correct, and plenty of orders were received although the

first examples could not be delivered before the middle of 1969.

Of the numerous published tests of the 365 GTB/4, that of l'Equipe (August 16, 1972) was perhaps the most interesting in that it gave precise comparison figures with the Lamborghini Miura, the Mercedes 350 SL, the Jaguar V-12 E-type, and the de Tomaso Pantera. At 278 km/h (172 mph), the Ferrari was the fastest of the five, ahead of the Miura (273 km/h) (169 mph) and the Pantera (241.6 km/h) (150 mph). The much greater power of the Daytona allowed a slightly "longer" final drive ratio than that of the 275 GTB/4 (10x33 in place of 9x32) (3.33 to 1 in place of 3.56 to 1). But the new Ferrari berlinetta also had the best acceleration, with a 13.8 second standing start 400 metres, and 24.3 second standing start kilometre, compared to 14.3 and 25.5 seconds respectively for the Miura, its closest competitor, which was also lighter (2745 lb vs. 3571 lb) than the Ferrari, and more powerful (385 hp DIN vs. 352).

Originally intended for the American market, the retractable headlights (vehicle at right) were standard on all production by 1971.

The first variation on the Daytona theme was the magnificent 365 GTS/4 spyder presented by Pininfarina at the Frankfurt Salon in September, 1969. The conversion was remarkably successful, and the sharp edge formed by the rear deck and the rear fenders harmonized perfectly with the rest of the design, which was not changed from the berlinetta. Only the Borrani wire wheels, which replaced the alloy wheels, were different, but then they were also available on the berlinetta as an option.

At the Paris Salon several weeks later Pininfarina showed a second variation on the same theme, a curious "special coupe" on which the roof was belted by a stainless steel arch. The top was fixed, but behind the arch, the wrap-around rear window was removable. Otherwise the treatment of the rear deck was similar to that of the spyder, with a slight elongation being noticeable, and the bumpers were more enveloping. This coupe remained a one-of-a-kind, but such was not the case with the spyder, which Scaglietti built in several limited series throughout the career of the Daytona. The 365 GTS/4 was, therefore, a sort of official successor to the NART spyder.

The first variation on the Daytona theme was the 365 GTS/4 unveiled in September, 1969, at the Frankfurt Salon. The adaption was perfectly successful, requiring a minimum of modifications to the original lines.

At the 1969 Paris Salon a few weeks later, Pininfarina
showed this special coupe, with removable rear window and
elongated rear, on its own stand.

By the end of August, 1971, the production of the 365 GTB/4 had reached the 500 examples required for homologation in Group 4 (Special Grand Touring) of the international racing code. At first Maranello had no intention of exploiting this opportunity. The Daytona was a touring vehicle, although it was certainly well conceived and executed. But to build a race car from a vehicle intended for the road was a practice that was diametrically the opposite of the traditional philosophy at Ferrari. Racing improved the breed, so to attempt to reverse the process was of no value. At the insistence of several enthusiasts, however, the factory somewhat modified this line of action although its involvement was always nebulous. In the beginning these enthusiasts were Charles Pozzi, the new Ferrari importer for France; Colonel R.J. Hoare, the importer

The weight of the Daytona entered in the 1971 24 Hours of Le Mans by Luigi Chinetti's NART was 3338 lb. This first attempt was completed by a brilliant 5th place overall, well ahead of all the GT class. But the 365 GTB/4 was not yet homologated in that class, so the team of Luigi Chinetti, Jr. and Bob Grossman had to content themselves with a first place in the class of "a good try."

for the British Isles and, for a number of years, racing as a semi-official Ferrari team under the title "Maranello Concessionaires," Jacques Swaters and Georges Filipinetti, who played the same role in Belgium and Switzerland with Ecurie Francorchamps and Scuderia Filipinetti, and above all Luigi Chinetti, the indefatigable force behind the North American Racing Team (NART).

In fact, it was Chinetti who first succumbed to the attraction of the Daytona as a race car, and entered one of the first examples (12467) in the 1969 24 Hours of Le Mans. An accident in practice cut short this first venture, but the fifth place won in the 1971 24 Hours by Bob Grossman, "Coco" Chinetti (the son), and the same vehicle certainly put the fire to the powder. A request for homologation in Group 4 was submitted by Ferrari, but without real conviction as the Daytona of record was a strictly production example. The range of allowable modifications was, therefore, rather restricted. The homologation was not to become effective until January 1, 1972, but the corner had been turned. Ferrari had agreed to enlist in the "Competition Daytona" operation.

The factory's involvement was not completely official, first of all because the cars were to be raced by

One of the three vehicles from the first series with aluminum body, plexiglas windows, and wheels of 8" and 9" was that of Scuderia Filipinetti (14437) with which Elford and Kingsland placed fourth in the 1971 Tour de France.

One of the two vehicles in aluminum with glass windows, for NART, was 14885 with which Luigi Chinetti, Jr. and Bob Grossman were classed 2nd in GT at the 1972 12 Hours of Sebring.

private entrants, and secondly because the cars were not constructed at the Ferrari racing shops at Maranello, but at the "Customer Assistance" facility on Viale Trento e Trieste, in Modena. We shall look at this interesting adventure which unfolded in three stages.

Work on the first three examples began in 1971, with that year's Tour de France, a competition in which the 250 GT had been particularly brilliant in earlier days, being the objective. With their homologation in Group 4 having not yet become effective, the 365 GTB/4s competed in Group 5, directly against the Matra 630 spyders, but a greater latitude was therefore allowed in their preparation. The mechanical preparation, however, was limited by the factory to a very careful assembly and some modifications to the tuning. The most important effort was directed toward saving weight, as the bodies were made in aluminum, with the hood, trunk, and doors in plastic as were the side and rear windows. Finally, wider rims (8 inches in front, 9 inches in the rear) were fitted with racing tires.

The results were heartening for the two examples that were actually entered in the Tour de France (the third car, 14429, was sold to a fortunate Italian customer for his personal use). The Scuderia Filipinetti car (14437) finished fourth, with Elford and Kingsland driving, and the car of Charles Pozzi (14407) finished ninth with drivers Andruet and Roure.

This first series was completed by two additional examples (14485 and 14489) which differed from the first three in having the standard glass windows. They were delivered to NART in early 1972 for the 12 Hours of Sebring.

At this same time a new "semi-official" series was begun, with the 1972 24 Hours of Le Mans being the objective. This series once again was comprised of five vehicles, 15225 for Scuderia Filipinetti, 15373 for Ecurie Francorchamps, 15667 for Charles Pozzi, 15681 (with right-hand drive) for Maranello Concessionaires, and 15685 for NART. This time the body-work was in steel, and the wheels were wider (9 and 11 inches) but the mechanical preparation consisted of very little more than that given the preceding series. During this same time, Luigi Chinetti was having additional examples prepared right and left, using normal examples as a base, to enlarge his team, 13367 and 13855 by Sport Auto-Modena, 14065 at Holman

and Moody, and 14141 at Traco, in the United States. The "works" GTB/4s remained, however, the best of the lot. At Le Mans, for example, of the nine Daytonas which started in 1972, the first four finishers in the Special Grand Touring class were all of the semi-official 1972 set. In the lead (and in fifth place overall) was the car of Team Pozzi (15667) driven by Andruet and Ballot-Lena.

Jarier and Young captured the Grand Touring class in the Watkins Glen 6-Hour race with the NART car (15685). Team Pozzi inscribed, for the eleventh time, the Ferrari name on the honor roll of winners of the Tour de France for automobiles with Andruet, "Biche," and 15667 again. Finally, Team JCB, who had acquired the Maranello Concessionaires car (15681), closed the 1972 season with a victory in Grand Touring class at the 9-hours of Kyalami, in South Africa.

These successes encouraged an even greater effort for 1973. A new series of five special Daytonas were put into production. With 450 horsepower they were obviously more powerful. They were 16343 for NART, 16363 for Charles Pozzi, 16367 for a Ferrari dealer in California, Francisco Mir, 16407 for NART again, and 16425, with right-hand drive, for Jacques Swaters' Ecurie Francorchamps. These vehicles comprised a synthesis of the experience gained with the preceding series, but also introduced some important innovations. The engine was fitted with special pistons, had a compression ratio of 9.9:1, was fitted with chrome rings, and had reinforced wrist-pins. The racing type connecting rods were machined from a steel billet, as had been done with the connecting rods for the GTO. Camshafts now allowed a greater opening, and the timing was sharper. The ram air intake was enlarged and the diameter of the manifolds was tuned to the length of the exhaust. Modification was made to the advance curve of the distributors, and special ignition drives were mounted. Four bendix fuel pumps, in place of the two used in 1972, were fitted, with the surge tank in the rear compartment. Several NART cars, and only they, received a special transmission cooling layout. The brakes were improved, with the disc calipers being enlarged to allow thicker pads, and forced air ducts were fitted to cool the discs, which remained covered. The ususal brake servo was omitted in favor of two master cylinders with independent dual circuits and an adjustable pedal. The suspension

After a victory in GT at the 24 Hours of Le Mans (Andruet /Ballot-Lena), the "Series 2" competition Daytona of Team Pozzi (15667) won, with Andruet and "Biche," the 1972 Tour de France.

The first outing for the "Series 3" competition Daytona of Ch. Pozzi (16363) at the 4 Hours of Le Mans in 1973. It would win another GT victory (Ballot-Lena/Elford) in the 24 Hours three months later.

mountings made use of Uniball joints in place of the traditional silentblocs, and the diameter of the front and rear stabilizer bars was reinforced.

Finally, in conformity with the new safety regulations, two special fuel intake passages that permitted venting of the tanks were installed at the rear, and the standard fuel reservoirs were replaced by two fuel cells.

In the interior the roll-over bar became a sort of cage with a large tube passing above the doors and windshield. The speedometer disappeared at this time from the dashboard, and cockpit ventilation was improved. The headlamps received quartz-iodine lamps and, on the cars for the French importer, the electrical installations were completely duplicated so as to prevent a total failure. A second windshield wiper motor was even fitted as a spare!

Throughout 1973, several of the 1972 cars received some of these same modifications, such as 16383 in the United States. None, however, were given the connecting rods and pistons that were exclusively used on the "Works" type engines.

The first success of the season, the second place of Minter and Migault at the 24 Hours of Daytona, was won by the "non-official" special (14141) of Luigi Chinetti, but it was above all at the 24 Hours of Le Mans that one expected to find the Ferrari successes. For the second time the victory went to the team of Charles Pozzi, who captured the Special Grand Touring class with Ballot-Lena and Elford in 16363, which was driven back to Paris following the race! This proved the incredible reliability of the Daytona as an all-around car. The epic of the Daytona was not finished, either, as is seen from the following table (p.   ) which summarizes its racing career. Final proof can be found in the second place overall won in the 1979 24 Hours of Daytona by Morton Adamowicz, and 16407 from 1973, seven years later.

At the end of 1973 the first 365 GT4/BBs were delivered, and with them the page of Ferrari belinettas with front engines was definitely turned by the men of Maranello. The Daytona continued to be heard from on the race tracks, but from this time on it will be totally the result of private initiatives. Such was the case notably for 16717, the last Daytona for Ecurie Francorchamps, built for the 1975 Le Mans race from a production berlinetta. It received all the proper modifications, but was entirely prepared in Brussels.

One should also recall the appearance at the 1975 Geneva Salon of a spyder built by Giovanni Michelotti to the order of Luigi Chinetti. This spyder was quite unusual, resembling in certain ways the Chevrolet Corvette, and was built from a production Daytona (15965). Its most remarkable features were undoubtably a removable roof and a rear window that could be lowered electrically. But the most astonishing fact was its entry in the 24 Hours of Le Mans that same year. It participated in practice, but unfortunately not in the race as a result of a regrettable argument which provoked the withdrawal of the entire NART entry just one hour before the start of the race.

Another special not lacking in originality was the "Sport Wagon" designed by an American architect, Bob Gittlemen, and built at the end of 1975 by Panther Westwinds, in England, to the order of "Coco" Chinetti and Gene Garfinkle. Only the hood and the windshield were saved from the berlinetta which was used as a base. The finish was particularly well done, but the primary innovation was the treatment of the rear, where two "butterfly" doors allowed access, from each side, to the luggage compartment. The turbocompressor originally intended for the car, according to the designers, would allow this "utility" vehicle to attain a top speed of 370 km/h (229 mph), but apparently it was never installed.

It is not known for certain how many examples of the Daytona were made. The serial numbers comprised between 12400 and 17000. A total figure of 1350 units (berlinettas and spyders) is probably close to the actual number and it will probably remain for a long time the best seller of the thoroughbreds from Maranello.

In 1974 Luigi Chinetti Sr. had Giovanni Michelotti build this "Spyder NART" destined for the actor/driver Steve McQueen.

Luigi Chinetti once again went to Michelotti in 1975 for the transformation of another Daytona (15965) which was even entered in the 1975 24 Hours of Le Mans.

WHERE ARE THEY NOW?

Series 1—1971

14407	Ch. Pozzi—C. Grandet—J. Serres (F)
11429	Dott. Mariani—M.A. Tippetts (I)
14437	Sc. Filipinetti—W. Felber (CH)—R. Ramsey, Jr. (USA)
14885	L. Chinetti—?
14889	L. Chinetti—D. Fong (USA)

Series 2—1972

15225	Sc. Filipinetti—N. Buhrer (CH)
15373	J. Swaters (B)—T.A. Robert (GB)
15667	Ch. Pozzi—G. Domet (F)
15681	Maranello C.—JCB—P. Dowell—G. Marsh—M. Neilan (GB)
15685	L. Chinetti—D. Fong—K. Starbird (USA)

Series 3—1973

16343	L. Chinetti—V. Loh—J. Crevier—E. Johnson (USA)
16363	Ch. Pozzi—J.C. Bajol—J.P. Delaunay (F)
16367	F. Mir—J. Levitt—R. Keller (USA)
16407	L. Chinetti—D. Carradine—J. McRoberts/W. Nicholas (USA)
16425	J. Swaters (B)—R. Gordon—H. Edgley (GB)

Competition Results

1969	24 Hours of Le Mans (15/16 June)				
	16	NART	12467	Grossman/Posey	DNS

1970	24 Hours of Daytona (31-1/1 February)				
	22	NART	?	Gregory/Pickett	DNF

	12 Hours of Sebring (21 March)				
	25	NART	?	Cluxton/Pickett	DNS

1971	12 Hours of Sebring (20 March)				
	24	NART	?	Cluxton/Grossman	12th, 5th Class

	24 Hours of Le Mans (12/13 June)				
	58	NART	12467	Grossman/Chinetti	5th

	1000 Kms of Paris (17 October)				
	9	Pozzi	14407	Andruet/Ballot-Lena	3rd

	16th Tour de France Automobile (17/25 September)				
	138	Filipinetti	14437	Elford/Kingsland	3rd
	140	Pozzi	14407	Andruet/Roure	7th

1972	6 Hours of Daytona (6/7 February)				
	18	Ring Free Team	12467	Grossman/Reynolds	15th OA, 6th Class
	19			Matthews	
	22	NART	14885	Posey/Bucknum	DNF

	4 Hours of Le Mans				
	39	Pozzi	14407	Ballot-Lena/Andruet	4th
	98	Cornet-Epinat	14049	Cornet-Epinat	

	Sebring 12 Hours (25 March)				
	22	NART	14885	Chinetti/Grossman	8th OA, 2nd Class
	21	NART	14889	Posey/Adamovicz	13th OA, 3rd Class
	18	Bakers Motors	12467	Ingle/Reynolds	19th OA, 5th Class
	1	K.F. White	14065	Hobbs/Scott	DNF

	Agaci/Montlhéry (16 April)				
	45	Pozzi	14407	Ballot-Lena/Rouveyran	18th OA, 6th Class

	24 Hours of Le Mans (10/11 June)				
	39	Pozzi	15667	Andruet/Ballot-Lena	5th OA, 1st Class
	74	NART	15685	Posey/Adamovicz	6th OA, 2nd Class
	34	Filipinetti	15225	Parkes/Lafosse	7th OA, 3rd Class
	36	Francorchamps	15373	Bell/Pillette/Bond	8th OA, 4th Class
	38	NART	13855	Jarier/Buchet	9th OA, 5th Class
	57	NART	14141	Chinetti/Gregory	DNF
	35	Filipinetti	14437	Chennevière/Vetsch	DNF
	37	Maranello C.	15681	Westbury/Hine	DNF
	75	Pozzi	14407	Migault/Rouveyran	DNF

	6 Hours of Watkings Glen (22 July)				
	22	NART	15685	Jarier/Young	6th OA, 1rst Class
		Baker Motors	12467	Di Lorenzo/Reynolds	11th OA, 5th Class
	21	NART		Hobbs/Posey	DNF

Competition Results

XVIIth Tour de France Automobile (14/24 September)

118	Pozzi	15667	Andruet/«Biche»	1rst
117	Pozzi	14407	Rouveyran/Migault	2nd
119	Filipinetti	15225	Elford/Stone	DNF

1 000 kms of Paris (Rouen, 15 October)

21	NART	14889	Jarier/Lafitte	9th OA, 3th Class
22	Pozzi	15667	Andruet/Ballot-Janet	10th OA, 4th Class
23	Pozzi	14407	Migault/Rouveyran	11th OA, 5th Class

9 Hours of Kyalami (4th November)

	J.C.B.	15681	Brown/Sytner	12th OA, 1rst Class

1973

24 Hours of Daytona (3/4 February)

22	NART	14141	Minter/Migault	2th OA, 1rst Class
21	NART	14889	Grossman/Chinetti	5th OA, 2nd Class
23	NART	16343	Ballot-Lena/Andruet	DNF
20	NART	15685	Merzario/Jarier	DNF

4 Hours of Le Mans (1st April)

32	Pozzi	16363	Andruet/Wollek	3th OA, 1rst Class
33	NART	14889	Migault/Guitteny	5th OA, 2rd Class
31	J.C.B.	15681	Green/Corner	6th OA, 3rd Class
46	Grandet	14407	Guenrie/Grandet	9th OA

1 000 kms of SPA (6 May)

42	Francorchamps	16425	Pillette/Bond	12th OA

24 Hours of Le Mans (9/10 June)

39	Pozzi	16363	Ballot-Lena/Elford	6th OA, 1rst Class
40	Pozzi	15667	Dolhem/Serpaggi	9th OA, 3rd Class
38	NART	14141	Chinetti/Migault	13th Oa, 6th Class
34	Francorchamps	16425	Andruet/Bond	20th OA, 12th Class
6	NART	16407	Posey/Minter	DNF
36	NART	14889	Grossman/Guitteny	DNF
33	J.C.B.	15681	Green/Corner	DNF
37	D & S.R.T.	16367	di Patma/Garcia-Veiga	DNF
56	Shark Team	14407	Gueurie/Grandet	DNF

6 Hours of Watkings Glen (21 July)

24	D. & S.R.T.	16367	Garcia-Veiga/Monguzzi	13th OA, 5th Class
8	NART		Posey/Migault	14th OA, 6th Class
9	Grossman		Grossman/Yenko	15th OA, 7th Class

1974

4 Hours of Le Mans (24 March)

30	C. Grandet	14407	Grandet	4th
29	H. Jones	13367	Mignot/Jones	7th

24 Hours of Le Mans (15/16 June)

71	Grandet-Pozzi	14407	Grandet/«Bardini»	5th OA, 1rst Class
54	NART	14141	Heinz/Cudini	6th OA, 2rd Class
56	NART	16407	Ethuin/Guitteny	11th OA, 5th Class
57	H. Jones	13367	Mignot/Jones	16th OA, 9th Class
55	NART		Paoli/Couderc	DNF

	6 Hours of Watkins Glen (12 July)				
	55	NART		Hiss/Cudini	DNF
	82	D.&S. (F. Mir)	16367	Garcia-Viega/Waco	DNF
1975	24 Hours of Daytona (1/2 February)				
	71	V. Loh	16343	Woodner/Phillips	7th OA, 1st Class
	0	NART	14141	Minter/Ballot-Lena/ Gagliardi	28th
	56	H. Jones	13367	Jones/Mignot/Grandet	DNF
	Sebring IMSA				
	87	H. Jones	13367	Jones/Mignot	9th
	Riverside IMSA (10 May)				
	4	K. Starbird	15685	Kline/Cord	16th
	24 Hours of Le Mans (14/15 June)				
	47	Francorchamps	16717	Andruet/Pillette/de Fierlant	12th
	48	H. Jones	13367	Mognot/Jones/Gurdjian	13th
	46	NART/Ward	15965	Faccetti/Bucknum	DNS
	45	NART	16407	Guitteny	DNS
1976	24 Hours of Daytona (21 Jan/1 Feb)				
	71	K. Starbird	15685	Minter/Cord/Adams	6th
1977	24 Hours of Daytona				
	64		14437	Minter/Forbes-Robinson /Newman	5th
	65		16407	Morton/Wood/Carradine	DNS
	66		15685	Barbour/Cannon/ Adamowicz	DNF
	12 Hours of Sebring				
			16407	Morton/Carradine Bondurant/Minter/ Smothers	10th
	Laguna Seca IMSA (1 May)				
				J. Cannon	DNF
	Belgium Championship		16617	M. Dantinne	
	French Hillclimb Championship		15225	N. Buhrer (Group 4)	1st
	SCCA Regional B Production Championship		13771	R. Donner	
1978	24 Hours of Daytona				
	94		13367	Henn/Sahlman/Satullo	
			13371	Henderson/Turner/Hillin	25th
			16407	Morton/Adamowicz/ Carradine	8th
			15965	Devendorf/Keyser/Kline	DNS
1979	24 Hours of Daytona				
	64		16407	Morton/Adamowicz	2nd

VI
More Power and Luxury
VI·A
The 275 GTS, 330 GTS
& 365 GTS
1964-1969

When production of the 250 GT Spyder California was ended in early 1963, there was no longer a Ferrari convertible available. The 275 GTS came along in October, 1964, to correct that state of affairs when it was displayed, along side the 275 GTB, at the Paris Salon. These two new vehicles, which were unveiled at the same time, were in fact very similar to each other. The berlinetta and the spyder used the same 2.40 metre wheelbase chassis and the same 3.3 litre engine, although the power rating of the engine used for the spyder was less, 260 horsepower @ 7000 rpm as opposed to 280 horsepower for the berlinetta. On the other hand, a shorter final drive ratio (10/33 as opposed to 9/32) gave the spyder a higher top speed.

The major difference was in the bodywork. For the 275 spyder, Pininfarina created a compact and harmonious design which recaptured, on a reduced scale, several of the characteristic traits of the 330 GT 2+2 coupe created barely a year earlier. The front, this time, had only two headlights, the rear fenders were marked by a slight rise over the rear wheel arches, and

(Left and below) For the 275 GTS which was unveiled at the 1964 Paris Salon, Pininfarina adapted the basic lines of the 330 GT 2+2 to the 2.40 metre wheelbase chassis.

Several modifications were made at the beginning of 1965,
and a hard top of original design was offered as an option.

the rear was shorter and less massive than that of the 2+2 coupe.

With an overall length of 4.32 metres, this luxurious spyder, whose bodies were actually built by Pininfarina at Turin, was even more compact than the berlinetta, but its lines were much less aggressive. In the interior, a new arrangement of the seats allowed a slightly larger chair for the passenger, making it possible to carry three persons in case of an emergency, but for only a short distance. This arrangement was, however, only seen on the very first examples.

Finally, the new cast light alloy wheels used on the berlinetta were not fitted to the spyder, which remained faithful to the Borrani wire wheels, albeit in the new diameter of 14 inches.

Several modifications appeared at the beginning of 1965, the most notable being the design of the engine compartment air outlets. The three vents introduced at that time were common to the GTS, the 330 GT 2+2 and the 500 Superfast. A hard top also became avaliable as an option at this same time, and the four rear exhaust outlets were set noticeably further apart.

Road & Track published, in September 1966, a detailed test of the 275 GTS. Weight as tested was found to be 3345 lb. At 7000 rpm it attained a maximum speed of 233 km/h (145 mph), and the standing start quarter mile was covered in 15.7 seconds. The figures published by **Car and Driver** a month later, after their test of an identical vehicle, did not completely agree. They gave 14 seconds for the standing start quarter mile, and 231 km/h (143 mph) for the maximum speed.

Production, which began in the final weeks of 1964, continued without major modifications until the end of 1965. At that time the rigid drive shaft of the GTB was also adopted for the GTS, and the wire wheels were replaced by the light alloy wheels identical to those fitted to the 275 GTB "Series 2." Before the 330 GTS came along to replace it, the 3.3 litre spyder was produced in about 200 examples, whose serial numbers (always odd) are found between 6000 and 8600.

The larger passenger seat was very quickly abandoned.

The 330 GTS appeared some time before the 1966 Paris Salon where it was first put on public display along with the 275 GTB/4, which we have already covered. The new spyder actually represented a convertible version of the 330 GTC coupe presented six months earlier at the Geneva Salon, and it used the coupe's mechanical base intact. This new GTS therefore differed in numerous points from the 275 GTS, although its body remained essentially unchanged other than the nose which was identical to that of the 330 GTC. The 4 litre engine of the 330 GT 2+2 was used, but the block had a new external design with only two chassis mounting points. The engine and the transaxle were united into a rigid assembly by the tube which enclosed the drive shaft, and this entire assembly was mounted to the chassis at four points, two on the transaxle and two on the engine. This mode of mounting, which very noticeably reduced the noise level in the cockpit, was hence forth standard in all Ferrari production cars, even in the 330 GT 2+2 which retained a gearbox attached directly to the engine, as we saw in Chapter IV.

It is interesting to compare the test which **Road & Track** conducted at different times of the two models of the GTS, the 275 in September, 1966, and the 330 in August, 1968. The figures in the following table very clearly demonstrate the improved performance brought about by the increase in power and torque:

		275 GTS	330 GTS
Acceleration: 0 to	40 mph	4.1 sec.	4.0 sec.
	50	5.7	5.5
	60	7.2	6.9
	100	18.8	17.1
	120	28.6	26.4
0 to	100 ft.	3.4	3.1
	500	8.7	8.0
	1/4 mile	15.7	14.9
Speed at end of 1/4 mile		91 mph	95 mph
Maximum speed @ 7000 rpm		144 mph	
@ 6600 rpm			145 mph

The titles used in **Road & Track** for these tests serve as a reminder of the pleasures experienced in driving these two Ferrari spyders. For the 275 GTS the title was already tempting: "Those Who Like Driving Owe Themselves At Least One of These." But for the 330 GTS it was even more alluring: "Go Ahead, Give Yourself a Treat, Buy One." The Americans did not fail to follow this advice, and the majority of the GTs were sold in that market. This, despite the vehicle regulations which, at that time, were being rendered more and more severe by the American government.

The 330 GTS was presented in 1966, shortly after the 330 GTC from which it adopted the basic design and the mechanical specifications.

At the end of 1968, the 330 GTS was replaced by the 365 GTS. Probably produced in some 100 examples, the 330 GTS was similar to two other Ferrari convertibles: the 365 California already discussed in Chapter IV, and the 275 GTS/4 NART discussed in Chapter V.

The 365 GTS which was written into the production catalog for 1969 faithfully followed the evolution of the GTC coupe by adopting the 4.4 litre two-cam engine born with the 365 California. This same engine was also mounted in the new 2+2 coupe, the 365 GT. The increase in displacement was accomplished by increasing the bore to 81 mm, and the published power rating was raised to 320 horsepower, still at 6600 rpm. The rest of the mechanical layout was unchanged from the preceding model, and only the change in location of the engine compartment air vents allowed external differentiation between the 365 GTS and the 330 GTS. These vents were removed from the flanks and placed, in the form of two flat grills, on the engine compartment lid. The hard top that had been created for the 275 GTS, plus the wire wheels, and the installation of air conditioning remained available as options, as had been the case with the preceding 4 litre spyder as well.

The 365 GTS had a very brief career. By the middle of 1969 it was phased out in favor of the 365 GTB/4, which was not really a replacement for it as the Daytona was a whole new species of Ferrari. In actuality, it was not until 1971 and the first deliveries of the Daytona Spyder that a Ferrari convertible was once again available.

The 365 GTS in all probability was not produced in more than 20 examples. The short time span for its production was not sufficient to explain this very low number. Part of the responsibility must be placed on the out-dated styling, particularly when compared to the Daytona, but the most profound cause can be traced to the United States. There the new safety laws were becoming very strict, requiring manufacturers to make extensive modifications and run expensive tests. Ferrari had become willing to play along with the regulations, but only with new models.

There does not appear to have been built, originally, any special bodies for the GTS. Nevertheless, there was the transformation built by William Harrah in the United States on a 330 GTS (10913). Following the "Targa" principle of Porsche, the American agent gave this GTS a solid stainless steel arch. A generous rear window enclosed the rear of the cockpit, covering a large part of the rear deck.

While it is not known for certain that it used the chassis of a GTS, a spyder built by Zagato in 1974 to the order of Luigi Chinetti does not want for originality (The creations by that Milanese bodybuilder that were applied to Ferrari chassis can be counted on the fingers of the hands). The extreme front of the Spyder 3Z seen in Chapter III was used here again, but the hand of Zagato was even more obvious in the mixture of curves and sharp angles which made up the balance of the design, a style often judged to be a bit too geometric.

The archives of Pininfarina recount a total of 320 of the GTS bodies being built in the three versions: 275, 330, and 365. This was a record that has not yet been equalled by any other series of Ferrari convertibles.

The 365 GTS which appeared at the end of 1968 was recognizable by the new air outlets for the engine compartment.

The geometric lines on this 1974 spyder are easily recognized as being by Zagato.

VI·B
The 330 GTC & 365 GTC
1966-1970

In 1966 the Ferrari range was composed of five models. The 330 GT was in its third year of successfully continuing the 2+2 formula. The 275 GTB was entering its second year, having undergone some very important modifications which allowed it to continue with even more elan the most ancient tradition of Maranello, that of the two-place high performance berlinetta. The 275 GTS was a direct derivative of the GTB, in convertible form and the 500 Superfast continued in its role of "Super Ferrari" for the select few, a combination of speed, luxury and comfort. There was no direct successor to the 250 GT "Lusso," whose production had ceased in 1964 with the introduction of the 275 GTB. The role of being an intermediate

between the sportive berlinetta and the 2+2 coupe was precisely that given to the 330 GTC coupe, which was unveiled at the Geneva Salon, in March, 1966.

The 330 GTC can be briefly described as a luxurious two-place coupe by Pininfarina, combining the four litre engine of the 330 GT 2+2 with the short wheelbase chassis of the 275 GTB and GTS. The engine (Type 209) was in fact the same four litre which had equipped the 2+2 since its appearance at the beginning of 1964. Its system of attachment to the chassis was, however, modified to adapt it to the architecture of front engine/rear gearbox inherited from the berlinetta. The rigid assembly of engine/gearbox was attached to the chassis at four points, two on the transaxle and two on the engine, using solid rubber mounting pads made by Saga. The engine block therefore had to be redesigned, and it was given the new designation of 209/66. Nevertheless, it retained all the dimensions and characteristics of the preceding version, especially

(Left and below) Intermediary between the 330 GT 2+2 coupe and the 275 GTB berlinetta, the 330 GTC appeared at the 1966 Geneva Salon with this harmonious design by Pininfarina.

the bore and stroke (77 x 71 mm) which gave it a total displacement of exactly 3967 cc (or about 330 cc per single cylinder). With the same Weber 40 DCZ 6 carburetors and the same 8.8:1 compression ratio, it was rated at the same power, which was 300 horsepower at 6600 rpm.

The chassis (Type 592 C) continued the general architecture and the 2.40 metre wheelbase of the berlinetta, the biggest innovation by comparison with the 2+2 being the four-wheel independent suspension.

To clothe this new coupe, Pininfarina created a compact design with great harmony of lines. It combined with great success the nose of the 500 Superfast, the rear of the 275 GTS, and a greenhouse agreeably lightened by a very generous amount of window area. As on the 2+2, the spyder, and the Superfast, the 330 GTC had its body built at Pininfarina itself, and as a result its finish was particularly well done.

The first test of the 330 GTC was published on November 19, 1966 by the English weekly, **Motor**, and it was signed by Paul Frere. This famous driver and journalist gave an interesting and very forceful opinion of this new Ferrari. "The greatest surprise is the silence of the engine" was his first comment. The new system of mounting the engine/gearbox group to the chassis had a profound effect in lowering the noise and vibra-tions transmitted into the cockpit, as effective as increasing the amount of sound-proofing insulation would have been. "In handling, the 330 GTC is exactly like all the Ferraris which I have driven before. . . It is close to being as neutral a vehicle as one could want, and if pushed to the limits of adhesion on a dry road (I did not have the opportunity to drive it in the wet), it is the rear which gently breaks loose first, in a marvelously controllable manner, and with slight variations possible in response to speed changes. . . I much prefer this discrete final understeer to the more decidedly understeering characteristic of the 330 GT. The 330 GTC also improves on the latter with a quicker steering, with just three turns lock-to-lock. . . But the most impressive feature of the handling of the new vehicle is the solidness with which it changes direction, particularly in the S-bends, where it tracks with about the same precision as a modern race car, and without the floating sensation that is the general characteristic of touring vehicles and the majority of production sports cars. . . The general refinement of the 330 GTC also applies to its comfort. . . The highest speed which I was able to attain in two attempts with the 330 GTC was 235 km/h (146 mph) at about 6600 rpm, this on a road that was flat and with practically no wind blowing, before traffic forced me to lift my foot. But at

Pininfarina built several examples of this 330 GTC Speciale, originally intended for Princess de Rethy. This design also inspired that of the 365 GT 2+2.

this speed the vehicle was still perceptibly accelerating, and without doubt it would have reached the 240 km/h (149 mph) mark and probably equalled the speed announced by the manufacturer of 242 km/h (150 mph)."

Some acceleration figures, 14.6 seconds for the standing start quarter mile, and 26.3 seconds for the kilometre, close this account rendered by a rare authority.

The 330 GTS which was presented at the Paris Salon, in October, 1966, was nothing more nor less than a convertible version of the 330 GTC, and the production line-up for 1967 was brought into harmony with this new two-place coupe, the proof of which we have already seen with the 330 GT.

While orders for special bodywork were becoming somewhat rare, the 330 GTC was, nevertheless, the object of an interesting exercise presented by Pininfarina at the Brussels Salon in January, 1967. This coupe combined with very remarkable elegance the streamlined nose of the 365 California cabriolet and the vertical concave rear window designed by Pininfarina in 1965 for the prototype Dino 206 S. Other than these innovations, the rest of the design was sober and somewhat rectilinear. This same inspiration will be found in the lines of the 365 GT coupe which prolonged the dynasty of the 2+2 starting in late 1968. On the nose of this special coupe, destined for the Belgian royal family, were found retractable fog lights similar to those of the 365 California. Several standard 330 GTCs were also equipped with a similar arrangement, and the special coupe shown at Brussels was itself copied by two or three additional examples.

The production of the 330 GTC continued without major change until the end of 1968, when it was re-placed by the 365 GTC. It was built in about 600 examples, whose serial numbers (always odd) are found between 8200 and 11700.

The 365 GTC which immediately took the place of the 330 GTC was not externally differentiated other than the repositioning of the engine compartment air vents (some late examples of the 330 were also so equipped). These vents were removed from the flanks of the front fenders and relocated in the hood, just in front of the windshield.

On the mechanical level, the most consequential change was the adoption of the 4.4 litre engine which was already being used in the 365 GT 2+2, introduced at the 1967 Paris Salon. The additional 400 cc obtained by increasing the bore to 81 mm allowed the power to increase from 300 to 320 horsepower, at the same engine speed of 6600 rpm, but the gain in torque, from 33.2 to 37 mkg (267 lb/ft) at 5000 rpm, was even more considerable. The maximum speed, therefore, was not increased, but the various acceleration times were noticeably improved.

Probably because of the same reasons mentioned in conjunction with the 365 GTS, production of the 365 GTC did not last for more than a year. The American market was being progressively closed to vehicles that were not designed specifically with that market in mind, as will be the case with the 365 GTC/4 in 1971. Therefore production of the 365 GTC ceased at the beginning of 1970, and its place in the Ferrari range was left vacant for the time being. Nevertheless, it was built in about 150 to 200 examples (serial numbers comprised between 11800 and 12700), demonstrating that the men of Maranello were treating the two-place coupes with the same care as the four-place coupes and the more sportive berlinettas.

The 365 GTC appeared at the end of 1968, at the same time as the 365 GTS. Like the latter, it was recognizable by the different air vents for the engine compartment.

VI·C
The 365 GT 2+2
1967-1971

(Left and below) The first 2+2 Ferrari with four wheel independent suspension, the 365 GT was introduced to the marketplace at the 1967 Paris Salon. Viewed from the front, the design by Pininfarina resembled that of the 500 Superfast. The more rectangular rear was reminiscent of that of the 330 GTC Speciale that appeared earlier in the year.

After the introduction of the 250 GTE 2+2 in 1960, the formula of a two-door four-place coupe became one of the specialties of Maranello, and was an unqualified success. In eight years the 250 and 330 2+2 coupes bodied by Pininfarina totaled almost 2100 examples produced, or more than 50% of Ferrari's production during the same time span. In other words, the production of just these two models represented a number greater than the production total of the eleven other models offered in the same period. With, among other improvements, even higher performance levels and much more refined comfort, the 365 GT 2+2 continued this success.

This 365 GT 2+2, which first appeared in public at the 1967 Paris Salon, was a very new 2+2 and not just because of the new bodywork. Most notable was the adoption of a 4.4 litre engine (Type 245) which was later also installed in the 365 GTC and GTS. As we have already seen, the 400 cc in displacement gained by increasing the bore from 77 to 81 mm resulted in a gain of 20 horsepower, but the increase in torque was even more considerable, rising from 33.2 to 37 mkg (267 lb/ft) at 5000 rpm. On the 330 GT 2+2 the carburetion was handled by three Weber 40 DFI/5 double-choke carburetors, and the compression ratio was 8.8:1.

As with the last version of the 330 GT 2+2, the gearbox was mounted in unit with the engine, with the intermediary of a single-plate dry clutch, and the driveshaft was contained in a tube which joined in a rigid manner the engine/gearbox assembly, on one end, and the rear axle differential case, on the other, this latter containing a plate-type limited slip. The rigid assembly thus formed was mounted to the chassis by means of rubber pads located at four points, two on the rear axle differential case. This, except for the location of the gearbox, was the system already in use on the GTC and also used on the GTB/4 starting a year earlier, with the advantage being a reduction of noises transmitted to the occupants.

The traditional chassis of welded steel tubes was, of course, retained, as was the 2.65 metre wheelbase of the 330 GT 2+2. The front and rear tracks were appreciably widened, but the most important innovation concerned the suspension. At the rear was found a new independent-type system using unequal length A-arms, coil springs and telescopic shock absorbers co-axial with the springs. To this point the system was quite similar to that introduced in 1964 on the GTB and GTS, and continued on the GTC. But here, to correct the variations in load inherent in a four-place coupe whose rear seats may or may not be occupied, it was also fitted with hydro-pneumatic devices which assured a constant static level no matter what the load. This was truly the first time that such devices were mounted on a high performance vehicle. Ferrari and Koni spent a great deal of time studying and perfect-

Several details were modified on the definitive version. Later, the perforated wheels were replaced by the five pointed star design of wheels as used on the "Daytona."

ing this new self-levelling suspension, and it undeniably constituted important progress.

Another innovation was the power steering installed as standard equipment on the 365 GT, another first for a product of Maranello and one which confounds those who think of Ferrari as nothing but a competition vehicle.

To clothe this high-speed palace, Pininfarina produced a design somewhat different from those of his preceding 2+2 coupes because of its increased agressiveness. There was the silhouette of the 500 Superfast, with its streamlined nose and slightly tapering rear, and also the design of the 330 GTC Speciale presented at the Brussels Salon at the beginnning of the year. On the 365 GT, however, the rear window was rectangular and only very slightly curved, and formed almost a single plane with the rear deck. Regretfully, there was a certain lack of harmony between the curves of the front and the sharp angles of the rear.

As for the interior, all was carefully planned to improve the comfort of the driver and his passengers. Therefore a system of air conditioning was supplied as standard equipment. Eye appeal was also not neglected, and refinements were found everywhere on these bodies which were built by Pininfarina themselves, at Turin.

When compared to the test of the 330 GT some three years earlier, the test of the 365 GT by Jose Rosinski, published in **Sport-Auto** in October, 1968, gave a measure to the progress achieved ". . . by this Ferrari from which all brutality has been carefully banished. But miraculously the vehicle has not by any means been emasculated or even corrupted. . . The expression 'glued to the road' could have been invented for the 365 GT." There followed some figures "established between two heavy downpours:" 240 km/h (149 mph) at 6300 rpm, some 20 km/h (12 mph) better than the 330 GT. The times for the 400 and 1000 (000 ft and 0000 ft) metres from a standing start (15.6 and 28 seconds) were however essentially the same.

During the production run the cast light alloy wheels originally fitted, and using the excellent new Michelin XVR tires, were replaced by wheels using the five pointed star design as on the Daytona. Borrani wire wheels remained, however, available as an option. This change probably occurred shortly after the berlinetta was introduced, during 1969, and was one of the rare modifications made to the 365 GT 2+2.

Between the end of 1967 and the beginning of 1971 the 365 GT 2+2 was produced in about 800 examples, whose serial numbers (always odd) ran between 10700 and 14100. This represented more than 50% of Ferrari's total production during the same period. At the beginning of 1971 the 365 GT ceded its place, at least on the assembly line, to the 365 GTC/4 that was introduced at the Geneva Salon. However, it will be necessary to wait until the 1972 Paris Salon for the appearance of a new Ferrari 2+2, the 365 GT/4.

Put at the disposition of the Course Marshall for the 1969 24 Hours of Le Mans, the 365 GT driven by Fernand Tavano brought in the skier/race driver Jean Claude Killy after the break-down of his Alpine.

Galleria

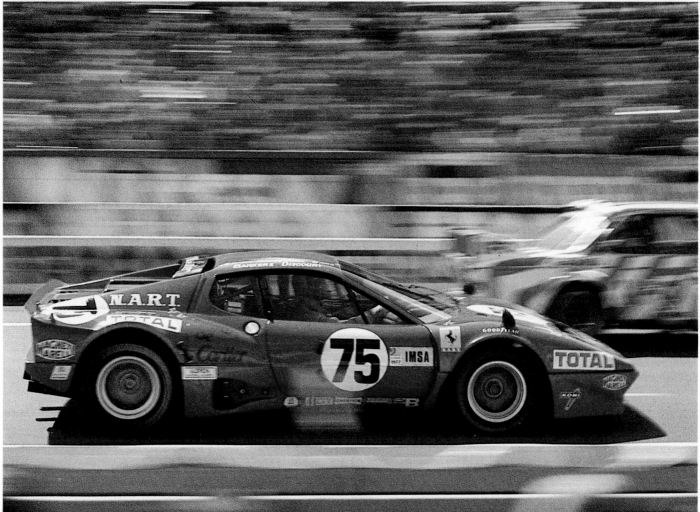

VI·D
The 365 GTC/4
1971-1972

Following the introduction of the 330 GTC in 1966, the range of touring Ferraris was composed of three basic models, each having a precise place in an exact formula. At one extreme was a two-place berlinetta of sportive character, at the opposite extreme was a 2+2 coupe, and between these two extremes, between the comfort and luxury of the 2+2 and the performance of the berlinetta, was an intermediate two-place coupe. This latter role was that assigned to the 330 GTC, and later to the 365 GTC. By its principle characteristics, and by the C in its designation, the 365 GTC/4 can perhaps be considered the last representative of this intermediate position.

(Left and below) Despite its appearance, the 365 GTC/4, shown here on the Pininfarina stand at the 1971 Paris Salon, was technically closer to the 365 GT 2+2 than to the Daytona.

In actuality, the 365 GTC/4, which was unveiled at the 1971 Geneva Salon, also became a replacement for the 365 GT 2+2 coupe, whose place it took on the assembly line. In appearance the 365 GTC/4 was closer to the Daytona whose career it paralleled. However, it was different in numerous areas, and it represented a radical evolution in comparison to the 365 GTC while it was not a true replacement for the 2+2.

The engine of the 365 GTC/4 retained the principle dimensions of the 365 GTB/4, most notable being the bore and stroke (81 x 71 mm) and therefore the total displacement of 4390 cc. Also retained from the Daytona were the four overhead camshafts, hence the figure "4" which came at the end of the model's designation. But the overall height of the engine was profoundly changed as a result of a completely new car-

buretion system, this consisting of six Weber dual-choke carburetors (38 DCOE) that were mounted horizontally instead of the more traditional vertical placement. These carburetors fed the combustion chambers through manifolds located between the intake and exhaust camshafts. As a result the engine lost several important centimeters of height, allowing a lower hood line and also freeing the space in the center of the Vee required for installing the anti-pollution equipment. This equipment was obligatory on vehicles destined for the North American market, where each year the rules were becoming more and more stringent. Another important difference found in comparing this engine with that of the berlinetta was the system of lubrication, the oil here being contained in a wet sump holding 16 litres, as on the 2+2. The compression ratio was 8.8:1, as with the Daytona and the 2+2, but, for the first time in the history of touring Ferraris, the power output was not revealed in the catalog. It has been estimated at between 330 and 340 horsepower, developed at 6800 rpm. Finally, the official designation of this engine as Type F 101 denoted a new system of numeration introduced with this model.

As with the 2+2, but contrary to the GTC and berlinetta, the five-speed gearbox was mounted in unit with the engine, with a single disc dry clutch. The four-point mounting system used to attach the rigid assembly of the engine/differential housing remained identical.

Although it was shorter, with 2.50 metre wheelbase, the chassis of the 365 GTC/4 retained all the characteristics of the 365 GT 2+2, notably the power brakes, the power steering, and the oleo-pneumatic self-leveling devices at the rear. On the other hand, the ventilated disc brakes came directly from the Daytona.

To clothe this ensemble, Pininfarina created a very unique body design. The very plunging hood line was shorter and lower than that of the Daytona and the curves of the fenders were widely acclaimed, as were the rear quarter windows which were extended to a point and gave the maximum of glass area. The impor-

tance of the greenhouse and the rear deck was increased and this gave the GTC/4 a more relaxed silhouette than that of the aggressive Daytona. A new trend advocated the suppression of chrome and this was noticed in the bumpers of the 365 GTC/4. At the front, they were made of a flexible resin colored flat black and were wholly integrated into the design, forming the periphery of the grill and signal lights. At the rear, the simple rectilinear blade bumper was also flat black, but made of metal.

The more generous dimensions of the greenhouse and rear deck allowed the placing of two occasional seats behind the front seats, and a greater volume was reserved for baggage in the trunk. In addition, the provisions for folding down the backs of the rear seats allowed a supplementary space for luggage. The more forward location of the cockpit required a more voluminous central console between the two comfortable front seats, and on the dash were gauges of a new style which henceforth were used in all new Ferraris. The circular visors disappeared in favor of round dials encased in flat black squares.

A refined and rapid vehicle, the 365 GTC/4 very successfully filled its niche. It was produced in 500 examples between the spring of 1971 and the fall of 1972, with serial numbers (always odd) comprised between 14100 and 16300. In this short time span, the 365 GTC/4 accounted for close to 50% of Ferrari's production of V-12 engined touring cars, the rest being taken care of by the Daytona.

The United States imported the majority of this production and a special version of the 365 GTC/4 was created for this market, characterized by the fitting of anti-pollution equipment. This also resulted in a loss of power, however, to 320 horsepower at 6600 rpm. Externally, the USA version was recognizable by the four side-marker lights recessed into the flanks at their extremities.

Production of the 365 GTC/4 was terminated with the introduction of the 365 GT4 2+2 at the 1972 Paris Salon.

The voluminous central console was dictated by the forward position of the cockpit, which allowed the fitting of two secondary seats, and by the gearbox mounted with the engine.

Its 4.4 litre 4-cam engine was recognizable by the six horizontal carburetors.

Giovanni Michelotti and Willy Felber successfully transformed, in only three months, a GTC/4 (16017) into this
unique "beach car" destined for an individual from the
Persian Gulf area.

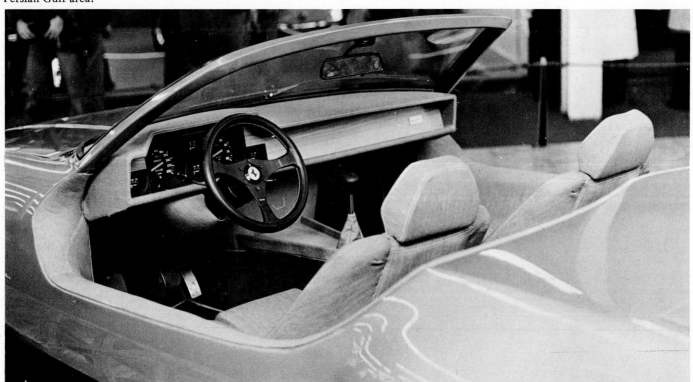

Another 365 GTC/4 was the basis used by the Felber/
Michellotti team for this three-door station wagon shown at
the 1977 Geneva Salon.

VI·E
The 365 GT4 2+2
1972-1976

The 365 GT4 2+2 retained the principal mechanical characteristics of the 365 GTC/4, but with an additional 20 cm of wheelbase.

After a lapse of a year-and-a-half, an all new 2+2 coupe was introduced to the market at the 1972 Paris Salon, under the logical designation of 365 GT4 2+2. This new coupe came to fill the void left by the cessation of production in the spring of 1971 of the 365 GT 2+2, but in fact it was directly descended from the 365 GTC/4 with which it shared numerous features.

The mechanical base of the new 2+2 was in fact identical to that of the GTC/4, the only exception being the wheelbase. Carried over without change was the 4.4 litre 4 cam V-12 engine with six horizontal carburetors whose power was again not specified in the catalog. As on the preceding coupe, this "sufficently powerful" engine was united with a five-speed gearbox,

and this unit was coupled to the differential case by means of a drive shaft tube. The entire rigid assembly was mounted to the chassis at four points. The chassis itself remained faithful to the Ferrari tradition, and to its credit continued the perfections found on the GTC/4: four wheel independent suspension, oleo-pneumatic self-leveling units at the rear, power brakes and steering, and ventilated disc brakes. The only difference was in the dimensions as the front track was appreciably increased, and the wheelbase was stretched from 2.50 to 2.70 metres; this permitted the building of the most spacious 2+2 in the history of the Ferrari/ Pininfarina association. This is well demonstrated by comparing the dimensions of the 365 GT 2+2 and the 365 GT4 2+2.

Length	4990 mm	(196.5 in)	4800 mm	(189 in)
Width	1790 mm	(70.5 in)	1800 mm	(70.9 in)
Height with static load	1335 mm	(52.6 in)	1292 mm	(50.9 in)
Wheelbase	2650 mm	(104.3 in)	2700 mm	(106.3 in)
Front track	1440 mm	(56.7 in)	1470 mm	(57.9 in)
Rear track	1472 mm	(58 in)	1500 mm	(59 in)
Front overhang	990 mm	(39 in)	937 mm	(36.9 in)
Rear overhang	1324 mm	(52.1 in)	1173 mm	(46.2 in)
Trunk capacity	0.455 mc	(16 cu ft)	0.486 mc	(17.2 cu ft)
Cockpit:				
Maximum width-front	1385 mm	(54.5 in)	1450 mm	(57 in)
Maximum width-rear	1320 mm	(52.0 in)	1430 mm	(56.3 in)

The principle novelty of the 365 GT4 2+2 was found in the body which Pininfarina built for it. As the above table shows, despite the more generous interior volume, the latest 2+2 was shorter than its predecessor. The design by the master coachbuilder of Turin was primarily responsible for this, most notably through the treatment of the greenhouse. The importance of this was underplayed, thanks to a sharply inclined windshield and rear quarter windows of remarkable finesse. The somewhat rectangular design of the body was lightened by a plunging hood line and a longitudinal molding, giving, according to some observers, "the impression of two superimposed shells." This effect was reinforced by the high position of the black polyurethane foam bumpers. At the front, the four headlights were retracted into the bodywork by electrical controls, leaving only the turn signal lights in the open. Daytime signalling by means of flashing was effected with the fog lights located behind the radiator air intake grill.

In the interior, as on the GTC/4, there was found a large central console, again dictated by the forward position of the cockpit, and the arrangement of the dashboard was very little changed. The car was a genuine four-place vehicle and the finishing was particularly well done.

Weight empty was given as 1500 kg (3300 lb), and in driving trim it rose to about 1950 kg (4290 lb). Finally, as on the 365 GTC/4, the light alloy cast wheels were fitted with Michelin XWX tires, size 215 x 15.

The only test which appears to have been published for this model was that which appeared in the English weekly **Autocar** on October 4, 1975. It was particularly interesting in that this latest 2+2 Ferrari was compared with several close rivals: the Aston Martin DBS automatic, the Jensen Interceptor, the Rolls-Royce Corniche, and the Jaguar XJ 12 L. Of the five, the Ferrari had the smallest displacement. It was, however, the fastest at 242 km/h (150 mph) but it lost in acceleration to the Aston Martin, which accelerated from 0 to 60 mph in 6.2 seconds, as opposed to 7.1 seconds for the Ferrari. This test reached the following conclusion: "Our own vehicles can all compete on one level or another. But none of them can compete with the Ferrari on all levels."

In the front, the cockpit was little changed by comparison with the GTC/4, but two true seats were now able to be located at the rear.

One of the very rare variations, probably the only one, to the design given to the 365 GT4 2+2 by Pininfarina was executed in 1975 by Fly Studio of Modena, the school of automobile studies founded by Giacomo Caliri, a former aerodynamic engineer at Ferrari. Using the mechanical base and the original body, this newest Modenese enterprise created a unique convertible with a removable two-part roof, the two panels being separated by a fixed central rib. The rear of the greenhouse was also restyled, with a flat, electrically controlled retractable window being inserted between the two sail panels, which extended onto the rear deck. Built to the order of the Moroccan leather tanner Etienne Aignier, one of the sponsors of Clay Regazzoni, this special remained a one-off, proving once again the problems encountered in attempting to change an existing design, particularly a design which was already perfectly successful.

Before being replaced by the 400 Automatic and GT at the 1976 Paris Salon, the 365 GT4 2+2 was built in 470 examples. This low production figure can be explained by the closing of the American market, Maranello having decided in effect to no longer attempt to conform their 12 cylinders to the legal requirements of that country.

The 365 GT4 2+2 was presented in a world premier at the 1972 Paris Salon. On the stand of the French importer, Charles Pozzi, it was displayed beside the Daytona competition which captured the Tour de France.

This strange, transformed 2+2 built by Fly Studio Modena is, to this day, the only known variation on the base of the 365 GT4 2+2.

VI·F
The 400 GT & Automatic
1976-

In October, 1976, the Paris Salon once again marked an important stage in Ferrari history with the presentation there of two new models, the BB 512 which we will examine in Chapter VIII, and the 400 which is our immediate interest. This occasion was particularly important as far as the 2+2 was concerned, for it marked the very first time that a Ferrari was offered with an automatic transmission. The press release issued jointly by Ferrari and Pininfarina explained that this was "the result of a different concept of the automobile which had developed and asserted itself especially in countries with a high density of automobiles, and which will find increasing favor in Europe in the future."

(Left and below) With the exception of a discrete spoiler in the front, the very elegant design by Pininfarina remained unchanged for the 400 Automatic and 400 GT. Note however the new method of attaching the wheels.

This response of Maranello to a rather rapid evolutionary turn at that time created something of a surprise. The manually operated gearbox, a component which had nearly always been manufactured in-house by Ferrari, was one of the most noble traditions of Ferrari and of almost the same rank as the V-12 engine. However, the idea of a Ferrari with an automatic transmission was not new. In **Cavallino**, the excellent American Ferrari magazine, it parentage was attributed to C.A. Vandagriff, a Ferrari dealer in California who, in 1971, had a 365 GT 2+2 fitted with a General Motors 400 three-speed automatic. He tested this experiment for several months before shipping it complete to Modena, along with a lengthy report. It remained apparent that there were some problems to be worked out, and Maranello did not class the project high on its list of priorities. For that reason, it appears unlikely that any of the Ferraris so equipped, usually the 365 GT 2+2, were originally made by the Ferrari factory itself. Nevertheless, the idea reappeared in

1976 with the 400 Automatic, and it was precisely this same transmission, the Turbo-Hydramatic 400, which was used. It was originally designed by General Motors for engines with less than eight litres capacity, and was used in the Cadillac, in light GM trucks, and in the Rolls-Royce and Jaguar automatics. It was very probably the best mass produced automatic transmission, and rather than design a new unit, Ferrari chose to use this proven unit, contenting itself with adapting it to the particular power and torque characteristics of the V-12 engine.

At the same time, and to obtain a more perfect match between this new three-speed automatic and the V-12 engine, the latter underwent several modifications. The stroke was increased to 77 mm, enlarging the total displacement to 4823 cc (about 400 cc per cylinder, hence the designation). The camshafts and valve timings were also modified and with the same six Weber 38 DCOE carburetors, the maximum power remained about 340 horsepower at 6500 rpm. Torque was increased from 43 mkg (319 lb/ft), at 4600 rpm to 48 mkg (347 lb/ft) at 3600 rpm.

The modifications made to the body style, already quite well known on the 365 GT4 2+2, were minimal. On the front chin a discrete spoiler was added, its primary function being a better channeling of air to-ward the engine compartment. A rear view mirror with interior control was mounted on the driver's door. The number of taillights on the truncated rear panel was increased from four to six. Finally, the Cromodora cast light alloy wheels retained the same dimensions (7.5 x 15 inches) and the same five-pointed star design, but their mounting was changed from the Rudge hub to the more traditional five bolts.

As far as Pininfarina was concerned, the most important modifications were made to the interior arrangements. The seats were redesigned for even more comfort and in order to facilitate access to the rear seats, the front seats slid forward when the backs were folded forward, thereby doubling the opening available for reaching the rear seats. The dashboard and the console were covered in leather, as were the redesigned door panels, replacing the flat material used earlier. Finally, a quadraphonic stereo radio was installed as standard equipment, and a second air conditioner was available on order.

A version with a manual five-speed gearbox was still available under the name of 400 GT, but the Automatic was in ever increasing demand, proving that at Maranello, evolution can be reconciled with the most noble traditions.

In the cockpit, only the decoration was changed, but the disappearance of the clutch pedal was quite obvious.

VII
A New Generation

The idea of a smaller, more affordable gran turismo that would allow a new group of enthusiasts to be introduced to the Ferrari experience was entertained around Maranello for a long time. The first physical manifestation of the idea appeared in 1959 after several experimental engines had been produced with this goal in mind. One of these engines was mounted in a Fiat 1100 chassis and bodied by Pininfarina with a coupe body that differed very little from similar bodies found on several Fiat models at the time. An official name for this unassuming vehicle is not known, but the press dubbed it "Ferrarina" and even "Tommygun" because an insignia bearing that effigy was located on the grill. The Ferrari name did not appear on any part of the car, but it was only necessary to look under the hood to dispel any doubts about its origins. The engine, an in-line four-cylinder of 850 cc displacement, could not hide its parentage particulary because of the design of the cam cover, on which the traditional Ferrari logo was merely replaced by the figure 854

(850 cc, 4 cylinders). The car was extensively tested, perhaps with different engines, and Ferrari himself used it for a long time as his personal transportation, but it appears that it was not further developed beyond the test vehicle stage.

A second venture, which can also perhaps be considered as the logical result of the first experience, appeared at the Turin Salon, in November, 1961, under the designation "Mille." It was also powered by an in-line four-cylinder engine and the displacement attained this time was 1032 cc, but the conception once again was typically Ferrari. This four-cylinder engine was very close to being nothing more than two-thirds of one bank of the 250 GT engine. The prototype was clothed with a very pleasant fastback coupe body designed by Bertone, but once again the Ferrari name did not appear on any part, although there was no other name. It therefore appears probable that Ferrari had no intention of selling this car under his marque, nor of building it at Maranello. In fact, it was

---

(Left and below) A miniature of the 250 GT Pininfarina coupe in the courtyard at the Maranello factory in 1960, the 850 cc conceived by Ferrari. It was never given an official name and did not go into production.

The appearance of the four-cylinder engine left no doubt as to its origin.

The four-cylinder engine of 1032 cc displacement could not again disavow its parentage.

Lorenzo Bandini, one of the Ferrari Team drivers, was of assistance to the launching of the ASA 1000 Bertone coupe, in 1963.

Nicolo de Nora, the son of an important Milanese industrialist and, also a regular client of Maranello, who acquired the rights to fabricate and sell the "Mille," and to accomplish this he created the Societa ASA (Autocostruzioni, Societa per Azioni).

A preproduction prototype was presented at the 1962 Turin Salon under the designation of ASA 1000 GT. Compared to the first prototype, there were very few changes, but the first deliveries were, nevertheless, not able to be made before the end of 1964. It was a bad start. By 1967 the ASA enterprise closed its doors, and production probably did not exceed 100 examples.

Meanwhile, the idea of a true little Ferrari to be built at Maranello was no doubt conceived. What is now known to have been, thanks to hindsight, the very first prototype was shown on the Pininfarina stand at the 1965 Paris Salon under the name "Dino 206 GT Speciale." The mechanical base was the Dino 206 S which was being built in a small series for the 1966 racing season. The engine was a V-6 with four overhead camshafts that was directly descended from the engine of the 1500 cc Formula 1 World Championship car of

1961. The name Dino, nickname of Alfredo Ferrari, the unfortunate only son of Ferrari who had died of illness in 1957, was first given to the Ferrari V-6 created at his initiative for the single seat Formula II car. This designation thereafter was given to all the V-6 and V-8 engines from Maranello with a new system of numeration, the three digits no longer indicating the single cylinder displacement, but instead the total displacement in decilitres for the first two digits, and the number of cylinders for the last digit. Thus the Dino 206 of the 1965 Paris Salon was equipped with a 2 litre (20 decilitres) 6-cylinder engine.

This show car was actually built on a racing chassis (serial number 0834) and the engine, located ahead of the rear wheels, contained no internal pieces. The most interesting feature of this car was its bodywork which established a new style. It was characterized by an extremely low line which dictated very pronounced humps above the wheels, resembling the contemporary P2 and, in addition, announced the design of the P3 which came onto the stage in 1966. This relationship was further reinforced by the cast light alloy wheels,

The very innovative "Dino 206 GT Speciale" presented by Pininfarina at the Paris Salon can perhaps be considered as the first prototype of a new generation of Ferrari.
(Above) The absence of a speedometer and the very short shift lever betrayed, however, the purely racing origins of this prototype (0834) directly derived from the Dino 206 Sport.

which repeated the design of the racing prototypes, a design which was also found, in 1966, on the 275 GTB, the 330 GTC/GTS, and the 330 GT 2+2.

The central location of the engine gave the greenhouse a slightly forward position. Also very low, it was also quite remarkable with its rear treatment where a vertical, concave rear window formed a unique hollow over the engine compartment. The sail panels extended as far as the rear of the vehicle above the rear fenders, following the principle inaugurated on the marvelous 375 MM of the 1954 Paris Salon (see page 109). Other original details were the four headlights protected under a transparent cover which uniquely terminated the frontal treatment, and the hollows located under the side windows which contained the door handles and, at the same time, served as air intakes for the engine compartment.

The essential components of this design were also found on two other prototypes which were shown at different salons in Europe in the autumn of 1966: the curious berlinetta with central steering shown at the Paris Salon, to which we will return in the next chapter, and the "Dino Berlinetta GT" shown at Turin, which interests us here. On the aesthetic level, the whole design was very similar to that of the 1965 vehicle with only the proportions and some details changed. With a higher roof, the new Dino was less streamlined and appeared more compact. At the front, the headlights were more traditionally located, under covers, at the ends of the fenders, and a small radiator air

intake made its appearance at the base of the front cover. The bumpers also contributed to a more functional appearance. Finally, the cast light alloy wheels used the five-pointed star design.

At the same 1966 Turin Salon, the Fiat "Dino" was unveiled, a cabriolet bodied by Pininfarina but whose "Dino" engine is of great interest to us here. As its name indicates, this V-6 was conceived at Maranello with the idea of using it in a Formula II single seater. But the rules of that formula stipulated that the engines had to be derived from mass-produced units. An agreement was entered into between Ferrari and the giant of Turin, Fiat, the terms of which allowed Fiat to build the engine in its factory and use it in a vehicle that could quickly attain a production of 500 examples as required for homologation. And so, there came about a Fiat with a Ferrari engine.

This engine actually represented a third generation of Ferrari Dino V-6 engines. Its design was developed by Engineer Franco Rocchi, and was characterized by the 65° angle formed between the two cylinder banks, and by four overhead camshafts. As for the rest of its architecture, it was typical of the products of Maranello, notably the over-square dimensions giving a displacement of 1987 cc.

Tested in 1966 in the Dino 206 S, it was later found, in various forms, in the Fiat Dino Pininfarina cabriolet, later in the Fiat Dino Bertone coupe, in the Formula II single seaters, of course, and finally in the Dino 206 GT reproduced at Maranello.

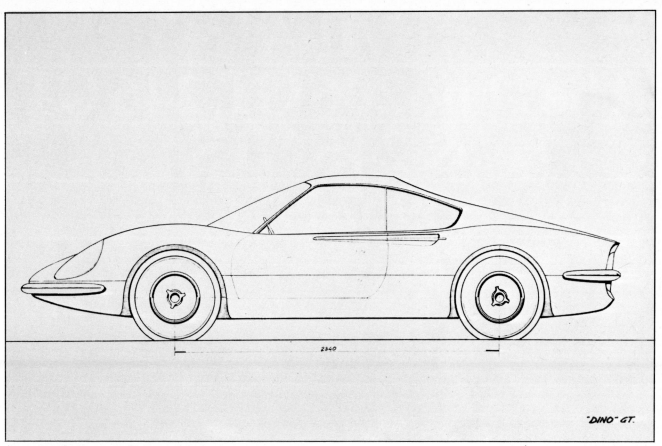

A second prototype, the Pininfarina "Dino Berlinetta GT," was shown at the 1966 Turin Salon. The lines approached those of the Dino GT, but the V-6 engine was still mounted longitudinally.

A third prototype of the Dino marque was unveiled at the Turin Salon one year later, in November, 1967. It presented an important evolutionary development on several levels, the most important, perhaps, being the position of the engine. The V-6 two litre unit, whose production was handled at Turin by Fiat, was now mounted parallel to the axis of the rear wheels and in front of them. This unusual placement required a completely new gearbox which was entirely constructed at Maranello. While nothing was changed on the engine block, the five-speed fully synchronized gearbox was redesigned so it could be located parallel to the crankshaft. To effect this a new sump was cast in the foundry, in the purest Maranello tradition, to be a single case for the gearbox and the differential which followed it, with hermetical sealing to insure separate lubrication systems for the engine and the transmission.

At Maranello, the V-6 originating at Turin was also submitted to some special treatment to give it even more performance. The compression ratio (9:1) remained unchanged, but the Weber 40 DCF carburetors breathing through the air intake located on the right side, plus a special exhaust system, and other specific tuning procedures, increased the output from 160 horsepower at 7200 rpm to 180 horsepower at 8000 rpm, and the maximum torque increased from 17.5 to 19 mkg (137 lb/ft) at an engine speed increased from 6000 to 6500 rpm.

The engine/gearbox assembly was mounted to the chassis by means of four silentblocs, and its new positioning allowed a reduction of 6 cm in the wheelbase

(Left) This third prototype, from 1967, had acquired the definitive form, and the V-6 engine was positioned transversely between the cockpit and the rear axle. But numerous finishing details were not yet finalized.

The V-6, with 1987 cc, was built by Fiat but all of the lower part, which housed the oil sump, the gearbox, the drive shafts and the differential, was built at Maranello.

(now 2.28 metres). The chassis, built at Ferrari, was also purely Ferrari. It consisted of a single unit made from electrically welded steel, and was equipped with four wheel independent suspension with coil springs and co-axial telescopic shock absorbers. There were, as well, four wheel ventilated disc brakes with brake servo and dual hydraulic circuits. The steering, as usual, was by rack and pinion, and Michelin XWX tires were mounted on cast light alloy rims of 6.5 x 14 inch dimension as opposed to the 15 inch wheels on the preceding prototypes. Mounted by Rudge center-lock hubs, the design of the wheels was that of the Fiat Dino.

Finally, the body itself underwent some important modifications, most notably on the aerodynamic level. The windshield was more steeply raked, the roof was made slightly longer with a tighter line, and to accommodate the taller engine/gearbox assembly the rear deck was slightly higher, which actually, was also an improvement in the aerodynamics. The reduced diameter of the wheels allowed a reduction in the hump of the fenders, especially at the front, and the transverse location of the engine permitted a sizeable rear luggage compartment (about 10 cu ft), the front compartment being completely filled by the spare tire. Three deck lids were provided, all opening at the rear

After Turin, in November 1967, this other prototype of the Dino 206 GT was shown on a Dino stand at the 1968 Brussels Salon.

and hinged at the front, one for the front compartment, one for the engine compartment, and one for the luggage compartment.

As for the interior, the typical finish and detail of Ferrari and Pininfarina gave the 206 GT nothing to envy in comparison with her big sister Ferraris.

In reality, the 206 GT shown at the 1967 Turin Salon was yet another prototype built by Pininfarina. Several prototypes were built at this stage, and deliveries of the production examples did not begin until the spring of 1969. The production versions, whose bodies were built in aluminum by Scaglietti in Modena, were recognizable by several finishing details, both interior and exterior, the most notable being the addition of vent windows on the doors and the elimination of the headlight covers.

The Swiss periodical **Revue Automobile** published, in its February 13th, 1969 edition, one of the rare tests to be conducted on the Dino 206 GT in its definitive version. The figures attained are eloquent proof of the success of this first-born of the new generation of Ferraris. For acceleration from a standing start, 100 km/h (62 mph) was reached in 7.2 seconds, 200 km/h (124 mph) in 33.8 seconds, and the kilometre in 28.2 seconds. A top speed of 230.7 (142 mph) was obtained in fifth gear at about 7700 rpm.

On these 206 GTs, which await their bumpers in an aisle at the Maranello plant, can be noted the definitive design, notably the vent windows.

The Dino came along to replace the 206 at the end of 1969. It varied not only by its displacement but also by a wheelbase increased by 6 cm. The Rudge hubs were abandoned at the beginning of 1970.

However, the 206 GT had an extemely brief career, and it does not seem to have been produced in many more than 100 examples before it was replaced, at the end of 1969, by the Dino 246 GT announced earlier in the year. Externally nothing distinguished the new Dino from the model which it replaced other than a door hiding the fuel filler on the right sail panel. Indeed, the "Dino GT" inscription on the rear remained unchanged. It was difficult to spot the fact that the wheelbase was returned to the 2.34 metres of the "pre-prototype," gaining some 6 cm, while the tracks (1425 mm front and 1400 mm rear),did not change.

The most significant innovation concerned the V-6 engine block whose displacement was increased to 2418 cc thanks to new dimensions for the bore and stroke (92.5 x 60 mm). Still built by Fiat, where it was also used in the cabriolet and coupe, it was no longer made of light alloy (Silumin) but in cast iron. Otherwise, its architecture remained unchanged. The vehicle thereby gained an additional 150 kg (331 lb) of weight, but its power was increased from 180 to 195 horsepower at a speed of 7600 rpm as opposed to the former 8000 rpm, and the torque was also increased to 23 mkg (166 lb/ft) at 5500 rpm. The sales brochure described it thusly: "Tiny, brilliant, safe..."

but added, a bit harshly, "almost a Ferrari." After the start of 1970 this slogan was changed to: "Tiny, brilliant, safe proof of the constant development of the smaller Ferrari cars." Actually, the Dino was, after all was said and done, a true Ferrari, the first Ferrari gran turismo with a central engine. By its performance, its aggressive lines, and the sound of its engine, it brought to a whole new clientele the profound pleasures associated with the products of Maranello. Its price also had a great deal to do with its success. In 1970 it cost $13,400 as opposed to $20,000 for the 365 GTB/4 Daytona.

Also in early 1970, the mounting of the wheels by means of Rudge center lock hubs was replaced by a new mounting with five bolts, while the design of the wheels was not changed. The cross-section of the Michelin tires also increased from 185 to 205, and the rear track was enlarged from 1400 to 1430 mm.

The 246 GTS appeared at the 1972 Geneva Salon. Thankfully, the remodeling of the greenhouse did not alter the basic lines.

With similar proportions, the dashboard of the Dino is
exactly that of the Daytona.

Between 1970 and 1971 production of the Dino almost doubled, and the appearance of the Dino 246 GTS, at the 1972 Geneva Salon, constituted a greatly appreciated addition to the Dino range by offering a roof with the central section being removable, leaving a fixed arch at the rear. Other than removing the rear quarter windows, Pininfarina retained intact the design of the 246 GT greenhouse and the effect was particularly successful. The 246 GTS reminded one of the Dino 206 S spyder, or better yet, with many of the same proportions, the famous 330 P4 prototype of 1967.

The success of the Dino 246 was no less important on the North American continent, despite the legal requirements of the United States (anti-pollution requirements and the use of lead-free gasoline) which cost the special versions made for that market about 20 horsepower. These versions are most easily recognized by the four rectangular side marker lights located at the extremities of the flanks.

In March, 1970, the monthly publication **Virage** published an interesting comparative test between the Dino 246 GT and the Porsche 2.2 litre 911 S. In all the principle areas, speed, acceleration, driving pleasure, etc., the advantage was given to the Italian car. But when Porsche introduced in 1971, a 2.4 litre version of the 911 S, some of the advantages changed sides. This was undoubtably one of the reasons which led Ferrari to study a larger displacement engine for the Dino. As a result the 308 GT4 came along to take the place of the 246 in 1974. Before going out of production, about 4000 examples of the Dino 246 were made, with about 1200 of them being spyder versions.

Some Dinos destined for the American market were equipped with these Campagnolo wheels. They are moreover recognizable by an increase in signal lights.

VII·B
The Dino 308 GT4
& 208 GT4
1973-

With the 308 (30 decilitres, 8 cylinders) Ferrari returned to the almost mystical 3 litre displacement of the 250 GT. This new 3 litre engine, full of "brio," stood up well in comparison to its earlier counterpart, benefitting from the significance of ten years of experience, progress, and success. In addition, while it cannot disown its noble heritage, the 308 wasted no time in making its own mark, whether it be because of its Bertone bodywork or its V-8 engine.

(Left and below) The Dino 308 GT4 was presented at the 1973 Paris Salon with the principal characteristics being a 2+2 body designed by Bertone and a V-8 engine.

The primary innovation of the 308 GT4, which was unveiled at the Paris Salon in October, 1973, was certainly the V-8 engine with the two banks of cylinders forming between them an angle of 90°. This configuration was not new to Maranello (it was first found in the 158 Formula One car, World Champion in 1964 driven by John Surtees) but this was the first time that it was found in a transverse position, and on a gran turismo. The Ferrari tradition was therefore very obvious in the new light alloy cast block coming from the foundry, with shrunk-in cast iron liners. But, in contrast to the engine for the preceding Dino, the fabrication of the new engine was handled at Maranello itself. As usual with Ferrari, the rods were mounted in pairs on the crankshaft, which turned on five main bearings. There were four overhead camshafts acting directly on the valves, which formed an angle of 40°

between themselves. A notable innovation was the driving of these camshafts by means of two toothed belts. This same principle was, moreover, adopted at about this same time for the 12-cylinder "Boxer" engine. The traditional, but noisier, camshaft driven by chains was thus only on the V-12 engines.

The four Weber 40 DCNF double-choke carburetors were located in the center of the Vee, in two rows, and the ignition was provided by two distributors driven off the intake camshafts, with the spark supplied by an electronic Marelli Dinoplex unit.

As on the preceding Dino GT, the oil used for lubrication of the engine was contained in the sump itself, and this sump consisted of one cast piece which also housed the five-speed gearbox, parallel to the engine, and the limited-slip differential.

With an unchanged compression ratio of 8.8:1, the power output of the Dino engine was increased from 180 horsepower at 8000 rpm for the V-6 to 250 horsepower at 7700 rpm for the V-8, and the torque increased from 23 kgm (166 lb/ft) at 5500 rpm to 29 kgm (209 lb/ft) at 5000 rpm.

As usual, this assembly was mounted at four points to the excellent chassis of welded tubes inherited directly from the 246, and also found were the same four-wheel independent suspension by means of transverse wishbones, the same servo-assisted ventilated disc brakes, and the same cast light alloy wheels fixed in place by five bolts, equipped with the Michelin XWX tires of 205 x 14 inch size. The tracks (1.46 metres) were wider and the wheelbase (2.55 metres) was appreciably lengthened with the dual objective of making

more room for the somewhat cumbersome new engine and allowing more room in the interior.

While mechanically the 308 GT4 did not lack innovations, its bodywork was something new, principally because of the signature it carried. This was the first time since 1953 that the design for a production Ferrari did not emanate from Pininfarina. The reasons which led Ferrari to abandon, only temporarily, his usual supplier for the neighboring Turinese firm of Bertone have never been precisely stated. For whatever reasons the change was made, there can be no doubt that the charge given to this other great name in Italian coachbuilding was very difficult: Reconcile four place seating with a central engine location, within a 2.55 metre wheelbase, with no wasted space! Bertone, however, was equal to the task and found the

Bertone was able to place four seats within the 2.55 metre wheelbase despite the central engine located just ahead of the rear wheels.

The V-8 engine with four overhead camshafts driven by toothed belts was a completely new production item for Maranello.

The 308 GT4 (08020) entered by Luigi Chinetti's NART in the 1974 24 Hours of Le Mans had undergone some substantial modifications.

solution, even if the design was not always aesthetically applauded, a criticism more often found coming from casual observers than actual users of the vehicle, however.

In order to reconcile all the apparently irreconcilable demands, Bertone designed a body noted for its plunging, pointed nose and sharply inclined but only slightly curved windshield that formed an almost flat angle with the hood. A very flat roof was also a characteristic of this design, as was the flat rear deck which, when viewed in profile, dips only slightly before joining the rear panel at an almost right angle, thereby reducing the rear overhang to a minimum. With a rather forward driving position, there was room for two supplementary seats in the rear. The 2+2 qualification, however, was not added to the name of the vehicle. The overall length came to 4.30 metres, 10 cm more than the 246 GT, which was quite astonishing.

At the rear the flat vertical window was recessed between the sail panels so as to retain the two deck lids,

one for the engine compartment and the other for the luggage compartment, with the spare wheel of reduced section being contained in the front compartment. At the front, the double headlights were retractable, a rectangular grill hid the radiator air intake and was placed below a black polyester resin bumper which incorporated the turn signal lights. The grill was flanked by two quartz-iodine fog lights which also served as flasher-signalling lights when the headlights were retracted.

The announced performance figures, with the standard final drive ratio of 17/63, gave 14.4 seconds and 26.2 seconds for the standing start 400 metres (1313

The 208 GT4 created in 1975 for the Italian market was recognizable by the absence of fog lights and by a single exhaust outlet.

feet) and 1000 metres (3283 feet) respectively, and a maximum speed of 250 km/h (155 mph) at 7400 rpm. These figures were generally confirmed by the numerous tests published, which also universally praised the astonishing flexibility of the 3 litre engine.

Luigi Chinetti could not resist for very long the temptation to transform this model for competition. Therefore, he modified one of the very first examples (08020) and entered it at Le Mans in 1974. This car had a large spoiler at the front, body panels and windows of plexiglas, a rear wing supported by two fins overhanging the rear, larger demountable Speedline

wheels, and a mechanical preparation in keeping with the car's intention. An early retirement did not allow an adequate judgement of the car's potential. Entered again at Le Mans, in 1975, it was unfortunately included in the general withdrawal of the NART entries.

In 1975 Ferrari announced two new 8 cylinder cars, the Ferrari 308 GTB to which we will return later, and the Dino 208 GT4, a 2 litre version of the GT4 "2+2" destined exclusively for the Italian market where vehicles of less than 2 litres displacement benefit from a reduced value added tax. To accomplish this the bore was reduced from 81 to 66.8 mm, giving an exact displacement figure of 1991 cc. With a 9:1 compression ratio and four 34 mm carburetors, the announced power was 170 horsepower at 7700 rpm with a maximum speed of 202 km/h (125 mph). Externally, the 208 GT4 retained the Bertone design, and it can only be distinguished from the 308 GT4 by

---

With the "Rainbow," for which no production was planned, Bertone was able to allow his imagination to run free. The 308 GT4 chassis (12788) was shortened to 2.45 metre wheelbase.

the absence of fog lights on either side of the grill, by a single exhaust outlet, and by the Michelin XDX tires. Finally, in the interior, the gauge surrounds were colored black, as were the spokes of the steering wheel.

For the design of the 308 GTB Ferrari returned to the services of Pininfarina, but Bertone fought back in presenting, at the 1976 Turin Salon, his conception of a spyder, a model lacking from the Ferrari range since the abandonment of the 246 GTS. Free of the constraints which had limited the design of the coupe, and believing that it would have no chance of going into production, Bertone treated the design with complete freedom and the result was quite surprising. The base was that of a 308 GT4 (12788) whose chassis was reduced by 10 cm (which still left it 11 cm longer than the chassis of the new 308 GTB) in order to give it a more aggressive and compact effect. The extremely low silhouette formed a true "wedge" and all curved lines were scrupulously banished, with even the design of the special Speedline wheels created for this design attempting to hide their inevitable curves. An interesting innovation (which was patented) was that which allowed the driver to swing the roof down behind the seats without having to leave his seat. This "rain-or-shine" versatility gave this strange creation its name: 308 Rainbow.

At the end of 1976 there appeared several modifications in the appearance of the Dino GT4 which came directly from Ferrari. The commercial name of Dino was dropped and the prancing horse replaced the Dino insignia on the nose, the wheels (whose design was also changed), and the center of the steering wheel. The interior finishing was modified and, at the front, the grill was expanded in size and adopted the traditional rectangular texture. It was also at about this same time that the ignition system was reduced from two to only one distributor.

With the abandonment of the Daytona in 1974, and the 365 GTC/4 in 1971, the Dino 308 GT4, and later the 308 GTB and GTS, were the only new Ferraris legalized for sale in the United States, and the requirements for getting them certified for sale in that market resulted in versions that were more and more different from the vehicles destined for all other markets. Because they were now adapted to the use of unleaded gasoline, these USA vehicles were, moreover, practically unusable in Europe where this type of gasoline was not sold. In 1978 the 308 GT4 "USA version" had, as a result, lost about 10% of its power, and added about the same percentage of weight. Externally it is always recognizable by the rectangular side market lights which occupy the extremities of the flanks, by the more voluminous retractable bumpers, and by the wider wheels with a five-pointed star design similar to those of the 308 GTB.

As of this writing, the Ferrari 308 GT4 and 208 GT4 were still being manufactured and sold.

VII·C
The 308 GTB & 308 GTS
1975-

The 308 GT4 which came at the end of 1973 to take the place of the 246 GT was not really a replacement. That role would be assigned to the 308 GTB which was unveiled in its world premier at, once again, the Paris Salon, in October, 1975, along side the 365 2+2, the 365 GT4 BB, and the Dino 308 GT4. Moreover, on the stand of the French importer, Charles Pozzi, at that same show, was displayed another prestigious 3 litre, the 312 T which, driven by Niki Lauda, won the Formula 1 World Championship in 1975. Thus, it was under the sign of that victory that the 308 GTB first appeared.

(Left) The 308 GTB was unveiled at the 1975 Paris Salon under the sign of victory acquired by the 312 T, the Formula 1 World Champion that year.

While it did not carry the Dino insignia, the newest Ferrari belinetta had to be considered as the direct descendant of the 308 GT4. The differences between these two vehicles, which were to be produced in parallel, concerned, in order of importance, the bodywork, the chassis, and the engine. For the design of the new body, Ferrari recalled Pininfarina. This master stylist successfully harmonized the lines of the 246 GT and the lines of the Berlinetta Boxer first presented in 1971. From the Berlinetta Boxer was taken the "double shell" effect created by the groove cutting the body at the level of the bumpers, the plunging nose which necessitated retractable headlights, and a somewhat square rear onto which the sail panels extended as far as the discrete spoiler above the rear deck. From the Dino 246 came the reduced proportions, the recessed concave rear window, and the scooped-out conical air intakes on the flanks, just ahead of the rear fenders.

As for all the 6- and 8-cylinder cars, the bodywork was built
by Scaglietti at Modena.

Actual construction was undertaken by Scaglietti of Modena, that carrozzeria having come under the absolute control of Ferrari. And the greatest innovation came with the use of fiberglass in its construction, or more correctly, with the remarkable results which were obtained with that material which, until then, had never been put to such good use. The finish was in fact irreproachable, even with metallic colors. (Later, all 308s would revert to metal bodies, however).

The chassis lost 21 cm of wheelbase (down to 2.34 metres) by comparison with the 308 GT4, but otherwise it retained the same characteristics with the exception of the wheels, which inherited the five-pointed star design from the Daytona albeit with a diameter of 14 inches and mounting via five bolts. The tires were still the excellent Michelin XWXs of 205/70 x 14 inch size.

The 90° V-8 engine positioned transversely between the cockpit and the rear axle differed only by its use of dry sump lubrication, which permitted an increase in the quantity of oil in circulation and helped reduce engine temperatures in hard usage. However, the U.S.A. version retained the wet sump of the Dino 308 GT4 and an exhaust system with four outlets, while the normal version was given a new exhaust system with a single outlet. The power remained the same as that of the Dino, being, according to the sales brochure, 255 horsepower at 7700 rpm.

Paul Frere was one of the first, in November, 1975, to conduct a test of the 308 GTB, using the Fiorano circuit and the narrow mountain roads overlooking Maranello. To the readers of the Belgian weekly, **Sportmoteur**, he summed up his impressions with "the most seductive model to ever come from Maranello" after having learned that "the performance is deceptive, the motor being so flexible and sweet in its performance." Tight turns revealed a slightly under-steering handling which was easily controlled with the accelerator pedal. The true element of the 308 GTB was

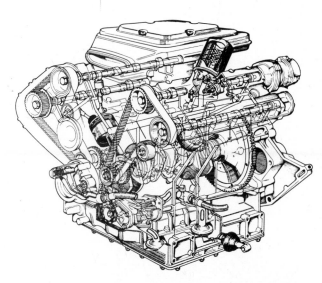

The V-8 engine of the GTB differed from that of the GT4 only by the use of dry sump lubrication.

Like its bodywork, the interior design of the 308 GTB was totally new.

It is not exactly known what modifications were made to
this 308 GTB/4 tested at Fiorano at the end of 1976.

the fast curves, which it took in a true four-wheel drift, with perfect balance. No less interesting was the impression of Tico Martini, Formula 1 constructor and former racing driver, delivered to readers of the new **Autohebdo** (No. 9) after several laps on "his circuit," Magny-Cours, one damp day: "It displays a little too much understeer in the wet, but remained very comfortable, manageable, and easy to catch. I remember quite well the joy of driving the vehicle, and found it necessary to only slow down to control the understeer. It was always handling itself in a perfectly safe manner, and, quite certainly, this tendency would be much less in the dry. . . And then there was the acceleration. . . To have acceleration like that, to bring out so many horses without thinking of the consequences! What a way to get into trouble with all of today's limits."

To deduce that the 308 GTB was conceived in order to one day give birth to a racing version is, perhaps, a bit premature. However, an example was seen at Fiorano in September, 1976, a "308 GTB/4" in tricolor livery (red-white-green) looking very official. The purpose of this may never be known. This "Group 4" vehicle (hence the 4 added to its designation) may have been used to test different engines, known and unknown. A short time later it was sold in Belgium, with a 90° V-8 engine that approached 300 horsepower. Several other 308 GTBs were also converted to racing usage, but in a manner that did not involve the factory itself. Such, notably, was the case of the vehicle of Karl Foitek in Switzerland, and even the case of the 308 used by Carlo Facetti to capture the 1978 Italian championship in Group 4.

An interesting novelty produced by the same Carlo Facetti and his team was the 308 BT which they prepared for certain events in the Group 5 World Championship of Makes, and the Italian championship in the same class. Their 308 "silhouette," whose major modifications were made by Carrozzeria Fratelli Moioli, was actually equipped with two KKK turbo-chargers, increasing the power to 710 horsepower at 9000 rpm. As of this date, however, the twin-turbo 308 had yet to make its first race appearance.

The 308 BT ("bi-turbo") announced by Carlo Facetti in 1978 has yet to appear in a race.

At the 1977 Geneva Salon, Pininfarina showed this "Study on the 308 GTB." Several of the innovations were later offered as options on the production vehicles.

The interior finish displayed more leather, and the dashboard was inspired by that of the BB.

At the 1977 Geneva Salon, Pininfarina presented on this stand a 308 GTB that had been revised and modified in the wind tunnel. The adoption of Michelin TRX tires, wider but of less height, required new 15 inch wheels and an enlargement of the wheel wells, which was achieved by the addition of aluminum panels. In the same way the rear spoiler was amplified and a wing was added between the sail panels, as on the Berlinetta Boxer. The light gray color of the pieces that were added gave this vehicle a unique red and gray two-tone effect. It carried, in the interior, the designation 308 T, in honor, certainly, of the 3 litre champion of the world in 1975. Also noted on this vehicle was the exhaust with four outlets, the reduced bumpers, a supplementary radiator vent in the front hood, and, under all of this, a more pronounced spoiler. This styling exercise remains a one-off, but it is interesting to note that several of the features which it introduced were later offered as an option on the normal 308 GTB.

The 308 GTS, presented at the 1977 Frankfurt Salon, repeated the formula which made a success of the Dino 246 GTS.

This was notably the case for the front spoiler, the lower profile tires (but Pirelli P7's, and on different rims) and the exhaust with four outlets which was standard equipment on the USA version.

At the Frankfurt Salon, in September, 1977, the 308 GTS was unveiled. It filled the void left by the disappearance, three years earlier, of the Dino 246 GTS. For this new "spyder," Pininfarina once again used the idea of a removable roof panel which, when the vehicle was "open," was stored behind the seats. Also the rear quarter windows were replaced by louvers intended to improve the rearward side visibility. Mechanically, the spyder did not differ from the berlinetta except for its return to the wet sump engine lubrication system as on the Dino 308 GT4.

The 308 GTB and GTS sucessfully continue to this day the path traced by this new generation of 8-cylinder Ferraris.

In 1978, a new painting department was opened within the Maranello plant.

VIII
The Last Large Ferraris?

The first Ferrari with a central engine, the 246 Formula 1 single seat, appeared at the 1960 Grand Prix of Monaco, and the first Ferrari sports/racer with a central engine, the 246 SP, appeared less than one year later. So when, at the 1963 Paris Salon, the 250 Le Mans berlinetta appeared it was a new demonstration of the firmly established principle of Maranello, of the veritable "golden rule" of Ferrari, which stated that research and development always follows the sequence of monoplace to sports/racing to gran turismo. While homologation of the 250 LM in the gran turismo category posed some grave probelms (it was granted in November, 1964, but for Italy only), Pininfarina, at the 1965 Geneva Salon, supplied adequate proof that the 250 LM could very well be a true touring car. Owners of other LMs did not hesitate to confirm this also, as we will see later.

The 250 LM berlinetta (6025) displayed by Pininfarina differed from its sisters above all by its much more refined finishing. Increased sound insulation, an interior decorated with leather, electrically powered side windows, bumperettes for protection, faired-in front signal lights, grills embellishing the rear fender air intakes, and an elegant paint job in the American

(Left) The 250 Le Mans berlinetta (6025) shown by Pininfarina at the 1965 Geneva Salon can undoubtedly be considered as the first touring Ferrari with a central engine.

Several 250 LMs were similarly converted. For example, 5903, in 1969.

racing colors, (white with longitudinal blue stripes) were all part of the modifications wrought by Pininfarina. The normal rear window was replaced by a vast, streamlined, thermoformed perspex window that extended almost to the rear spoiler, creating an enclosed expanse above the engine compartment. Finally, in order to facilitate entry which was somewhat difficult because of the very large door sills, two supplementary "butterfly wing" doors were fitted into the roof.

This superb attempt at "civilizing" the 250 LM did not, however, deter others from similar endeavors. In 1966 the amateur Italian race driver Roberto Benelli attempted to adapt his LM (5995) to a mixture of both touring and competition usage. And in 1969 Tom Meade, the American stylist living in Modena, attempted similar modifications to another LM (5903) to which he even gave a partially removable roof. It was to Pininfarina, however, that credit had to be given

The second touring Ferrari with a central 12-cylinder engine was the 365 P, an experimental berlinetta with three places and central steering presented by Pininfarina at the 1966 Paris Salon.

for creating what must be considered as the first touring Ferrari with a central engine, the 1965 Geneva Salon 250 LM.

Passing over the first two prototypes of the Dino 206 GT, that of the 1965 Paris Salon and that of the 1966 Turin Salon, both of which were already discussed in Chapter VII, the next creation to be considered was the "365 P Berlinetta Speciale" of the 1966 Paris Salon. This was another special creation by Pininfarina, and a second touring Ferrari given a centrally located V-12 engine. The basic layout of the design was so surprising—three seats, with the driver in the center slightly advanced and two passengers, one on either side—that the exact technical specifications of this astonishing exercise are often completely ignored. As for the aesthetics, except for the altered proportions, it appeared to be another prototype of the future Dino 246 GT. But if one relies on the second ex-

ample, (8815, the last or next-to-last?) which was delivered some time later to the President of Fiat, for technical innovations, the surprise was no less great for the assembly was quite original. With a wheelbase of 2.60 metres, the chassis was unique for that era. At the front it resembled that of the 250 LM, and at the rear, that of the contemporary 365 P. With a 4.4 litre V-12, it appeared to be derived from the 365 California, another contemporary. There are a number of questions which remain unanswered concerning this unusual series of two or three examples, most notably the idea that a more extensive production series might have been envisaged. Remember that it was at about this same time that the Lamborghini Miura first appeared!

The Dino 206 GT went into production at the time of the 1968 Turin Salon. It was the first gran turismo with central engine to be mass produced by Maranello, but it was not always considered as a true Ferrari, "al-

The next exercise was entitled "P6" and was unveiled at the
1968 Turin Salon, still be Pininfarina. But this time the engine compartment, certainly large enough to house a V-12,
was empty.

most a Ferrari" said the sales brochure. At this same salon Pininfaina unveiled a new styling exercise, the P6, but without an engine this time. Considering the high rear, the four tail pipes, and the curious vent louvers in the shape of an arch, it certainly possessed the possibility of housing a 12 cylinder engine, perhaps even a V-12. The rest of the design was very seductive. It would be shown again, three years later, at the 1971 Turin Salon.

When one recalls that for Ferrari, the principle of a flat ("boxer") 12-cylinder engine was born in 1965, in 1500 cc in the single seat 512 Formula 1, that it, in 1969, catapulted the 2 litre 121/E spyder to the European Hillclimb Championship; that it was reutilized, in 3 litres, on the 312 B for Formula 1 and then, in 1972, on the 312 P spyder which won the World Championship of Makes, then one can realize that once again the "golden rule" of Ferrari development has been respected, and that the Berlinetta Boxer, the first Ferrari to be put into series production with a central engine, was not conceived in haste.

The first presentation of the Berlinetta Boxer was exactly
three years later, at the 1971 Turin Salon. Certain lines
resembled those of the P6, but the greatest innovation was
the use of a flat 12-cylinder engine.

VIII·A
The 365 GT4 BB
Berlinetta Boxer
1971-1976

The Berlinetta Boxer was unveiled in its world premier on the Pininfarina stand at the 1971 Turin Salon. Found on this exhibition portotype were numerous aesthetic traits shared with the P6 also presented here some three years earlier. This was especially true of the frontal treatment, but the centrally-located flat 12-cylinder engine allowed an even lower silhouette for the sleek body on which one of the innovations was a groove cutting the bodyshell at mid-height. All of the frontal lower part, which generously overhung the front wheels, constituted the front bumper in which was incorporated a radiator air intake decorated by a traditional grill of rectangular texture. Above, the hood and fenders formed an almost flat surface

into which were set the covered turn signal lights, the retractable headlights, and an air outlet for hot radiator air. The large hood and the steeply raked windshield almost formed a single plane. The side windows were given generous proportions and extended onto the sail panels, which were themselves stretched into two fins extending the length of the rear deck. The rear window was recessed vertically between these two fins, and a multi-purpose wing was located across their top. Following a principle experimented with by Pininfarina as far back as 1965, this created a zone of depression above the engine compartment which was used here to supply air for ventilation and carburetion. This permitted the removal of the lateral air intakes that up

(Left) Several prototypes were subjected to lengthy testing before the BB was launched on the market at the end of 1973. This one is recognizable by the radio antenna. In the background an unpainted body revealed its composition: In white, the aluminum; in gray, the steel; and in black, the reinforced resin.

From the first production examples the radio antenna was imbedded in the windshield.

to this time, had been found on all the central-engined Ferraris.

At the rear, the lower part of a very short overhang was also made to function as a bumper in which were placed the exhaust outlets. Above, the truncated rear panel contained a large ventilation grill on which were attached the taillights and the support for the registration plate.

The choice of materials used was exceptionally varied. The opening parts were in aluminum, notably the massive front and rear covers which incorporated the fenders. Bumpers were of reinforced resin, and the tubular chassis, as well as the rest of the body, was in steel.

Particular care was taken to conserve the best ratio of weight between the front and the rear. Therefore the radiator, the spare wheel (of reduced dimensions), and the space reserved for luggage were placed under the front. The same care was also given to noise and heat insulation, as well as the aerodynamic studies conducted in Pininfarina's new wind tunnel, in collaboration with the Turin Polytechnic Institute.

While it was apparently complete, the Berlinetta Boxer shown at Turin in 1971 was in reality only an exhibition prototype. It was necessary to be content with dreams and be patient for two years until the production cars were presented, as the success being garnered by the Daytona made it unnecessary to hurry events. Meanwhile, the "Boxer" engine continued its career in Formula 1 with the 312 B, and in the World Championship of Makes, with the 312 P which won the championship in 1972.

The commercialization of the Berlinetta Boxer was begun at the 1973 Paris Salon. It was only then, after having experimented with several prototypes, that the definitive technical characteristics of the 365 GT4/BB, as the type was officially called, could be detailed.

It was, of course, the 4.4 litre flat 12 cylinder engine which first captured the attention. Based on a block of light alloy (Silumin), it was a magnificent piece of foundry art (a skill in which Maranello had acquired a specialty over a number of years) with shrunk-in cast iron cylinder liners having a bore center dimension of 95 mm. Also found was a magnificent crankshaft machined from a solid billet of chrome molybdenum steel, another masterpiece found in all Ferrari engines. This crankshaft turned in seven main bearings, and the forged connecting rods were paired

on the six throws. Finally, if the dimensions of the bore and stroke (81 x 71 mm) of the light alloy pistons (the same as those of the 4.4 litre V-12 engine) are considered, then the list of common points with preceding production engines from Ferrari has been exhausted. Here the cylinders were no longer disposed in a Vee, but in the same horizontal plane (180°) as the crankshaft. Thus the name "Boxer," which however, is questioned by some who allege that the term designates engines with opposite pistons working in different directions. This, of course, was not the case with the Ferrari, since the paired connecting rods dictate that the directly opposing pistons travel in the same direction. Whether or not this engine merits the name "Boxer," this layout had for its principle advantages a considerable reduction in height, benefitting both the aerodynamics and, because it permitted a lower center of gravity, the road holding.

The vertically located light alloy cylinder heads each contained two camshafts, directly actuating the valves which formed an included angle of 46°. An innovation was the cylindrical caps which served as an intermediary between the lobes of the camshafts and the stems of the valves.

Another important innovation was the toothed belts driving the camshafts. Quieter than the preceding chains, and resulting in an appreciable saving of weight and of work involved in casting the block, they represented an important advance for which Ferrari is certainly known as the innovator on vehicles of this category. The same system was also found on the 308 GT4 8-cylinder engine presented beside the Berlinetta Boxer.

Fuel was supplied by two electrical pumps to the four triple-choke Weber 40 IF 3C carburetors located vertically above the cylinder heads. A total of 120 litres (32 gallons) of fuel was carried in two light alloy tanks located in the flanks between the cockpit and the rear wheels.

The twelve spark plugs were supplied by a single two-stage distributor driven by the right intake camshaft (on the prototype shown at Turin in 1971, it was the right exhaust camshaft). Lubrication was by wet sump, with one oil filter per cylinder bank and a heat exchanger replacing the oil radiator.

Because of space limitations the transmission could not be placed at the rear of the engine, as on the prototypes. So the five-speed fully synchronized gearbox

An additional row of ventilation louvers appeared later on the engine cover.

The flat 4.4 litre 12 cylinder engine was rated at 380 horsepower at 7700 rpm.

was located under the engine, along side the oil sump, and therefore slightly offset to the right of the longitudinal axis of the vehicle. It was driven, following the single plate dry clutch, by a cascade of three pinions—the same principle already used on the Dino—located on the rear face of the assembly. The limited slip differential was located in the same ensemble, following the gearbox, and almost level with the next-to-last throw of the crankshaft, in order to satisfactorily locate the engine as we shall see later. In fact, the case for the gearbox, the engine sump, and the differential constituted a single cast piece, of silumin, but the lubrication of the gearbox and that of the engine were, of course, separated.

This impressive ensemble had a power rating given at 360 to 380 horsepower at 7700 rpm, and maximum torque was rated 42 mkg (303 lb/ft) at 3900 rpm. As a result of the "Boxer" configuration, the crankshaft was found to be about 50 cm above the ground. Unfortunately, the accessories which were mounted above the engine reduced the major advantages of a flat engine. But the only other possible solution with a 12-cylinder engine was that of a V-12 mounted transversely with the gearbox running parallel. This had been the Miura's "solution," with its known inconveniences, the main one being the amount of noise transmitted throught the bulkhead by such a powerful engine. The advantages of the Berlinetta Boxer on this point are well known.

The entire engine/drive train ensemble was positioned longitudinally behind the cockpit and, in order to not extend the wheelbase to more than 2.50 metres, the engine noticeably surrounds the axis of the rear wheels, as we have already referred to in discussing the positioning of the differential.

The chassis repeated the principle composition that had been born with the Dinos: a framework of square-section tubes covered on the two faces by welded sheet steel. At the front and the rear, two cradles of tubing also of square section were added, and joined with the mounting pillars for the windshield and the roof. The engine/drive train ensemble was attached to the lower framework by means of four silentblocs, with the mounting points no longer being part of the engine block, but of the sump/gearbox/differential case.

The suspension was four-wheel independent, and as usual was by means of superimposed wishbones, telescopic shock absorbers with co-axial coil springs, and stabilizer bars. Here, however, there were found four shock absorber/coil spring units at the rear.

Checking the weight distribution found 44% on the front and 56% on the rear. The brake system was by ATE and consisted of four ventilated discs of 28.8 cm (11.02 in) diameter at the front and 29.7 cm (11.7 in) at the rear. They were activated by a hydraulic cylinder with co-axial plungers, pneumatic brake booster and vacuum pump. As in the past, the front and rear hydraulic circuits were separate.

The cast light alloy wheels with Rudge hubs were of the same five-pointed star design, and the same dimensions of 7.5 x 15 inches, as those of the Daytona. They also were mounted with the same Michelin XWX 215/70 VR 15 tires.

By comparison with the prototype of the 1971 Turin Salon, the body, whose building was entrusted to Scaglietti, underwent a few detail modifications. The door hiding the fuel filler was relocated. On the rear grill, the four optical groups of taillights were replaced by six similar elements, and the rear skirt was redesigned to contain the voluminous exhaust system with six tail pipes grouped three-by-three. All the vehicles were delivered in standard two-color trim, with the lower "shell" and the roof wing, as well as the carburetor cover, being uniformly flat black. Finally, the electrical antenna embedded in the immense windshield and the pantographic wiper which swept the windshield in case of rain also merit mention.

Without doubt the Berlinetta Boxer did not lack allure. Very low (1.12 metres) (3.68 feet), wide (1.80 metres) (5.91 feet), with a length of 4.36 metres (14.3 feet) and a purposeful stance, it had the air of a true "prototype." By comparison, the Daytona seemed to be from another period of time.

The German bi-monthly, **Auto Motor und Sport** (April 10, 1976), gave some figures comparing the Lamborghini Countach, the De Tomaso Pantera GTS, the Maserati Ghibli, and the Porsche Turbo. From a standing start it was the Porsche which most quickly reached 180 km/h (112 mph) (15 seconds), ahead of the Countach (16 seconds) and the BB (17.1 seconds). For the standing start kilometre, (.62 mile), it was the Countach which was fastest (24.3 seconds), ahead of the Porsche and the BB (25.2 seconds). Finally, in maximum speed the Ferrari was second (281.3 km/h) (174 mph) behind the Lamborghini (288 km/h) (178 mph) but ahead of the Porsche (250 km/h) (155 mph).

In order to take the wider wheels and the lower profile Pirelli
P 7 tires, the wheel arches of this 365 GT4/BB (17779)
were modified in a manner almost imperceptible.

The English weekly **Motoring News** (July 18, 1974) added: "Other so-called exotic cars we have driven through the years. . . have invariably disappointed us. The Maserati Ghibli felt like a supercharged Bedford 5-tonner, a Ferrari GTC needed a servo on the accelerator pedal, a Lamborghini Miura felt hot, noisy and uncomfortable, an Aston Martin (a wonderful car, we hasten to say) had such a heavy clutch pedal that our left leg twitched all day after a drive in the rush hour. But in the space of three hours, the Berlinetta Boxer revealed no such shortcomings, and on the contrary was one of the easiest, most pleasurable cars we have ever driven."

If, however, the test figures that were published were not very different from those of the Daytona, it was because the progress made with the Berlinetta Boxer was on a completely different plane. Paul Frère explained in **Sportmoteur**: "The session on the Fiorano circuit was a true pleasure, the available power always being sufficient to exit the corners with a great deal of acceleration, after breaking the rear wheels loose in a well-controlled slide. . . Without being particularly light, the rack & pinion steering was very agreeable, moderately demultiplied and very precise. In this respect the BB is certainly a great improvement over the Daytona which, because of the weight of the engine on the front wheels, had a harder and slower steering and therefore was slightly more tiring. On our circuit of our favorite mountains, the Appenines, the BB was a veritable joy, not the least of which was the roads being sufficiently wide to not handicap a vehicle some 1.80 metres in width.

"On the comfort level as well the BB illustrated the progress made in later years by the fastest vehicles: a lower center of gravity, a better distribution of weight, and a modern suspension all permitting the adoption of relatively soft springing without harming the handling on the good surfaces while assuring not only adequate comfort but also better road holding on the mediocre roads."

While there can be no doubt that Ferrari and Pininfarina were remarkably successful in adapting to a tour-

Luigi Chinetti was the first to attempt to prepare a BB for racing. Here 18095 during practice for the 1975 24 Hours of Le Mans.

vehicle the solutions previously reserved for racing cars, the opposite process of transforming the BB from a touring vehicle into a race car was not so simple. This, however, was no deterrent to Luigi Chinetti, who attempted the experiment with several BBs that were modified to varying degrees, but without ever posting any convincing successes.

In the spring of 1976 a new Berlinetta Boxer of 5 litres displacement was announced for the Paris Salon in October. The production of the 365 GT4/BB therefore ceased before the summer. In a little less than three years it had been produced in close to 400 examples.

In 1977 the modifications were more extensive. Migault and Guitteny finished 16th.

VIII·B
The 512 BB
1976-

A spoiler at the front and a redesigned rear
that was wider and longer, were the principal modifications
given to the design of the BB.

When it was officially presented, at the 1976 Paris Salon at the same time as the 400 Automatic, the new 512 BB had already been in production for several months. The new designation of 512 BB—5 litres, 12 cylinders, Berlinetta Boxer—revived memories of the 5 litre sports/racing cars of 1970 and 1971. Yet while its aesthetic appearance was little changed, it represented a very important evolution. The displacement was increased to almost 5 litres (4943 cc) thanks to a slight increase in the bore dimension (from 81 to 82 mm), but especially due to a new crankshaft which allowed lengthening the stroke by almost 10%, from 71 to 78 mm. A comparison of the sales brochures for the two BBs surprisingly revealed that the maximum power (360 horsepower) was not increased although the compression was higher (9.2:1). However, this power was now attained at a slightly lower engine speed (6800 rpm in place of 7700). Also noted was the adoption of dry sump lubrication, but it was the gain in torque, of close to 10%, which was the major point, and which indicated the accent given to improving the driving pleasures.

The rear wheels were increased to 9 inches width, and were now equipped with Michelin XWX tires size 225/70 x 15 inch, this dictating an enlargement of the rear wheel wells by about 2 cm each. This was accompanied by discrete modifications in the design of the rear, which gained 4 cm in length. The ventilation of the engine compartment was augmented by three rows of supplementary vents, and the grill in the rear

panel was replaced by oblique blades. The six taillights were replaced by four, as on the first 4.4 litre prototype, and the exhaust system was also returned to four outlets of larger diameter. The NACA ducts located on the lower flanks were intended to improve the ventilation of the rear disc brakes, and the spoiler integrated into the front overhang of the vehicle improved the handling characteristics.

As with the 4.4 litre, the 512 BB was not intended for a racing career. There were, however, several interesting attempts on the part of the French importer, Charles Pozzi, as well as Luigi Chinetti and Jean "Beurlys," to race the 512 BB, the first with two vehicles, the other two with one vehicle each. The first three vehicles were prepared at Modena, at Viale Trento e Trieste, with the official assistance of the factory, for the 1978 24 Hours of Le Mans. The weight was reduced to about 1100 kilograms (2425 lbs) and a more careful engine assembly and tuning raised its power to some 460 horsepower. As for the aerodynamics and handling, the cars were fitted with a spoiler of increased size, an aerodynamic duct on the front deck, wider rims equipped with Michelin racing tires, and a wing overhanging the rear as on the 312 Formula 1. Prepared at Brussels by the Garage Francorchamps team, the vehicle for "Beurlys" had these same specifications although there was some differences in the aerodynamic artifices. The BB demonstrated an interesting potential at the Le Mans track, appreciably bettering the times set by the "Daytonas" several years earlier primarily due to a faster speed through the curves. But the race was not a success for the vehicles due to a breaking of the gearboxes.

A second series of vehicles were immediately put into production, under the same conditions, but this time the preparation was to be more extensive. The adoption of indirect fuel injection allowed a power rating on the order of 480 horsepower at an engine speed of 7200 rpm, with an even greater gain in torque and flexibility. The transmission was reinforced by square-cut gears and its lubrication, moreover, was improved with the installation of an independent oil radiator. An important amount of work was also devoted to the suspension and the brakes. An aerodynamic study undertaken in the wind tunnel by Pininfarina resulted in a completely redesigned front and a long rear on which the wing was carried by two fins. The total length had thereby gained about 40 cm

In early 1978 a 512 BB Competition tested on the track at Fiorano. The lateral blue-white-red band indicates the initiator of the project, the French importer Charles Pozzi.

At the 1978 24 Hours of Le Mans the three BBs built at Maranello appeared in the same form. The covered nose could be mounted on all these vehicles.

The wing was that which was normally mounted at the front of the 312 T3.

Built in Belgium, the BB of J. "Beurlys" received different aerodynamic equipment.

while the saving of about 100 kilograms reduced the weight to about 1075 kilograms (2370 lbs). Finally, the adoption of even wider rims (10 and 13 inches) had dictated a very noticeably widening of the fenders.

Three vehicles were entered in the 24 Hours of Daytona in 1979, the two vehicles of the Charles Pozzi team, directed by Daniel Marin, and the vehicle of Luigi Chinetti. But the very special strains imposed by the famous banking at Daytona on the tires and suspension very quickly posed unknown problems. During practice one of the Pozzi vehicles left the track after a tire burst. The damages were repaired in time for the race but after only six hours the same problem under the exactly identical circumstances had the same consequences for the Chinetti vehicle, at the time being driven by Jean-Pierre Delauney. It was immediately decided to withdraw the other two BBs from the race as a measure of prudence.

At the 24 Hours of Le Mans, in June, 1979, the same three cars were entered plus an additional one for Jean "Beurlys" that was identical to the first three. After a long renovation and a serious preparation, the two vehicles of the French importer were in peak condition. But the first disaster struck shortly after 7 a.m. when Michel Leclere collided with a slower competitor in the wetness at Hunaidierres. The other BB, driven by Jean-Claude Andruet and Spartaco Dino was then in 8th place overall, and all hopes rested with it. The final blow came at about 9 a.m., some six hours before the end of the race, when the loud speakers announced the slow-motion passage of Andruet at Mulsanne. The engine of the second French BB had lost its soul, apparently the victim of a failure of lubrication. It was in third place at the time!

For 1979 the transmission was modified (straight cut gears) and fuel injection replaced the carburetors.

The short experiences of the competition 512 BB are misleading. What can its future be? It seems obvious that in this era the competition cars are more and more different from the touring vehicles, and so the transformation of a vehicle conceived for the road into a vehicle capable of competing on the track demands more and more work. For the men at Maranello this increased work load is probably not the best use of their time, which is already well filled by the demands of production and of Formula 1 racing. The victory of Ferrari in the Formula 1 World Championship for 1979—this was being confirmed as these lines were being written—serves to console this state of affairs. Finally, there remains the 512 BB, the last descendant of a lineage of unequalled prestige. The last of the large Ferraris? Until the next Ferrari. . . .

Pininfarina effected important work on the aerodynamics. The experience of the 512 BB Competition remains to be followed.

The 275 GTB of 1966, the 365 GTB/4 of 1969, and the 512 BB of 1976 symbolize ten years of prestigious Ferrari-Pininfarina berlinettas. Will the 512 BB be the last? Until the next. . . .

Annex

Which Year?

Serial Number	Year	Serial Number	Year
001		4135	
	1948		1963
005		5255	
	1949		1964
023		6591	
	1950		1965
0123		08111	
	1951		1966
	1952		
0263		09441	
	1953		1967
0321		10853	
	1954		1968
0387		11985	
	1955		1969
0467		12999	
	1956		1970
0607		13983	
	1957		1971
0843		14811	
	1958		1972
1241		16283	
	1959		1973
1631		16609	
	1960		1974
2171		17523	
	1961		1975
3157		18195	
	1962		1976
4135		18737	

Achevé d'imprimer
sur les presses de Berger-Levrault,
à Nancy, le 1er juin 1981.
Dépôt légal : 2e trimestre 1981.
779159-6-1981
Imprimé en France.